SOUVENIRS

SOUVENIRS

AROUND THE WORLD IN NINETY YEARS

A BOOK OF MEMOIRS

⊰⊱

ZOLTAN OVARY

⊰⊱

INDIA INK PRESS
NEW YORK

Book Design and Composition: Andrew Sihler
Jacket Design: Angelo Marfisi
Printing and Manufacturing: Webcom, Toronto, Canada

India Ink Press
PO Box 655
Murray Hill Station
New York, New York 10156-0604

First Edition 1999
This book is printed on acid-free paper.

Library of Congress Catalog Card Number: 98-92391
International Standard Book Number: 0-9662878-1-9
Printed and bound in Toronto, Canada

10 9 8 7 6 5 4 3 2 1

TO ORDER:

Write to India Ink Press or
Call (212) 663-9042 or
Fax (212) 263-7533 or
Send e-mail to ovaryz01@popmail.med.nyu.edu

CONTENTS

Acknowledgements   vii

About Zoltan *by Lloyd J. Old*   ix

Preface   xiv

I	Kolozsvar	1
II	The Chocolate Hussar	15
III	Guest Family	25
IV	Street of the Wolf	39
V	Latin Quarter	48
VI	Cat's Hair	53
VII	Ambassadress Cerruti	64
VIII	Back to Transylvania	69
IX	India Ink	80
X	The Day of Saint Anna	85
XI	The Blue Spot	96
XII	The Beating Heart	107
XIII	America	115
XIV	Hypersensitivity	124
XV	Experiments	131
XVI	Music for a While	136
XVII	Addictive but Not Habit Forming	146

XVIII Fountain of Chance   163

  XIX Enthusiasts   180

   XX A Visit to the Pallavicini Palace   188

  XXI The Fifth Slave   194

 XXII The Silver Shop   202

XXIII Serendipity   208

 XXIV La Caravelle   214

  XXV Once Upon a Time   220

 XXVI Students and Teachers   235

XXVII *Isten Hozta*   242

INDEX   257

◆◊·◊◆

acknowledgements

I DEDICATE THESE PAGES to my friends who have so often urged me to write down the encounters and journeys of my life.

Many colleagues and friends read the manuscript and gave me good advice. Some worked page by page to suggest improvements or point out errors. In this regard I am specially grateful to David Longmire, William J. Simmons, Jeanette Thorbecke, Jan Vilcek, Byron Waksman, Frank Dabell, Jay Weisberg, and Andrew Sihler.

For almost fifteen years now, New York University Medical Center has been holding an annual Zoltan Ovary Symposium, a gathering of scientists, students, and special guests from around the world, who discuss their latest discoveries in immunology. A reception at the Century Club in Manhattan followed last year's symposium. The fifty or so guests gave me a touching gift during the reception. At the instigation of my colleagues Jeanette Thorbecke and Suzy Zolla-Pazner, they had all contributed to a fund to help me finish my book of memoirs. The only condition was that each one of them would get a copy of the book. Like it or not, I thought, I would have to come out with the book!

Others have given me special help during all these months.

Angelo Marfisi designed the lovely book jacket. It has been a privilege for me to work with an artist of Angelo's patience and imagination.

Csaba de Szalay provided my photo for the book jacket.

Vincent Nebrida gave help and advice on the business of publishing.

Art historian Frank Dabell, editor Carolyn Fleg, and writer and scientist Tomio Tada gave me kind permission to excerpt passages from their letters.

It is a deep honor for me that my friend Lloyd Old, a scientist and artist I respect greatly, wrote the introduction.

Two friends labored intensively for months on the book, and I couldn't thank them enough for all the dedication and intelligence they brought to their work:

Andrew Sihler designed the book and showed that typography is an art form in the right hands. It was an exciting adventure to go through his array of font proofs to choose from them, and to see how his beautiful design evolved.

It was my writer-producer friend Gil Quito who finally persuaded me to sit down and write these memoirs. He stayed the whole course, working with splendid skill to edit the manuscript and produce the book.

◆◊·◊◆

about zoltan

Zoltan Ovary's worlds of friends and colleagues were delighted to know that he was setting down his memoirs for all of us to share. Zoltan's life has been so full and remarkable that, despite years of far-ranging discussions with him, I realized that much remained unknown to me, not because of any reluctance on his part to relate his experiences, but because there was so much to tell. Now in publishing his memoirs, he has given us a unique gift, something both grand and precious.

In his inimitable way with a story, he recalls his extraordinary life, one framed by the great political, cultural, and scientific transformations of the twentieth century. His idyllic childhood, painted with a fine evocative brush, was prelude to a life of remarkable adventure and achievement despite a century dominated by political chaos and wars, a life filled with the unexpected and the exceptional, and one graced with the deep friendship of many extraordinary people. Three great cities, Paris, Rome, and New York, have been home to Zoltan during different phases of his life. Paris provided him with his medical education and his first exposure to research at the Pasteur Institute. Rome gave him safe harbor after World War II, where he practiced medicine and began his immunological work. And New York, his home for the past forty years, is where he has conducted his celebrated research at the New York University School of Medicine.

Zoltan is considered one of the legendary pioneers in

immunological research. During his lifetime, immunology has evolved from its origin in the study of infectious diseases to one of the most powerful disciplines in modern biology. Astonishing progress has been made in our understanding of the complex and surprising ways that our body responds to attack by bacteria, viruses, and other infectious agents, and this new knowledge gives much hope for more effective vaccines, as well as for new immunologically-based therapies for cancer, autoimmune diseases, and allergic disorders.

The study of allergy has been the primary focus of Zoltan's lifetime research, and he has made contributions of enduring importance to the understanding of this perplexing aspect of the immune response. Whereas we usually associate immunity with protection against disease, allergic responses have the opposite effect—they cause diseases, such as asthma, brought about by immune responses against certain foreign substances called antigens. The substances that can cause allergies are legion, and the symptoms of an allergic reaction can range from the annoying—such as sneezing, itching, and hives—to the debilitating and, in the extreme case, to shock and death.

The modern study of allergy can be said to have begun in the early 1950's when Zoltan and his collaborator Guido Biozzi introduced a new technique called Passive Cutaneous Anaphylaxis, or PCA, which Zoltan developed and refined over the years into a powerful analytical tool. For the first time, using skin reactions in guinea pigs, the antibodies that cause allergic reactions could be studied, quantitated, and isolated.

His work established a number of fundamental principles underlying the development of allergies, and many investigators around the world have built on the solid foundations that Zoltan created. This line of inquiry, initiated by Zoltan, directly led fifteen years later to the identification of a novel class of antibodies, called IgE, that is now known to be the mediator of most allergic reactions. A number of other seminal concepts in immunology also had their origin in Zoltan's experimental work with PCA. In an intuitive leap he called the bridging hypothesis, Zoltan correctly predicted that two antibody molecules on the surface of an immune cell needed to be brought into close proximity in order to trigger the release of substances mediating allergic reactions. This was a very prescient idea that has since been shown to be true for a range of other biological signaling systems.

Another milestone in immunological research was the result of a collaboration between Zoltan and his good friend Baruj Benacerraf, whom he met in Paris in the early 1950's and who was instrumental in Zoltan's coming to New York University. Through a series of classic experiments, Zoltan and Baruj discovered that different families of antibodies had different biological functions, a finding that disproved the longstanding belief, known as the unitarian theory, that all antibodies had the same activities.

Another landmark discovery came from his investigations of the antibody response to small chemical compounds called haptens. Haptens by themselves cannot elicit the production of antibodies. However, if attached to a foreign carrier protein, such as egg albumin, they do. Zoltan and Baruj found that the immune system retained a "memory" for the type of carrier protein used in the first immunization, because if animals are reimmunized with the same hapten attached to a different protein, the antibody response is far weaker than if the original protein were used. This phenomenon, called the "carrier effect," is now known to be due to complex interactions between two of the main actors in the immunological drama—the B cell, which is the source of antibodies, and the T cell, which provides help to B cells through the production of small regulatory molecules referred to as cytokines.

More recently, Zoltan has focused his attention on the

way T cells regulate the production of antibodies that mediate allergic reactions, particularly the way that their production is suppressed by subsets of T cells and their products. Thus, in his current work, Zoltan continues to pursue with vigor and passion the research he began fifty years ago in Rome. The only precedent I know for such persistent and distinguished scholarship in the field of immunology is Michael Heidelberger, the father of immunochemistry and a dear friend of Zoltan's, who continued his research until the age of 103.

Despite Zoltan's intense dedication to research, his interests and scholarship extend far beyond the borders of science. His erudition is astonishing, encompassing vast segments of Western history as well as the worlds of art and music. With boundless generosity and enthusiasm, he has shared his knowledge with countless students, friends, and colleagues around the world. Many of us first learned of the true grandeur of the Renaissance by wandering through great museums at Zoltan's side. Zoltan's pantheon of human achievement is amazingly vast, full of unsung or forgotten masters. However, I should mention that there are notable and passionate exclusions from this pantheon. His friends know that a very short list would include such established names and movements as Picasso, Schönberg, Freud, and Abstract Expressionism.

Finally, there could be no accounting of the man without celebrating his extraordinary capacity for friendship. In Zoltan's hands, friendship is a high art form, and in his memoirs there are wonderful accounts of his friendships with Ambassadress Cerruti, Princess Pallavicini, and Alice Tully, three extraordinary patrons of the arts; Pierre Grabar and Guido Biozzi, two distinguished immunologists; Hugues Cuenod and Albert Fuller, dear friends of Zoltan's from the world of music; and the many, many others who have had the splendid good fortune of knowing Zoltan. This book will be treasured by Zoltan's countless friends around the world. He has given all of us, those who know him and those who will meet him here for the first time, the opportunity to journey with him through a life of great and unique distinction.

Lloyd J. Old, MD
Director
Ludwig Institute for Cancer Research

preface

M ANY TIMES, friends approach me with questions. What is it like to be past ninety and still working full time? Tell us about life before the First World War. And Paris in the 20's—what was it like before cars began to crowd its avenues?

Then there's Transylvania, where I was born. Everyone seems to be interested in Transylvania, even though most people know it only as Dracula's domain.

As it happens, the historical Dracula, or Prince Vlad, lived not in Transylvania, but across the Carpathian mountains, in Wallachia. He often impaled his enemies, thus the title "the Impaler" that history and legend have attached to his name. Wallachians, seeking refuge across the Carpathian mountains, carried into Transylvania their accounts of the bloodthirsty Vlad. These stories formed the basis of the vampire legends that Bram Stoker popularized in his novel.

But there is another Transylvania. A world that has vanished yet is very much alive in my mind. It was a Transylvania of curious scientists and dreamy artists who attended the university my grandfathers directed and who came nightly to my mother's salon. It was a Transylvania of baroque palaces, lazy streets with horse-drawn coaches, and bold new ideas. A Transylvania of manners and rituals that have disappeared but still keep the power to sustain. This is the Transylvania that will be found in this book.

But Transylvania was only the start. Chance and fortune have led me to migrate to more places than I had ever expected when I was a small boy hearing about the world from *habitués* of my mother's salon.

This is not an autobiography, but a book of *memoirs* in the original French sense of the word: a collection of events and anecdotes regarding a subject or theme as personally recollected by the author. My boyhood encounters with people who loved science, music, and the arts affected me deeply and forever. They led me to choose the life of an immunologist and to seek out the friendship of artists and scientists. It is my experiences with these extraordinary people that I want to write about. Many of them have died, but for me they will always remain vibrant and alive.

The International Union of Immunological Societies says that I'm the world's oldest immunologist now working full time. Often, people ask me why, at the age of 91, I still go to my office and lab seven days a week, drop in on seminars, collaborate with students on scientific papers, and teach my students about worlds beyond science.

I have always loved the worlds of science, music, and the arts. I have learned not to allow time to diminish the passion. It is this passion that I would like to leave behind in this manuscript.

NEW YORK, NEW YORK   Z.O.
APRIL 1998

Author's note on Hungarian accents: Hungarian is full of written accents, and this is a book full of Hungarian names. In an English text, the overabundance of diacritical marks (acute accents, umlauts, and the like) can be quite distracting, like too many exclamation points. I am therefore omitting the Hungarian diacritics in the text. The index, however, lists the names with the proper accents. Kolozsvár, for example, is the entry in the index for what stands in the text throughout as Kolozsvar.

Se non è vero, è ben trovato.

Ma è vero!

Old Italian saying: *A good story, even if it's not true, is something to cherish.*

Me: *But it* IS *true!*

· I ·

kolozsvar

I WAS BORN ON APRIL 13, 1907, in Kolozsvar, the capital of Transylvania in the kingdom of Hungary. Kolozsvar, with its spires rising above centuries-old buildings and the Szamos river flowing through, was the second biggest city in the kingdom.

Kolozsvar had one of Hungary's two universities. It was a young and lively university, founded in the second half of the nineteenth century. Students came from all over the kingdom to join the excitement. My paternal grandfather was its chairman of the Philosophy of Law, and my maternal grandfather its chairman of Internal Medicine.

Kolozsvar's principal square was named Saint Michael's but everyone just called it main square. The older buildings, built between the 14th and 18th centuries, clustered in this area. In the middle of the square stood Saint Michael's, the city's fourteenth-century gothic church, its spire rising taller than anything else you could see.

Were you to look for Kolozsvar on today's maps, you would not find it. That is because the name that was on the map for hundreds of years was changed to Cluj when Transylvania was torn away from Hungary after the First World War.

I was born in an apartment at the northwest corner of the main square. On the streets below our second-floor windows, horse-drawn carriages clattered by, full of people, packages, fruits and vegetables. Women in long dresses and men in hats crossed the square all day long, their shadows hurrying right at their heels. There was a haberdashery downstairs, especially busy before the carnival balls when young men had their first tail coats made. It was a comforting world of old certainties and civilities. Most people did not know it would vanish soon.

Around the square were book stores, old palaces, a cafe, milliners, a florist, modistes, a jeweler, toy stores, pharmacies, perfumeries, a tobacconist, and a pastry shop. There were four banks and two hotels, the Hotel Central and the Hotel New York. Two food shops, Veres and Szele, sold rare and expensive delicacies like caviar, French cheeses, pineapples, bananas, macaroni, and catsup, which was a special import from England.

Our apartment was in a building owned by the piano teacher Valeria Donogan. The *maestra* had her own apartment next to ours and gave her piano lessons there. In Hungary, elderly ladies were always called Aunt, so I called her Aunt Valeria though she was not a relative. She had studied at the Ferencz Liszt Academy in Budapest with Arpad Szendy, the most famous piano teacher in Austria-Hungary. He considered her one of his best pupils. Her own students came to Kolozsvar from all over Transylvania, eager to try out her Boesendorfer piano and to learn her secrets. I did not have to leave our apartment to listen to the serenades and sonatas spilling out of her quarters. Thanks to Aunt Valeria, I heard music played well from the day I was born.

Passers-by would sometimes linger to hear the music as carriages hurried by in the street. At that time, no buses, cars or trams existed in Kolozsvar. People just walked, ran, or strolled to their destinations. Some families owned horses and coaches, but most people hailed horse-drawn carriages-for-hire called *fiacres*, a French word no one ever bothered to translate into Hungarian. My father Elemer, a lawyer, took a *fiacre* every day. He liked giving huge tips and because of this, the union of *fiacre* drivers elected him honorary president, a distinction he savored.

My sister Baba and I went every day to play in the garden of my maternal grandmother, Paula. This was on 15 Monostori Avenue, five long blocks away from our apartment on main square. My other grandmother, Polyxena, lived on 9 Monostori Avenue. Wedged between their houses were a small house (number 13) and a shop (number 11) that sold cooked hams and sausages. My grandparents' gardens curved and joined behind the shop and the neighbor's house so that we could go from one garden to the other just by climbing over a fence.

We preferred to stay in our grandmother Paula's garden as it was larger and more interesting. It was like a little park with a sandy playground and had different areas filled with flowers, trees and bushes where we could play hide and seek with our friends. Moreover, grandmother Paula liked giving in to us and, as some older people said, spoiled us. Our other grandmother Polyxena was the opposite. She believed in strict discipline and we were always a little afraid of her.

I was not a well-behaved boy by most accounts. Once when I was three (and my sister still in the crib), I was brought to play in grandmother Paula's garden. At the end of the day, it was time for her to take me home. I told her I was too tired and I wanted to go home in a *fiacre* like my father always did. She smiled at me then asked someone to hail a *fiacre*. And we rode happily to my parents' apartment.

The next day, it was grandmother Polyxena's turn to take me home. I told her I was too tired and wanted to go home in a *fiacre*. She said, "No! We will walk home."

I started crying. My grandmother dragged me kicking into the street. I wailed as she pulled me along the sidewalk. My screams got louder with every *fiacre* that came along. People stared out their windows. As we passed by the home of my godmother, the Baroness Karola Bornemissza, her mother leaned out of their second-floor window. "What's happening?" she cried out, "That child is shrieking like the devil! Oh God, what's happening?!" All the fuss got me wailing even louder.

My godmother looked down from behind her and saw me. "Oh, it's only the little Ovary boy! Don't worry," she told her mother. "That's routine with him!"

◆⦙⦙◆

At the turn of the century, Hungary had two universities. The older Pazmany Peter University of Budapest was established in 1653. The Ferencz Jozsef University of Kolozsvar was founded only in 1872. Professors at the Kolozsvar university were always working feverishly, as many of them wanted to get promoted to the Budapest university. On the other hand, those in Budapest seemed generally more content and sedate. My mother used to say that our university was like Saturday (then a working day), and that the university in Budapest was like Sunday.

My two grandfathers early on became my role models. One for his knowledge of medicine, the other for his passion about cultures and languages.

My paternal grandfather Kelemen Ovary, the university's chairman of Philosophy of Law, was known throughout the country for his erudition and the number of languages he spoke.

The classics were still the heart of university courses at that time. It was therefore not very unusual that professors like my grandfather could read and speak classical Greek and Latin. The Austro-Hungarian empire was a polyglot world and my grandfather was among those who made it their business to know its major languages. In addition to Hungarian, he spoke German, Romanian, Czech, Slovak, Serb, Croat, and Polish. His interest in other languages and cultures seemed inexhaustible. In addition to the Central European languages, he studied Russian and English, as well as the Latin tongues—Italian, Spanish, and French.

How my grandfather could ever find the time to learn all those languages, deal with obscure points of law, and support a wife and three children, was a mystery, I think even to himself. Not so for my grandmother Polyxena, who was endlessly running the household and taking care of his needs. As she saw it, she simply managed it so that he could have all the time to do what he wanted.

My grandmother dominated him as she did everyone else, but he enjoyed her company. After she passed away, I would often visit my grandfather in his house in the early afternoon, usually for about half an hour. He would be sitting at his desk and I would be standing the whole time, as was common practice. It was at this time that we got closer to each other. I would often ask about his travels and he would tell me about the interesting people he met and the great libraries he visited in many places around Austria-Hungary.

My maternal grandfather, Zsigmond Purjesz, was the university's chairman of Internal Medicine.

I sometimes wondered why the waiting room outside his office always had so many visitors. People were arriving from as far away as Austria, Germany, and Romania to see him. My mother and grandmother would tell me about his accomplishments matter-of-factly, as if they were the most natural things in the world. But I thought he might be doing something extraordinary. I learned more about him as I grew up.

One day, he was in his office preparing a lecture when his students came and told him that a critically ill patient had been admitted to the hospital. The doctors had already made all the tests but could not find out what was wrong. He went to the ward and examined the patient. Then he said to the chief resident, "But you missed the most important test. You did not look in his blood for malaria!" They made the blood smears and, sure enough, they found the malaria parasite, and immediately gave the patient the quinine my grandfather had ordered.

My sister and I sometimes had our midday meal at my grandfather's house, though we were never allowed to eat with the grownups. We either ate in a separate room or at a small table in the dining room, out of the way of the grownups. We would then run out to the garden and play, and would be admitted back to the dining room only when the grownups were having their black coffee after the meal. Every now and then, my grandfather would break a piece of his cube sugar and feed it to me on a spoon. Somehow, I always felt safe and secure in his presence.

I learned from my grandmother that he wrote the first book on internal medicine written in Hungarian, which became the standard text for doctors throughout Hungary. At the time he was writing the book, there was a cholera epidemic in Transylvania. Hundreds were dying weekly, which was not unusual at a time when modern sanitation was still in its infancy. The authorities enlisted him to supervise the fight against cholera. He ordered immediate steps for sanitation and strict quarantine, and with these measures, Kolozsvar was saved from the epidemic. King Ferencz Jozsef awarded him the Iron Crown, a decoration coveted in the kingdom above the golden ones. But the honor that really touched him was the title of "Honored Citizen" that Kolozsvar created especially for him.

Not too long ago, a friend sent me a newspaper article from Hungary about my grandfather. It included contemporary accounts, among them one by Miklos Jancso, his adjunct and successor at the university:

There came a time that no prominent person in Transylvania was not a patient of Purjesz or to whose bedside

Purjesz was not called. It didn't matter what sort of disease the patient had. When Purjesz arrived, he had such an effect on everyone, not only the patient but the whole family became happy and tranquil. As long as Purjesz saw the patient, people knew they had done the best that could be done. The patient died tranquil even if Purjesz could not help him. At least, this was the impression people had."

(*Szabadság*, April 3, 1997)

One time, a gentleman from Dezs, a town two hours away from Kolozsvar, came to seek his diagnosis. My grandfather, who did not care about anybody's religion, got distracted and, at the end of the visit, forgot the patient was Jewish. He noted in his prescription that the patient could eat "ham, but lean ham only."

The gentleman went home and showed the prescription to his wife. At that time in Hungary, there were two kinds of shops that sold meat. There was the regular butcher shop and then there was the *hentes,* which sold only sweet hams, cold cuts, and sausages.

The gentleman's wife went to the *hentes* with my grandfather's prescription and told the proprietor, "You know that I have never bought ham before, so you must help me. Look, it says here lean ham. I say, if Professor Purjesz advises it, there must be a special reason." The whole town soon learned about her purchase from the shop owner.

The following week, at my grandfather's next consultation, a dozen or so Jewish gentlemen from Dezs were waiting to see him. My grandfather opened the door and there were greetings all around. Then one of the men approached him and, honorarium in hand, exclaimed, "Doctor, no visit is necessary! Just give us the diet you prescribed for the rabbi!"

Shortly after my grandfather retired and moved to

Budapest, the professors at the university decided to install a bust of him in the university hospital's first courtyard. They commissioned Gyorgy Vastagh, a famous Hungarian sculptor born in Transylvania, to create a bronze bust. Local papers noted that the only other civilian bust installed in a public place while the person was still alive was the one in Oslo of the writer Henrik Ibsen.

The professors did not tell him about their plans until about two weeks before the unveiling. He did not want to have anything to do with it, but my grandmother persuaded him.

The city held a whole day of festivities attended by the mayor; the bishops of the Catholic, Calvinist, and Evangelist churches; and the mayor of his birthplace, Szentes. At the banquet, he gave 10,000 gold crowns, double the cost of the festivities, to help pay for the schooling of poor medical students. This last bit of information I learned only recently, from the same newspaper article I quoted above.

The bust was unveiled in 1912, when I was only five years old, but I still recall being pulled along by my governess Miss Pedley through a huge crowd of people. A man gave a very long speech and suddenly pulled a cloth off something. It looked very much like my grandfather, though with a difference. Unlike the bust, my grandfather had a smile.

◆◦§◦◆

A short walk from the university, in the middle of the main square, stood Saint Michael's, the town's principal church. It was an early gothic church begun in 1321 and completed 120 years later. Over the main entrance was a renaissance sculpture of Saint Michael bearing the arms of the fifteenth-century king Sigismund. Inside, slender pillars rose and curved into the vaulting. In early gothic manner, the church was left free of paintings or heavy decorations. Some Hungarian and Latin phrases were inscribed on the columns. There was a renaissance sacristy portal embellished with gay *putti* and the likeness of the donor, a man by the name of Johanes Klein, staring out from under his hat. Above the porch was a choir with an organ where my grandmother Polyxena sang as soprano soloist on holidays.

The songs, as well as the common prayers, were always in Hungarian. Latin, the language of the Mass, was understood by many congregants, since it was still in daily use in such professions as medicine, where protocols and death certificates were still being written in Latin; and law, where many books of precedents were available only in Latin.

On the south side of the church stood the monument of Mathias, who was born in Kolozsvar. He was, along with Stephen I, who founded the kingdom of Hungary in 1001, the greatest of Hungarian kings. His reign from 1458 to 1490 has become known as Hungary's golden age.

Mathias was born in a simple, two-story mansion located a block away from our apartment. The mansion was still standing and had been converted into a history museum by the time I was born. Unlike King Mathias' house, another of Kolozsvar's old landmarks had completely vanished. This was the castle mentioned in documents as early as 1213 by medieval settlers. By the time King Charles Robert granted Kolozsvar the status of a free royal city in 1316, this castle had been destroyed in the region's battles. But it remained part of the city's name, as *vár* is the Hungarian word for castle, and Kolozsvar means "castle of Kolozs." (The family name Ovary has the same root word, combined with *ó*, an ancient Hungarian word for old, and means "from the old castle.")

Kolozsvar was the seat of government of Mathias' father, Janos Hunyadi, who was royal governor of Transylvania when he won several important battles against the Turks. His fame as a general culminated in the victory of Belgrade in 1456, a turning point for the Christian world, still reeling from the fall of Constantinople three years earlier. To commemorate this victory, the Pope ordered that all bells in the Catholic world should ring daily at noon. They ring still today, in Hungary and elsewhere, though few people know why.

Janos Hunyadi's son King Mathias consolidated Hungary and became known as one of the great renaissance rulers. He and his wife, the Aragonese Princess Beatrice from Naples, invited and sponsored numerous humanists and artists from Italy, bringing about the renaissance flowering in Hungary. History records him commissioning works, now lost, from Verocchio and Filippino Lippi.

Mathias was also called Corvinus, as his coat of arms contained a raven (*corvinus* meaning "of the raven" in Latin). His huge library of classics, the *Bibliotheca Corviniana,* was famous throughout Europe, and at that time was second only to the library of the Medici. The *Corvinas,* the illuminated books he commissioned, have become even more fascinating owing to their gradual disappearance through the centuries. Those that remain are now the coveted possessions of libraries and museums. A few years ago, I was finally able to see two of the *Corvinas* at the Pierpont Morgan Library in New York. Other visitors in the gallery were commenting to their friends about the magnificence and artistry involved in producing the illuminated pages on display. For me, seeing the *Corvinas* was more than just inspecting some old pages. It was the fulfillment of a childhood dream.

The Mathias monument at Kolozsvar's main square was unveiled in 1902. It shows the king in full armor astride his horse, his followers rallying around him. The Hungarian sculptor Janos Fadrusz had won the contest to create the sculpture, and it became celebrated before it was installed in Kolozsvar, when its model won the Grand Prix at the 1900 Paris World Exhibition.

As a small boy passing through the main square with its sparrows, people, and shadows all fleeting by, I found the Mathias monument an amazingly constant presence in rain or shine, at dawn or dusk. Perhaps because of this, I developed a fascination for equestrian sculptures and have since found some supreme examples in Donatello's "Gattamelata" in Padua, the Capitoline Marcus Aurelius, and Verocchio's "Colleoni" in Venice.

The square around the Mathias monument was also the site of the daily *corso*. For about an hour each at noon and before dusk, young women and men would come and parade themselves on the side where the Banffy palace stood. The moon-gray palace seemed to be just the right backdrop, its row of baroque sculptures, pilasters, and urns giving the *corso* a theatrical air. The procession meandered back and forth from the Banffy palace to two other sides of the square. Why it didn't just go round all four sides, no one knew, but as far as everyone could remember, it had always been that way.

There were two pharmacies at the main square. The older one had been there since the 1500's when it first opened as an apothecary shop. It was called Hintz, after the original Saxon family that started and still owned it.

The other pharmacy was a relative latecomer. It was called Biro's, after the Jewish family that first opened it in the 1800's and still owned it. At that time, our good family friend Doctor Geza Biro was running it and lived in the family apartment on the floor above. Unlike the other pharmacy, Biro's was on the one side of the square that missed the *corso* with its daily parade of young women. Every now and then, I would hear Doctor Biro exclaim despondently, "Oh, I would give up anything … anything!… for the *corso* to pass by this side of the square!"

◆§§◆

On Good Fridays, the center of activity would shift from Saint Michael's church to Saint Peter's at the western edge of the town. There was a belief that if you went there on Good Friday and made a wish, it would come true, on the condition that you did not speak or greet anyone before you got back home. Thus, many well-bred people would go to Saint Peter's on Good Friday and seem like the rudest creatures, ignoring friends and relatives alike. Walking home from the church was a strange experience, as if a spell had been cast on the city. Everyone had lost the power of speech, and all you could hear were footsteps, horses galloping, and carriages clattering.

In the afternoons of Good Friday, it was a custom to walk to the end of Monostori Avenue, the town's major road leading east from the main square. *Monostori* in Hungarian means "from the monastery." There had been, just outside Kolozsvar, a monastery founded in 1061. It was a center of pilgrimage, and this was the road that led to that monastery. Long before I was born, only the name of the road and some ruins survived as a reminder of the once rich and famous monastery. It was a tradition to go to these ruins and pray on Good Friday afternoons. It took about an hour and a half to walk from the main square to the ruins and back. The journey back was more animated than the one from Saint Peter's, as there was no superstition against greeting anyone.

One Good Friday, my grandmother Polyxena invited some friends to her house on Monostori Avenue for a snack after the sometimes exhausting walk to the ruins. That was how it all started. By the time I was a little boy, my grandmother was already holding an open house. People streamed in and out of her house and were welcome even if she had never met them. She served all sorts of refreshments, alcoholic and non-alcoholic. The tables carried huge helpings of *kalács*, a special sweet bread of flour, milk, and eggs, similar to the Italian *panettone*. There were also plenty of rolled cakes in the shape of a horseshoe, that came in two varieties, the *mákos patkó* filled with poppy-seed paste, and the *diós patkó*, with nut paste.

I thought there was something strange in this, as all these cakes and breads were made for Easter and Christmas, not for Good Friday, when people were supposed to be fasting. So one Good Friday afternoon, I asked my grandmother, "Why are you serving them when it's not yet Easter?"

My grandmother, in her usual terse and authoritarian manner, answered, "So what? Easter or not, they're still good!"

Saint Michael's church took center stage again on Easter Sunday. To the pealing of bells, the parish priest would take out the golden monstrance and parade it outside the church, a long procession of devotees trailing him. As in most of the Christian world, Easter Sunday was the highlight of the Holy Week, the day families spent together over the thankful feast. My father liked young lamb with tarragon, a rare delicacy, and it was a must on our Easter table. We also had good helpings of the cakes and sweet breads seen at my grandmother's house on Good Friday, as well as *kürtös kalács*, a glazed bread cooked in the form of a horn.

For youngsters in Kolozsvar, Easter Monday was even more special. The night before this day, many a girl would lie sleepless in bed, get up and look herself over in the mirror, then try to sleep again.

For it was on Easter Monday that young men carrying bottles of rose-water would go to the houses of all the girls they cared about. The girls would be waiting in the drawing room, wondering who might be visiting them that day. The boys would come knocking, and as soon as they entered, they would make a declaration that went like this: "There are

some lovely flowers in this house. I have come to sprinkle
them so that they may remain fresh." Or just simply, "I
would like to water you."

The girls would all burst out giggling and the boys would
sprinkle them with rose-water, causing the girls to erupt in
even greater convulsions of merriment and feigned surprise.
Then the girls would serve the Easter breads and cakes and
sometimes a boy would pay special attention to a certain
girl.

The girls would then give their guests Easter eggs to take
home. Traditionally, Easter eggs had been painted only in
solid red. By then, the girls had already strayed from tradition and were decorating the eggs in all kinds of colors,
which many an old lady claimed had caused shock and dismay not too long ago.

· II ·

the chocolate hussar

ACROSS THE SQUARE from our apartment stood the huge 18th century Banffy palace. The Baron and Baroness Banffy lived there and set aside a small portion of the palace for commercial and civic use. On the ground floor was a military officers' club, a bank, and Layda's, the best pastry shop in the whole city.

My sister Baba and I loved to run across the square to this destination where we learned the words for the most interesting smells and visions, like macaroons, linzer tarts, Sacher tortes, candied pineapples, *dobos tortes* (a Hungarian specialty of glazed crust and chocolate cream filling), and *krémes béles* (the Hungarian version of Napoleon cakes).

One day, when my sister was eight years old, she and her friend Margit spent the afternoon treating themselves at Layda's. However, when they asked for the bill, they found out they didn't have enough money.

"Stay here while I go home and ask for money," my sister told her friend.

In the meantime, the friend, whom everybody called Kicsi Margit, "Little Margaret," to distinguish her from my cousin "Big Margaret," decided she wanted to order another pastry. So when my sister got back, they still didn't have enough to pay the bill.

"I shall go home and get more money," said Margit to my sister. She ran home to her mother, the Countess Horvath-Toldy. But when she got back, they still didn't have enough as my sister had meanwhile eaten more cookies.

So my sister told her friend, "I shall go get my parents. But listen," she warned as she left, "you must stop eating!"

My sister came back with my parents right behind. My parents paid the bill. They were so amused they couldn't bring themselves to scold the girls.

◆◦§◦◆

On the floor above Layda's pastry shop, also in the Banffy palace, was the gentleman's club where my father Elemer went every afternoon to read the foreign journals and play a game of cards or chess.

My father had a passion for chess. Before he got married, he traveled all over Hungary to play with the masters, and became known as one of the best chess players in the country. He taught me chess even before I learned to read and write. Every now and then, he would tell me stories of the great chess masters. He gave me my own chess set and I would often bring it to the playground in my grandmother's garden to find someone to play with.

There were many avid chess players at the gentlemen's club, but no one could beat my father. So anyone who played opposite him was seen as the underdog and naturally got everybody's support.

My father also loved to play practical jokes. There is a term for this in Hungarian, *ugratás*, "to make people jump." One day, my father thought of collaborating on an *ugratás* with his cousin Marci (pronounced Már-tsee). Uncle Marci, a judge and my father's cousin, was also a member of the gentlemen's club. In all the years he went to the club, he never played chess, as he did not know even the basic moves.

My father proposed to teach Uncle Marci not just the moves, but also one of the most spectacular chess games ever, one played by the chess master Paul Morphy, who lived in New Orleans in the mid-nineteenth century.

My father told me that Morphy was one of the greatest chess players in history. On a couple of occasions, Morphy faced eight professional players simultaneously. He played with a handicap: unlike his opponents, he was blindfolded. He won the match without touching any of the pieces. He stunned the chess world when he beat all three European grand masters in the space of six months, then at the end of the last match stood up and announced that he was retiring from championship chess.

The Morphy game my father wanted Uncle Marci to learn was a complicated one that took hours to play. As Uncle Marci didn't know chess to begin with, it took him months before he could even start to memorize the Morphy game.

In the meantime, they began performing their rehearsed dialogue at the gentlemen's club. My father would challenge Uncle Marci to a chess game, and he would dismiss my father with a wave of his hand, saying, "Why should I? I'll surely beat you. So why waste my time?"

This seemed strange to everyone, as no one had ever seen Uncle Marci play chess. They would say, "Beat Elemer? You must be joking!"

"Well, if you really want a match, so be it," Uncle Marci finally said.

So it was arranged that he and my father would face each other in a chess game at the Banffy palace.

But as the date drew near, Uncle Marci was having trouble remembering the game, so my father had to devise secret signals to give him. I would watch my father teach him the signals, which became almost as complicated as the chess moves themselves. For example, if my father tapped on the table and said, "I can't believe it," Uncle Marci should move the knight backward, or if my father scratched his cheek twice and said "Oh, God!" it would mean moving the castle so many squares to the side.

The night of the game arrived. My father and Uncle Marci wanted to put on a big show, but Uncle Marci became very worried about mixing up the moves. My father was concerned that all the months of preparation would come to nothing, the elaborate *ugratás* would fall flat on its face.

I wanted to see the game, but it was impossible. No child or lady was ever allowed to cross the threshold of the gentlemen's club. So I waited all night to find out what happened.

My father came back. He said that as expected, the crowd rooted for the underdog. They cheered Uncle Marci as he won piece after piece in the first hour of the match. Then the match started to go the other way. People patted Uncle Marci on the back, urging him on. But he just kept losing pieces, to the crowd's disappointment.

"Don't worry, I'll still win this game," Uncle Marci said.

Then, Uncle Marci lost the queen. The crowd groaned.

Suddenly, Uncle Marci moved a pawn, revealing Morphy's elaborate trap. It was a checkmate.

The crowd was speechless.

Then the hall burst out in cheers.

"Incredible!"

"Finally! Someone who could beat Elemer!"

"When is the next game!?"

Everyone was cheering the victor, but it was my father who was the happiest of all. The *ugratás* was a success!

Then, Uncle Marci stood up and, wiping the sweat from his brow, declared, "This is my last chess game. I want to retire a champion!"

◆⟩§⟨◆

When my maternal grandfather Zsigmond Purjesz, the physician, retired from his position in the university, he and my grandmother Paula moved to Budapest and left their house on 15 Monostori Avenue to my mother. So we moved when I was five from our apartment by the main square to our new home five blocks away.

It was an L-shaped townhouse of natural off-white stone. Its tile roof had turned brown with age. Like most houses in Kolozsvar and in countries like Italy and Spain, its front wall was also the house wall, with the windows of the elevated first floor looking down directly on the street. One gained entry through an iron grill gate that led to a side driveway and the house portal. A foyer opened into the drawing room with its huge fireplace and windows that looked out to the courtyard and garden which were behind the house, as was the case with all townhouses in Kolozsvar. Fresh-cut flowers and Caucasian and Persian carpets brightened the rooms.

Three connected rooms facing the street became the office of my father, my father's bedroom, and my mother's bedroom. Books lined all four walls of my father's bedroom. In winter, a fireplace burned warmly in my mother's bedroom, where a whole wall was also lined with books.

A huge mahogany table stood in the middle of the dining room. There was a lion-topped silver coffer containing cubes of sugar that I filched every now and then. A room beside the dining room became the children's room, that is, my sister Baba's and mine. It was connected to another one that looked out to the courtyard, and this became the room of our governess, Miss Pedley.

The foyer had a staircase leading to an elevated basement that had windows all around. I would sometimes climb down and prowl through its storage rooms of potatoes, cabbages, flour, carrots, firewood, coal, and my father's old documents; pass through the bedrooms of our cook Ilona, and our manservant's; watch a chair being repaired in a carpentry shop; or wait at the kitchen table for the first bite of a pastry from Ilona.

Behind the house was my grandmother's garden. When my grandmother moved into the house, she worked with a man who had laid out big gardens in Transylvania, and demanded of him something that looked like a park.

I would slip out to the garden through a dining room door to a terrace and run down some steps that led to a courtyard with a round flower bed half as wide as the courtyard and filled with tropical cannas and other blooms. A tall, perfectly symmetrical linden tree presided from a corner of the courtyard. At the courtyard's southern edge grew clumps of Japanese quince and lilac trees that were arranged like a half-parted curtain to reveal a lawn. The lawn was one of the most popular places in the garden for my playmates and me, as it was a wide open space where we could run and fall unimpeded. In the middle of the lawn stood a broad round group of rose trees (not bushes, as they had long trunks and grew to up six feet tall). On either side of the lawn were gravel walks that continued all the way to the end of the garden.

A band of pine trees dripping with ivy brought up the rear of the lawn. To the right of the pine trees stood a swing with two seats in the middle of a sand-filled playground. When we were not dodging children screaming on the swing, my friends and I would be building castles in the sand or playing hide-and-seek in the thicket of pine trees.

I would always leave the playground at around 5 o'clock and run through a pathway skirting the pine trees. I would reach the other side of the garden, in a clearing surrounded by pine trees, where my mother and her guests would be seated on wooden benches and chairs around a stone table that held my destination—the plate of homemade cookies that my mother always served with the tea.

It was my mother's practice to hold tea every day, including Christmas and Easter. At least a dozen guests were always on hand. On cold or rainy days, she served tea in the drawing room. Otherwise, she always held it at the stone table where the honey smell of the cookies mixed with the pine. I would take two or three cookies and eat them standing up before running back to the playground.

Beyond the pine grove, jasmine and rose bushes stood in a semicircle around wooden benches. On a fine summer day, their scent would drift through the rosemary, parsley, and tarragon clumps in the adjacent patch of herbs and vegetables. A cluster of yellow cherry, apple, and pear trees cast shadows in the middle of the patch. A band of red cherry trees brought up the rear of the garden. It was here on these trees that I would often climb and nibble away a red and yellow summer afternoon under the clear blue sky.

My sister and I often found plenty of playmates in the garden, as my parents welcomed the children of their friends, many of whom resided in apartments without gardens. Eva was one of the children who often came to the garden. Her father, Miklos Krenner, a writer and professor of Hungarian literature, was a classmate of my father's. Eva's mother belonged to an old aristocratic family whose fortunes had disappeared. She died while Eva was still a toddler. So Eva's father brought his daughter to the house every day and she became for us a sort of younger sister whom we enjoyed trundling around.

Another girl who often came to our garden was Irenke. Though she was my aunt, she was actually only a few months older than me. After Irenke's father died, her mother remained despondent for months and hardly left her house. My grandmother Polyxena, who was the lady's cousin, went over and urged her to stop lamenting. She offered to take Irenke to our house in the meanwhile, and that was how I first met her.

Irenke was a very musical child and later went to Budapest to study with Bela Bartok. He offered her a teaching position at the Ferencz Liszt Academy but she chose to come back to Kolozsvar to marry and to teach music. She has remained in Kolozsvar since then. We are now both in our nineties and we still write each other regularly. I send her coffee beans and chocolates every three months. In exchange, I get the loveliest letters from her, often about relatives and friends who have passed away but who come to life again through her memories. Irenke's are the only handwritten letters I can read easily without the aid of my glasses, for her handwriting remains firm, flowing, and precise, like that of a youthful woman.

Another of my playmates was Denes Banffy, the son of the Baron and Baroness Banffy. The Banffys were both past forty when their only child Denes was born, and of course right away he became the darling of the family.

Denes Banffy was unusually cultured and intelligent. He was not, however, friendly with other children. I was an exception, even though he was two or three years older than me. One reason was that we both had English governesses. There were hardly any other English persons in Kolozsvar, so our governesses often saw each other, with Denes and me in tow.

When Denes reached his tenth year, he wanted a hussar soldier made of chocolate for his birthday. Nothing was easier than to go to the pastry shop on the first floor of his parents' palace and order it.

When he went to pick it up the next day, he rejected it.

"But this is not a hussar!" he exclaimed. "The uniform is all wrong!"

"Well," the proprietor said, "come back tomorrow and we'll have it for you."

But every time, for almost a month, he refused what they gave him. There were always mistakes, in the hat, the sword, the anatomy, or some other detail.

Finally, the pastry chef brought out a chocolate hussar that was unbelievably detailed.

"It's perfect!" Denes exclaimed.

"I'm so happy you like it," the proprietor told him. He came back with a box and said, "You must be very careful when you take it home."

"Oh, no!" Denes stopped him. "Please don't pack it. I will eat it here right now."

◄◌§◌►

Miss Pedley, our governess, was a warm-hearted lady with long brown hair and a heart-shaped face. She was small in stature and looked frail but she was actually a courageous young woman with a strong will. She desired to see the world, but not having the means, she chose to take postings as governess, which enabled her to travel to foreign countries.

Most of the governesses in Kolozsvar were German-speaking ladies from Austria or Germany. There were a few French governesses, most of them stationed with titled families. Aside from us, I knew of only two other families with English governesses.

Miss Pedley did not speak much Hungarian. My sister and I had to learn English, as she had many interesting stories to tell. She would relate things she heard when she was a girl in England, about a boy who found a house made of cookies, or a girl who almost got eaten by a wolf. At other times, she would tell us about London, where she lived, and how it had a river full of ships that went to all parts of the world where the English lived with the natives, to India and Africa, Arabia and Malaya, Persia and China.

Miss Pedley went back to England when the First World War broke out. She married an Englishman and settled in London. My mother always made sure that my sister and I wrote her regularly.

Decades later, after two World Wars and the Communist takeover of Eastern Europe, my sister settled in Italy, and

I in the United States. Miss Pedley outlived her husband and had no children.

One summer, my sister invited Miss Pedley to her seaside house in Formia, between Naples and Rome. I went to fetch her at the airport in Rome. I was afraid I would not recognize her. But when she arrived, I immediately saw the same dreamy look she had as a young lady in Kolozsvar. My sister and Miss Pedley held each other's hands as soon as they met, and I remembered the time when my sister and I could leave the house only by holding onto Miss Pedley's hand.

Miss Pedley came back to Formia several times. We would often sit on the terrace overlooking the sea, warm ourselves with tea to the sound of the crickets, and every now and then tell each other about the Kolozsvar that we knew.

· III ·

guest family

At the turn of the century, Kolozsvar was a center along with Budapest of *belle époque* cultural life in Hungary. Budapest was the grander and more frenetic city, whereas Kolozsvar was considered the more graceful and felicitous.

My mother had a knack for gathering professors, scientists, and artists, and she became known for her literary and artistic salon in Kolozsvar. At our house on Monostori Avenue, there was an implicit invitation that anyone who came for tea could stay right through dinner. And so it became the practice of our cook Ilona that at five o'clock every day, she would send somebody to get the number of people staying for dinner that night.

One of the visitors to our house was the Hungarian painter Marcel Vertes, who later settled in Paris where he became successful as a lithographer, decorative painter, and illustrator of books that included the first editions of *La Vagabonde* and *Chéri* by Colette. One time before the First World War, he sent my mother a card from Paris, an original design by him. The card was addressed simply to "Olga, Kolozsvar." At the turn of the century Kolozsvar, with its 60,000 citizens, was by no means a small city. Still, the card made its way to my mother in due time. Vertes' little experiment succeeded, showing how good the postal service was at the beginning of the century in Kolozsvar. With the postal service nowadays, you may write the full name and the complete address, but if you go wrong on just one digit, chances are your letter will not make it or will do so only weeks or months later, after a detour back to the sender.

My mother, *née* Olga Purjesz, was one of the few Hungarian women found under her own name in the Hungarian Encyclopedia that came out just after the First World War. Her entry listed her as "Mrs. Elemer Ovary," something at which many women today would take umbrage. The encyclopedia cited her as the woman who created a lively salon in Transylvania, similar to those found in France in the nineteenth century, that became known as a second home to writers, scientists, and artists.

The life of her salon still resonates now, in guidebooks of the city and in newspaper articles such as the one in the April 3, 1997 issue of *Szabadság:* "In this house on Monostori Avenue, she created a literary and artistic salon, increasing the wide circle of friends of her father and mother. Here the poet Ady, Bartok, Dohnanyi, Moricz, Aladar Kuncz, and Sandor Hunyadi came very often. Even between the First and Second World Wars, the salon was very much frequented."

When I was about five years old, I started calling all these friends "guest family." Others picked up the name, calling each other members of the same "guest family." The name stuck and later entered Hungarian literature through the memory book *Családi könyv (Family Book)* by the novelist Sandor Hunyadi.

Without knowing it, I learned religious tolerance early in childhood from the "guest family."

Anti-Semitism, for centuries a simmering presence in Europe, had reached a boiling point in the late nineteenth century with the Dreyfus Affair, when a Jewish French army officer, Alfred Dreyfus, was convicted of treason as a spy for Germany and imprisoned in Devil's Island in the Atlantic Ocean. Many people were convinced he was innocent and,

years later, were able to prove their case and obtain his ac-
quittal. In the meantime, the affair whipped up a new wave
of anti-Semitism across Europe. Even after Dreyfus' exon-
eration, many anti-Semites clung to their hatred of the Jewish army officer and his defenders. For other people, the
whole affair exposed the irrationality and injustice of the
anti-Semitism that most of society had always taken for
granted.

In Austria-Hungary, the emperor Ferencz Jozsef, far
from being anti-Semitic, promoted and ennobled many Jews.
The empress Elisabeth took her lessons in Hungarian language and tradition from Miksa Falk, an eminent Jewish
scholar. Many of their subjects followed their enlightened
example, even though Ferencz Jozsef himself was as unpopular in independence-loving Hungary as his pro-Hungarian
wife was universally loved.

At my mother's salon, no one ever asked about the religious background of any person who wanted to join. Much
later, in the thirties, I learned that nearly half of our guest
family were Jewish or of Jewish origin.

We often had evenings of chamber music in our house.
The most popular works were string quartets by Beethoven,
Schubert and Mozart. Though Kolozsvar had a resident
orchestra, it played only for operas, not symphonic music. It
was before the era of the phonograph and the radio. The
only way for people in Kolozsvar to get acquainted with
symphonic music was to play it on the piano. Symphonies
were transcribed for piano for four hands and sold as music
sheets. The music available in stores was almost totally from
the romantic and classical periods, hardly anything from the
baroque. My mother and her friends used to play duo-piano
arrangements of Brahms symphonies together. The first
time I heard Beethoven's Ninth Symphony was as a work
for piano for four hands.

To listen to orchestral performances, one had to go to

Budapest. Nonetheless, famous soloists and chamber groups made their way to Kolozsvar. It became a custom that any prominent musician who gave a recital at the Kolozsvar Theater would pay a visit to our address on Monostori Avenue. This was how I met such musicians as Pablo Casals, Ernest von Dohnanyi, Bela Bartok, and Zoltan Kodaly.

Dohnanyi was a man of medium height but he always appeared taller in his well-tailored, impeccably-pressed suits. Even before he became famous as a composer, he had already made several tours throughout Europe and the United States as one of the world's top pianists. He had a prodigious musical memory and always played by heart, an extremely unusual practice for pianists before the First World War.

Dohnanyi became very much in demand as a composer, after the success of his "Variations on a Nursery Theme." The nation often commissioned him to write pieces for public celebrations. Dohnanyi also worked as conductor, teacher and music school director. He was so busy, he would sometimes mix up schedules and repertoires. Once, after a recital at the Kolozsvar theater, he was meeting his well-wishers in the backstage area when a lady shook his hand and exclaimed, "Maestro it was wonderful!"

"Thank you!" he said.

"Well, the carriage is waiting outside, whenever you're ready," the lady said.

"I'm sorry, I don't quite understand. Ready for what?"

"Remember, maestro, you're having an after-concert supper at my place!"

"Oh!" Dohnanyi exclaimed, "But I am already having supper at Mrs. Ovary's!"

My mother and I happened to be backstage as well. Overhearing Dohnanyi and the lady, my mother helped them avoid embarrassment by going to the lady and saying warmly, "But of course you're always welcome at my house!"

So the lady ended up taking supper with the maestro in our house instead.

Once, at another recital, Dohnanyi came out and sat down at the piano. He paused, then asked the stage manager, "Please, could I have a copy of the program."

The stage manager gave him the program and he read it. Then he told the audience, "I'm sorry, but I just arrived from a long trip. And I just want to make sure that I am not mistaking tonight's program with another!" Then he amazed everyone by performing the whole night's recital with nothing but the program in front of him.

Bartok, who was five years younger than Dohnanyi, also played everything from memory, with the exception of his own music, for which he always used a handwritten or printed score.

In contrast to Dohnanyi, Bartok seemed to me a remarkably closed and distant man. I never heard him start a conversation, though he would always answer politely whenever anyone asked him something.

In Hungary, people who knew each other well used the second person (like the French *toi*) instead of the customary third person (the equivalent of *vous* in French). I never heard Bartok use the second person. My cousin, a composer named Sandor Veress, who now lives in Switzerland, was a student of Bartok's. He told me that even with his students, Bartok always used the third person, which no other professor did.

Bartok always seemed full of hesitations and worries. But whenever he sat down at the piano, it seemed that all traces of self-consciousness would vanish. I remember him playing his piano piece, the *Allegro Barbaro*. I had never heard this kind of music before and was struck by its audacity. It was in complete contrast to the shy man I knew. I find it interesting that people nowadays still find the piece audacious.

Bartok gave his first recital in Kolozsvar in the early 1920's when he played some sonatas by Domenico Scarlatti.

It was the first time Scarlatti was heard in Kolozsvar as far as anyone knew. The recital was a great success. It got many people wondering if there were any other composers from Scarlatti's time who were also forgotten and needed to be rediscovered. At that time, much of the music from the baroque period had disappeared from concert programs, and it was thought that they were arcane works, primitive and inexpressive. I would hear the Scarlatti sonatas in many different incarnations in later years, including some excellent authentic period interpretations on the harpsichord. Yet Scarlatti will always be associated in my mind with this sad-eyed composer from Transylvania who is the very exemplar of modernism.

I found Pablo Casals to be a gentle, good-natured man. He always seemed a little nervous just before a recital. But once he began, he gave the impression of total command. His reputation preceded him. He had traveled all over Europe and the United States and was hailed as the greatest cellist of the time and perhaps of all time. He had discovered new ways of making sounds from the cello. For example, he started the practice of using two fingers (the shift) instead of one (the slide) in order to produce a cleaner legato. He also found a way of using the bow to make the cello's higher registers comparable to the violin's in lightness and intensity. As a soloist and as part of the famous Cortot–Thibaud–Casals Trio, he was responsible for rediscovering and establishing many great works in the chamber music repertoire. I had the privilege of hearing Casals play Bach's six unaccompanied cello suites. At a time when available music was almost totally from the romantic and classical periods, hearing the older baroque music, with its cleaner, more sober lines, seemed to me a very modern experience.

Despite his reputation, Casals was the exact opposite of the flamboyant soloist. He saw himself more as an interpreter than a virtuoso, which was an innovation at the beginning of the century. Many musicians were to follow his example, and in this way Casals deeply influenced the course of music in the twentieth century.

Casals was intensely attached to his Spanish homeland, and in particular to his birthplace, Catalonia. I always saw him as a mild-mannered man except whenever he talked about Spain. His opposition to Franco and his decision to leave Spain is well known. But he once told me something that made me see another side of his nationalism. It was during the Spanish civil war and we happened to be both on the same train going to Hungary, he for recitals and I for vacation from medical studies in Paris. Casals was carrying a newspaper with front-page stories about the war in Spain. He turned to me and exclaimed, "What is happening in Spain is horrible! Both sides don't understand that with all this fighting, they are destroying Spain itself!"

Zoltan Kodaly, so admired for his *Psalmus Hungaricus* and solemn ballads, I found a light-hearted and witty person. He was often on the lookout for ways to tease others. Once, there was a major Kodaly celebration held at the Kolozsvar Theater. A distant relative of mine, a beautiful soprano named Elizabeth Torok, sang Kodaly songs in the first part of the concert. During the intermission she came to our box, where Kodaly was sitting, and I made the introductions. She was dying to find out what the composer thought of her performance. But Kodaly kept a stone-faced silence.

Then she asked, "Maestro, I sang badly!?"

An uneasy silence hung in our box as Kodaly refused to answer her. My cousin drooped with disappointment. Suddenly, Kodaly's face lighted up in a smile. He grasped her hands warmly and exclaimed, "It's you, not I, who said it!"

⟡

Another remarkable member of the "guest family" was my
godmother, the Baroness Karola Bornemissza. (The name
Bornemissza has become well-known internationally because of the art collector, Baron Johan-Heinrich Thyssen-
Bornemisza, who not too long ago sold his art collection to
the Spanish government for $350 million. The baron's father
had married into the same family, but somewhere along the
way this branch had dropped an "s" from the name and
found its way to the Netherlands and Switzerland.) The
Bornemisszas were of the high Transylvanian aristocracy,
descendants of the princes who ruled Transylvania after the
Battle of Mohacs in 1526, when Transylvania separated from
Hungary and became an independent principality.

Everyone found my godmother a striking person. Although her features were somehow too angular, she radiated
not severity but soft beauty. She was known as one of the
most elegantly-dressed women in all of Austria-Hungary.
She had exceptional knowledge of literature and the arts. She
spoke Hungarian, German, French, English and Italian. She
spent the two hottest months every year in her favorite city,
Venice, where all the old Venetian families received her.

I had no idea of her aristocratic background until I grew
up. This was because she always related to me in an informal manner, which was unusual between an adult and a
younger person at that time. And as a small boy, I was less
impressed by all her knowledge and culture than by one of
her adventures.

In 1912, when Louis Bleriot, the French airplane inventor,
visited Budapest she went there to witness the first airplane
flight in Hungary. She then told her husband, the Baron
Elemer Bornemissza, that she would like to fly up with
Bleriot.

The Baron went and spoke to Bleriot. However, Bleriot
could not imagine taking up a private person and, of all the
most bizarre notions, a woman at that! He didn't want to

make a direct refusal, so he quoted the out-of-this-world charge of 10,000 crowns in gold.

The Baron said that he was not in the habit of carrying this amount of money, but if Bleriot would wait for half-an-hour, he would send somebody to his bank. Bleriot could not believe it, but in half-an-hour, he got the sum he quoted. This was how my godmother became the first woman in the world ever to fly. At that time, this was seen as a great leap forward for women's rights!

When the First World War started, my godmother decided to train in nursing. So she went to the head of the surgery department of the university, whom she knew, as they were both members of the guest family. A few weeks after volunteering, she was already assisting the surgeons as an instrumentalist nurse. The instrumentalist nurse's job, as the title implied, was to anticipate the surgeon's moves and hand him the correct instruments without any loss of time, a crucial job when scores of wounded and dying people were waiting outside the operating room.

She enlisted in the field army hospital and was sent to the Russian front. She stayed there for two years and afterwards got highly decorated. As was typical of her, she never boasted about this, or mentioned any of the hardships she had gone through.

We had an extendable dining table at home so that it could accommodate whomever of the guest family would stay for dinner. My mother sat at one end and my father at the other. I would always sit at the left side of my father; and my sister Magda, whom everyone called Baba, at my mother's left or, when there were many guests, at my father's right. The seating arrangement was a very important part of the ritual, and something I have punctiliously carried over from the old world, which some friends find amusing in these more informal times.

My godmother loved coming to the discussions at the

dinner table. Some people in town criticized her for not staying at home in the evening, like a proper woman. But she had very strong beliefs about the rights of women and of individuals. By the 1920's, she was coming to dine with us every single night except when she was away in Venice or Budapest. My mother always reserved the place of honor for her, the seat to the right. She became so much a part of our evenings, our other guests would ask about her health whenever she could not be with us for dinner.

Jolan, another regular member of the guest family, worked as a clerk at the Hungarian agricultural office. She had a beak-like nose and unusually small eyes that were always red. She never got married. After work, she would often come to our house to be with others who shared a passion for art and literature. She and my sister became the closest of friends.

Jolan lived with her mother and half-sister in a house two blocks away from ours. When the half-sister got married, the mother gave her the house. It became too crowded for Jolan and she decided to move out.

Facing the courtyard to the left of our house, there was a small separate building. It had three modest one-room apartments that my mother rented out. Jolan moved in as soon as one became available. Like the Baroness Bornemissza, Jolan took her dinner every night with us.

Jolan was one of those people who never made a living out of her outstanding talents. She worked for a pittance at the agricultural office and after work threw herself into her reading, music, and dance. She took piano lessons from the Maestra Valeria Donogan, who declared her to be one of her best students ever. She would often go to the parlor in the afternoon and play a Mozart serenade or Chopin nocturne just for herself, and everyone would stop what they were doing to listen. She was also an accomplished classical dancer. Unfortunately, there was no ballet troupe in town for her to join and develop her talent. At a time when phonographs were almost non-existent, it was not easy to find music to dance to. This did not stop her, and I would often find her in our courtyard joyfully dancing in silence.

Another member of our guest family, the Count Miklos Banffy, was of the same clan (but a different branch) as Denes Banffy of the chocolate hussar. Count Banffy was what people would call a renaissance man. He was an able architect and designed, with Karoly Koos, an elegant Calvinist church on Monostori avenue. It was built in 1913, and like all Calvinist churches in Hungary had a cock instead of a cross on its steeple, recalling the three times that St. Peter betrayed Jesus before the cock's crow. That same year, Count Banffy got a post as intendant (a combination of impresario, artistic director, and administrator) of the National Theater in Budapest. When Charles IV, the last king of Hungary, was crowned in Budapest in 1916, he and Karoly Koos organized the pageantry.

One of the guests at the crowning ceremony was the Countess Agnes Teleki, whom everyone in Kolozsvar called Aunt Ani. She lived across the street from us and was the mother of my childhood playmate Adam. She was a good friend of my mother but was not a member of the guest family. Meetings at my mother's drawing room always happened in the evening, and she, like most women of the time, considered it her duty to be in her own home. However, her son Adam, who later studied to be a Calvinist pastor but did not practice, became a regular member of the guest family.

For the crowning ceremony in Budapest, the Countess Teleki naturally wanted to look her best. She took out an heirloom, an antique pearl necklace, and wore it to the event. It so happened that her pearls were much larger and more brilliant than those of Queen Zita, the wife of Charles IV. At that time, it was a sacred anathema for ladies to ever wear costume jewelry. Until cultured pearls appeared on the market after the First World War, perfectly round pearls were extremely rare. They were more valuable than diamonds, for many centuries. Queen Zita was very much displeased about the Countess Teleki's necklace and told her ladies-in-waiting how uncomfortable it made her feel during the ceremony. Afterwards, the ladies-in-waiting told the Countess how upset she had made the Queen. They all laughed and relished this little footnote to the coronation.

The pageantry that Count Banffy organized was a great success. However, no one knew then that Charles IV would become the last of the Habsburg rulers. After the First World War, Banffy became the Hungarian Foreign Minister. He was good at drawing and painting, and he showed me the instant sketches and caricatures he made of the heads of state at the first conference of the League of Nations in Geneva. I was in awe of the endless ways he could express himself. He published many books as a writer, including one of the best Hungarian novels, the trilogy *Megszámláltattál, Megmérettél, Könnyűnek találtattál* (*Ye Have Been Weighed in the Balance and Found Wanting*) which chronicled the decline of the Hungarian aristocracy.

Count Banffy raised horses that were very well looked after. Whenever he sold a horse, he would always make a contract that when the horse got injured or became too old and the owner did not want to keep it anymore, the horse must be returned to him. He kept these useless horses in his estate since, as he put it, "They are also members of my family."

Not all the writers in the guest family were as well-placed as Banffy. In fact, most of them were the ever-proverbially struggling artist. And they liked gathering together, if not always for the company, for the meals and the drinks. After the First World War, they and some other writers founded the Helicon of Marosvecs, a free association of Hungarian writers in Transylvania. They got the name from the castle owned by one of the members, Janos Kemeny, where they held a conference every year.

The Helicon was very active and a number of its members eventually went on to publish successful books. In addition to Miklos Banffy, the group included writers who are now part of Hungary's literary pantheon, most notably Karoly Koos, Aron Tamasi, Iren Gulacsy, Sandor Hunyadi, and Aladar Kuncz.

Kuncz, a great admirer of French literature, was one of the struggling writers. He came often to my mother's salon and he gave me my first copy of Marcel Proust's *Du Coté de Chez Swann* as my graduation gift from college in 1924.

Some years later, when I was in Paris, I managed to repay him for introducing me to French literature. I was a young doctor working at the Pasteur Institute in the early thirties when I met Jacques de Lacretelle, an influential writer and later a member of the French Academy, and I got him interested in the work of Kuncz.

Just before the First World War, upon receiving a scholarship to study French literature, Kuncz left Kolozsvar for Paris. He was holidaying in Brittany when the war broke out. At that time, Hungary and France were not yet at war, and Austro-Hungarian nationals were promised safe passage to Switzerland. But they were instead placed in a prison camp on Noirmoutier ("black monastery"), an island in the Atlantic named after a monastery established in the seventh century by monks in black cassocks.

Kuncz and other Hungarian civilians spent the next five years in stifling captivity. He later wrote a novel, named *A fekete kolostor (Black Monastery)*, based on his experiences. It is a moving work that shows how some of the civilian captives discovered spiritual strength and how others broke down and lost their sense of reality.

I translated the first chapter of Kuncz's novel and gave it to Jacques de Lacretelle. It excited him and he found a publisher for it.[1]

Unfortunately, Aladar Kuncz died before the French edition was published. Members of the guest family lamented that this lover of French literature could never see the French edition of his novel, but took solace in speaking of him with pride.

---

[1] The novel was later translated into English as *Black Monastery*. The *Oxford History of Hungarian Literature* cites *A fekete kolostor* as "one of the greatest narratives of captivity written in any language."

· IV ·

street of the wolf

SUMMERS IN TRANSYLVANIA before the First World War, I would travel with the rest of the family to our country house in the Banffy mountains, some fifty miles from Kolozsvar. The journey took a whole day, in horse carriages for the first forty miles, then atop small mountain horses for the last ten. One time, my father hired an automobile for the first part of the trip. It caused a sensation. Everyone stopped what they were doing and ran out into the streets to watch the horseless carriage that moved at the incredible speed of 20 miles per hour.

Our country house was part of a community founded by some university professors and other citizens from Kolozsvar. Everybody knew everyone else and felt completely safe with each other. The community, called Magura, smelled of pine. The houses stood in the middle of pine forests and were all made of pine wood. There was an artificial swimming pool that held the reflection of pine trees. But it mostly remained empty, for even in summer it was usually too cold to swim.

Our family always spent a whole month in the Banffy mountains each summer. I took my toys and books with me from Kolozsvar. My father continued working with his law business even while on holiday. We would often take long walks in the woods in the afternoon or twilight, learning to distinguish edible mushrooms from poisonous ones, and gathering flowers for the house which was decorated with original Toulouse-Lautrec posters. These were huge lithograph posters, about 12 by 10 feet, that my father got when he visited Paris before his marriage.

The entire community, including our house and the Toulouse-Lautrec posters, was burned down by Romanians soon after Transylvania was given to the Romanian kingdom by the Treaty of Trianon in 1920. None of the owners ever got anywhere with their legal claims. The new Romanian government was aware the houses had been owned by Hungarians and it refused to follow up on any investigations.

⋘§⋙

There was then a small colony of Armenians in Kolozsvar and in some other pockets of Transylvania. These Armenians had found their way to Transylvania through Turkey, where they prospered but then had to flee Ottoman persecution. My paternal grandmother Polyxena descended from these Armenian immigrants.

Very near Kolozsvar was a small city, Szamosujvar, famous for two things: its Armenian garlic sausage, and the Rubens Madonna that could be seen in the town's principal Catholic church. The painting was given to the Armenian community by Maria Theresia, "King of Hungary."

How the Empress of Austria became the King of Hungary was due to the maneuverings of her father Charles III. Charles had no male heirs and the Hungarian constitution did not allow for female monarchs. He therefore issued a decree that his eldest daughter was the equivalent of a male heir. (Yes, kings are different from you and me.)

As for the painting, the Armenians had lent some money to Maria Theresia that she could not pay back. She proposed that they should ask for a favor instead. So they asked her to give them the Rubens painting. Maria Theresia was not amused and gave up the painting only with the greatest reluctance.

There was a Catholic church in Sepsiszentgyorgy, another city near Kolozsvar with a huge Armenian settlement. On the outside of the church stood several baroque statues of saints, like ghostly guards. The hands of all the saints were turned inwards, in a gesture not of giving but receiving. People would describe the proverbial frugality of the Armenians with the saying "Even the saints at Sepsiszentgyorgy have their hands turned inwards." The Armenians, most of whom were prosperous, all spoke Hungarian; hardly anyone knew Armenian. Most of them were intense Hungarian patriots, but until late in the 19th century, they all intermarried among themselves.

There were exceptions of course. My grandmother Polyxena Vikol being one, as she had married Kelemen Ovary, who was Hungarian. Another example was the Countess Rhedey, who was pure Armenian and married the Hungarian Count Ladislas. Their daughter Claudine married Alexander, Duke of Teck, and this union produced a son who became the father of Mary, the future wife of England's King George V. The English reigning family therefore has some Hungarian-Armenian blood.

In the early twenties, Eva Laszlo, a second cousin of mine on the paternal side, sent a letter to Queen Mary. She wrote that the Countess Rhedey's mother, and therefore the queen's great-great-grandmother, was buried in the land that Eva's family had owned. This land, which was thousands of acres in size, had however been expropriated, along with the family mausoleum, by the new Romanian government, after the Treaty of Trianon transferred Transylvania to the Romanian kingdom in 1920.

Eva pointed out to Queen Mary that they had a common ancestor in Countess Rhedey's mother. She was asking Queen Mary to intervene so that the mausoleum and the land it stood on should be given back to its former owners. Eva did not expect that her letter would be read, but when one is desperate, one tries everything.

Queen Mary had distinct connections to Queen Marie of Romania. Both grew up in the same circles in England and were both about the same age. Marie had been promised to become the wife of the English prince George, who was not in immediate succession to the throne. However, George ended up marrying Mary, Princess of Teck, after the ambitious Marie chose the crown prince of Romania instead. To Marie's dismay and regret, an unforseen death then brought George and Mary the crowns of the British Empire.

In any case, Queen Mary wrote to Queen Marie about my cousin's request. Queen Marie intervened and, as a result, the mausoleum and the land it stood on were returned to my cousin's family. So my cousin got her wish. But not in the way she meant in her letter to Queen Mary. For the only land that was given back was the piece on which the mausoleum itself stood. She got nothing else, not even a portion of the surrounding land. So here was my cousin, with a mausoleum she now had to maintain at her own expense, and without any of the compensation she had hoped for.

Both Eva and my grandmother came from the same sprawling Armenian family. My grandmother's grandfather and Eva's great-great-grandfather, Simon, had become prosperous by manufacturing cigars. At one time, he owned 72 houses in Kolozsvar that he rented out. He had three wives in succession and fathered thirty-two children.

It was said that Simon got so accustomed to having new children it came to the point that the announcement of an addition to his family ceased to agitate him. One day, he was playing cards in the gentlemen's club at the Banffy palace when a servant came rushing in.

"Sir, your wife is giving birth!" she exclaimed.

"Well, it's all happening as expected," Simon said. "Please go home, and thank you for letting me know." And he went on playing cards.

Soon after, the servant returned breathlessly. "Oh Sir, your wife is giving birth to another baby!"

Simon told everyone in the club, "Please calm down. Everything will be all right," and went on playing cards.

Then the servant came back, exclaiming, "Sir, your wife is giving birth to a third baby!"

Simon slammed down his cards on the table. "I must go! Otherwise, she will never stop!"

One of Simon's granddaughters married a distant cousin, also of Armenian descent, who owned a large estate near Kolozsvar. They became the parents of my cousin Eva and two other children. Theirs was the same estate that Eva and her family would lose and fail to reclaim. I often went to visit their country mansion on weekends. One member of their huge household was their oldest housemaid, Mary. She was a small, gracious lady who seemed to have all the time for everyone. She was about sixty, but her hair was still naturally black. My cousins treated her like a member of the family, and we all called her Mary *néni* (Aunt Mary).

She came to my cousin's family as a young girl, the un- wanted child of a family with too many children. Schooling was not yet obligatory when she was growing up, and she never learned to read or write. Most members of my cousins' household married and left to start families of their own. This was not the case with Mary *néni*, who lived into her nineties as part of my cousins' family.

Movies came to Kolozsvar just before the First World War and, as elsewhere, caused a sensation. There was then only one movie house in Kolozsvar, located on a street that led from the main square to the university. It showed Hun- garian, German, American, and French movies, all with Hungarian intertitles. For me, movies were not like real life as they were all black and white and silent, which somehow made them all the more glamorous.

One day, we brought Mary *néni* to her first movie. It was called *Les Mystères de New York*. It was a French crime and suspense movie shot in Paris with sets standing in for New York skyscrapers.

After we came out of the movie house, we asked Mary *néni* how she liked the movie.

"Oh, it was just wonderful!" she exclaimed.

When we got home, one of my cousins who did not see the movie asked her, "Please tell me, what did you see?"

Mary *néni* said, "Well, it began with a princess who lived in a tall palace with her father, the king. Somebody killed her father and so she had to flee from the palace and work on a farm. Then a beautiful prince came and saw her and fell in love. The prince caught and punished the people who killed her father. Then the prince married her. He took her to a big palace and she became queen. It was just wonderful!"

◀§◆▶

It was a bright summer afternoon when I heard about the beginning of World War I. My sister, a few friends, and I were playing in the sand-filled playground in the garden when I saw our cook Ilona in the distance, carrying the tea tray. I left my half-filled pail and ran through the path by the pine grove. I reached the stone table where my mother and about a dozen guests were chatting gaily. Ilona left the tray of tea and cookies on the table. Steam was still rising out of the honey cookies and I took one. I was nibbling at the cookie when another of my mother's guests arrived, half-running.

"The king has just declared war on Serbia!" he said.

A dreadful silence followed.

Then someone exclaimed, "My God, what shall happen to us now!?"

My mother looked at me with great tenderness. I took another cookie and ran back to the playground.

I was seven years old then and too young to grasp what they looked so worried about. I didn't know that the Austro-Hungarian empire had declared war on Serbia after the assassination of the Archduke Ferencz Ferdinand by Serbian nationalists in Sarajevo. It was an irony because the Archduke was intensely pro-Serbian and was, moreover, very unpopular in Austria and even more so in Hungary. It was said that the only person who liked him was his wife.

At the beginning of the war, only the younger men got conscripted, and so my father was not sent to the front until the last two years. For the children, life went on pretty much as before. I went to school as before and played with my friends in the sandy playground with our pails and toys. There was one exciting change. Every afternoon, all of us would run to the gates to watch the soldiers march.

There were then in the old section of Kolozsvar three secondary schools, or gymnasiums, as they were called in Hungary. Kolozsvar's population was ninety percent Hungarian and all three schools taught in Hungarian. The students studied for eight years, and after graduation could go on to university. Like all schools of the time, the gymnasiums emphasized the classics, especially Latin.

Two of the schools were on the old *Farkas utca* (Street of the Wolf). One was the Catholic school run by the Piarists, a teaching order like the Jesuits. The other, a block away, was the Calvinist school. On another street just three blocks away was the Unitarian school.

When I was about to enter secondary school in 1916, the University of Kolozsvar established a new sort of gymnasium that emphasized science over Greek and Latin. After long discussions with friends and professors in the university, my parents decided to enroll me in this new school. It was here, thanks to its outstanding teachers, that my interest in the natural sciences developed rapidly.

Unfortunately, the new school went out of business in 1920 when Transylvania was given to Romania by the Treaty of Trianon and the new authorities took over the school. All the students, including Catholics like myself, were transferred to the Calvinist school. For instruction in religion, the Catholics would then go once a week a block away to the school of the Piarists.

After finishing gymnasium in 1924, I wanted to become both a doctor and university professor at the same time, like my grandfather, who had moved to Budapest after retiring from his post at the University of Kolozsvar.

If I were to graduate from a university in Romania, I could not practice medicine in Hungary. If I were to graduate from a university in Hungary, I could not practice in Romania. It was decided therefore, that I should study in the University of Paris and determine later where I would pursue my career.

So one afternoon in 1924, I said goodbye to my parents, my sister, our cook, and the rest of the household on Monostori Avenue. With two big suitcases, I rode a horse carriage to the train station, then journeyed to Budapest, passing through the high mountains of northeastern Transylvania.

I broke my journey in Budapest, staying for one day with my grandmother Paula at her home on Elizabeth Ring across the road from the Abazia Coffee House, a popular meeting place of intellectuals in Budapest. Then I took the train for Paris, making stops in several cities and towns including Vienna, Zurich, and Lausanne. One saw mostly horse carriages and stone buildings then, none yet of the car traffic and glass-and-steel buildings that have come to dominate, and often oppress, most cities. It was truly another world. More people should have noticed its heartbreaking charms, but who would have known it would disappear so quickly?

· V ·

latin quarter

My train arrived on an autumn afternoon in 1924 at the Gare de l'Est in Paris. I was too tired to take heed of the fabled beauty of the city. What struck me immediately was how big the city was, how indifferent were the people rushing off on some business or another, how much faster everyone seemed to move.

In Paris at that time, French students and those who were from a country that had a building at the *cité universitaire* could live in that building. Being neither, I rented a room in a small hotel in the sixth *arrondissement*. It was a four-story building from the time of Louis XVI, with a massive portal and staircases flanked by heavy wrought iron. It was owned by a man who had just married a pretty, much younger woman. The location was very convenient, on rue Jacob, near a variety market at the corner and the School of Medicine. Like many other students, I did not eat at home, taking my meals in small restaurants in the Latin Quarter.

Some other students lived in the hotel, as well as an elderly, friendly American. He once asked me if I wanted to go see the art collection of an American woman named Gertrude Stein, who lived around the corner. He said she had plenty of works by artists like Picasso, Braque, and their contemporaries, who were then doing a lot of cubist paintings. I declined his offer, as I disliked (and dislike) this type of painting and, in any case, it was not difficult to come across them. Right outside our hotel on the Rue Jacob, and on the nearby Rue de Seine, there were several boutiques, one beside the other, very tiny shops with one or two chairs in their front rooms. Canvasses by Picasso and others cluttered their walls from top to bottom. The back rooms had stacks of rolled canvasses by these painters.

An ordinary middle-class family could still afford paintings by impressionists like Monet and Cezanne, although one had to go to galleries like Durand-Ruel near the Madeleine, or the small auction houses. Once, there was a minor auction where I became entranced by a large watercolor of the Mont Saint Victoire by Cezanne, going for the price of about 500 US dollars today. As I was only a student on a stipend, I just watched the bidding go by.

Another person who lived in the neighborhood of Rue Jacob was Raymond Duncan, the brother of the late Isadora Duncan. He gave interesting talks on dance that I sometimes attended. He, his wife, and his students all wore homespun togas. It was quite a sight, them skipping about in their peplums and togas in the tiny streets and shops, but the people in the *quartier* got used to them.

I often went out with my friends from Kolozsvar, Ella, Paul, and Joska (diminutive of Joseph). We would go to museums or small restaurants on the Left Bank and exchange the latest news from Kolozsvar.

Ella Farkas was studying art history at the Sorbonne. She was the eldest child of the richest man in Kolozsvar, Moses Farkas, whom all his acquaintances called Mozsi. He and my father became friends when they both worked as apprentices to a well-known lawyer in Kolozsvar. Going to law school was the fashionable thing to do at the turn of the century for young men from the upper classes who did not have a special vocation, like Mozsi.

An exceptionally resourceful man, Mozsi quickly discovered that his career, though elegant, was not very profitable. He therefore left the law profession and bought a small leather factory from its Saxon-Hungarian owner, renamed it Dermata, from the Latin word *dermis* for skin, and soon turned it into the biggest and most important leather factory not only in Transylvania but in all of Romania as well.

Mozsi was very proud of his daughter Ella, who combined beauty and intelligence. She would sometimes walk in the *corso* and people would say, "There goes the beautiful Ella." She had an aptitude for languages and the arts, and this led her to study at the Sorbonne under Professor Focillon, the foremost art historian in Paris.

Paul Savet was also enrolled at the Sorbonne, pursuing a course in mathematics. I first met him in 1920 when I was a schoolboy at the Calvinist College in Kolozsvar. For Catholic religious instruction, I would walk two blocks every Monday at noon to the Catholic Gymnasium run by the Piarist priests. I was assigned to sit at the bench on the left end of the first row. This was Paul's regular seat. As he was Jewish, he did not take the Catholic lessons. I would arrive at the end of Paul's class and he would give me his seat. At the end of my class, I would give the seat back to Paul.

While studying at the Sorbonne, Paul got an offer to join the faculty from his professor, who was impressed by his brilliance in mathematics. For a student to teach at the Sorbonne was indeed a flattering prospect!

Paul went to his professor's office right away to sit down and discuss the offer. The discussion went very well until the professor took out the list of members of the mathematics faculty. He went down the list murmuring, "So and so has a daughter but she's engaged … so and so has no daughter … so and so has two daughters but both married."

The professor put down the list and told Paul, "I am sorry, but at the present moment, no member of the faculty has an available daughter. Therefore, I am unable to offer you a position."

Paul was speechless.

He soon learned that this was one of the obscure traditions at the Sorbonne, unchanged since the middle ages. It was not unlike what happened to Handel in 1703 when, as a young musician trying to make his way in Germany, he was refused a job as organist at Saint Mary's Church in Lübeck because he was unwilling to follow tradition and marry any of the five daughters of the church's current organist and composer, the famous Dietrich Buxtehude.

Two years later, a young and penniless Bach walked for two days from Anstadt to Lübeck for the sole purpose of meeting this same Buxtehude and hearing him play. Bach admired Buxtehude's musicianship so much that he trebled his stay in Lübeck. As Buxtehude was known to have been himself impressed with Bach, it is presumed that the aging organist also offered his position to Bach and that the young man also declined, not willing to marry any of the daughters.

Could you imagine what would have happened if such were the reason for withdrawing a job offer in present-day America? Lawsuits galore! But times were very different as recently as the period before the Second World War, when paternalism was the order of the day in European university, civil, and home life, when the word of a superior had the weight of the Commandments. In any case, Paul did not care to marry any professor's daughter as he was interested only in Ella Farkas who, unlike Buxtehude's daughters, had no difficulty in attracting admirers.

The other member of our group from Kolozsvar, Joseph Kory, was studying ceramics and graphic arts at the Ecole des Beaux Arts. Like the three of us, he came from an upper-middle class family, called the *lateiner* class in Hungary. The word *lateiner* came from an old German term based on the word "Latin," as members of this class were all supposed to speak Latin.

Often, families of the *lateiner* class, though very well-educated, earned little. This was the case with Joseph's family. Joseph, who was five years older than me, was a good graphics artist. As a very young man, he often came to our house to listen to discussions about art, and he became a member of our guest family.

Joseph's parents could barely support their big family. So Joseph enlisted at eighteen in the Romanian army in order to make his way in the world. He soon realized that life in the military was not for him. He somehow managed to be discharged and then declared dead so he would never have to be drafted again. He also managed to find his way to Paris to study at the Beaux Arts. He lived in a tiny room, and I often invited him out for dinner as he was often nearly starving.

Joseph, like Paul, fell in love with Ella. She chose to marry Joseph. Ella's father Mozsi refused. He was not pleased with his daughter's decision to marry a starving artist. Moreover, his daughter was Jewish and Joseph was Catholic. Ella was a strong-willed young woman. She and Joseph got married. Mozsi refused to see his daughter from then on.

Returning to Kolozsvar, Joseph introduced Ella to my mother. They came to my mother's drawing-room almost every night to join others who were passionate about art. This was how Ella became almost another daughter to my mother. My mother later sat at Ella's bedside the whole night Ella was giving birth.

Ella had a charming little boy, Laszlo, whom we called Laci (pronounced Lát-see). He came almost every day to play in our garden. One day, my father met Ella's father Mozsi in the street. My father said to him, "Mozsi, Mozsi, why don't you forgive your daughter? You have such a charming grandson and I see him every day. You should enjoy the company of your grandson and your daughter while you can!"

Mozsi burst into tears on my father's shoulder. He made peace with his daughter.

· VI ·

cat's hair

Back in the latin quarter, I continued with my medical studies. The principal preoccupations of the internist then were diagnosis and prognosis, and great internists were sought after for their experience and intuition in this discipline. But the fact is that there was no treatment for most diseases. And usually the most the internist could do was to diagnose the disease accurately, predict its duration, and advise the patient what actions to avoid (inappropriate diet, for example) and what measures to take regarding hygiene, the few medications available, fresh air, and the like, while the disease took its course.

I began my medical studies at a time when research was beginning to ask many basic questions about diseases. It offered greater opportunities than internal medicine to discover something new. This was why I became interested in research. In addition to my medical studies at the University of Paris, I enrolled at the Sorbonne for courses in basic sciences like zoology, botany, biochemistry, biophysics and microbiology.

Medicine then was extremely different from what it has become. It was before Gerhard Domagk's discovery of sulfonamides, compounds that are not toxic to humans but could kill disease-producing microbes. And it was well before the real transformation of therapeutics with the discovery of penicillin by Alexander Fleming. These two developments would lead to the invention of modern drugs that would make it possible for the physician to treat many illnesses once thought incurable except through divine intervention.

Many of the most exciting breakthroughs were being made at the Pasteur Institute at the time I decided to go into scientific research. With my diplomas from the University of Paris and the Sorbonne, I applied for work at the institute, and thankfully was accepted. I soon met many remarkable scientists at the institute. Some of them were a bit eccentric but nevertheless gave me inspiration in my new life as a medical researcher. Among them was Ernest Fourneau, the great French organic scientist. Fourneau had studied in Germany and developed great respect for German biochemists. Later, when he and his student Daniel Bovet synthesized the first French sulfonamide, Fourneau refused to be the first author, in deference to previous work done by the Germans. Fourneau became known around the world when he synthesized the first French arsenical compound effective against syphilis. He called it Stovarsol, after "stove," the English translation of *fourneau*.

He was basically a kindly man, but strict and introverted. Anne-Marie Staub, another student of Fourneau's, told me that the first day she entered his laboratory, Fourneau showed her around, then asked if she had any questions.

"Well, yes," she replied. "What about vacations?"

"Mademoiselle," was the response, "we don't take vacations here. When we get exhausted, we drop dead and recuperate."

"Well, I found out," Anne-Marie told me, "that on or about Bastille Day (when all France goes on vacation), everyone was so exhausted we had no choice but to close down the laboratory and recuperate."

Fourneau's students Daniel Bovet and Anne-Marie worked on antagonists (inhibitors) of histamine, the compound released naturally by the body during allergic reactions. Their studies resulted in the first anti-histaminic drug used in human allergies, which they called Antergan.

It was for his work on curare that Bovet earned the Nobel Prize. Using curare, a resin-like substance from a South American plant that Indians used for poisoning arrows, Bovet was able to produce muscle relaxation in fish to a degree never previously observed.

When he was doing these experiments, Bovet never envisaged that they would later become the basis for the synthesis of artificial curare and other drugs that now permit complete muscle relaxation. Without them, heart or lung surgery would not be possible. This is but one example of how seemingly useless basic research can have very practical, if unforeseen, results.

Bovet married Philomena Nitti, daughter of the famous Italian politician Francesco Saverio Nitti, who was then in exile in Paris. Everybody at the Pasteur Institute admired Philomena's intelligence, though many found her domineering. Nothing describes Philomena Nitti-Bovet better than the reply I received after I sent a congratulatory telegram to Daniel for the Nobel Prize. The reply was a printed card from the Bovets containing one sentence: "Philomena Nitti-Bovet thanks you for your congratulations and the kind words you sent her husband for the Nobel Prize."

Many of the scientists at the Pasteur Institute had been schooled in the old way, that is, they valued art and music as much as science. Anne Marie Staub was one such scientist, as passionate about music as she was about her groundbreaking research in the laboratory. She was a good amateur singer with an affinity for baroque music, and she often gave impromptu performances after a day's work in the laboratory.

Another inspiring scientist at the Pasteur Institute was Jacques Monod, who later won the Nobel Prize for his discovery of the operon, a part of the chromosome essential in the activity of microorganisms.

Among Jacques Monod's publications was the best-selling book about science for the non-scientist, *Le Hazard et la Nécessité* (*Chance and Necessity*, Alfred Knopf 1971). He also happened to be a talented musician. During the war, he got an offer to become the conductor of a Canadian orchestra. He turned down the offer as he had decided that his place was in Paris with the Resistance.

Not long after I started working at the Institute, I bumped into Jacques at a baroque concert in the Salle Gaveau. He told me how sad it was that we did not have enough baroque music in Paris. He was thinking of recruiting some volunteers from the Pasteur Institute who would contribute a small amount of money and time to rent a room one evening a week and sing the choral part of Bach's "Christmas Oratorio."

We managed to gather a group together and the singing went so well that Jacques got the idea of presenting the full oratorio in public, and at the Salle Gaveau, no less—the most important concert hall in Paris before the Salle Pleyel was built a few years later. Jacques named our group *La Cantate*. He hired the best musicians and soloists, including the French soprano Madame Malnory-Marseillac and the Swiss tenor Hugues Cuenod, who was the student and collaborator of Nadia Boulanger, the renowned pioneer of this century's baroque music revival.

We enjoyed singing the oratorio and the concert-goers responded warmly. The journals gave us rave reviews and one critic wondered why no one had ever heard of our group, and when we would hold another concert. Well, they did not know that we had been rehearsing this oratorio for more than three years whenever we could get time off. Needless to say, there was no other concert by the *Cantate*.

Paris before the Second World War was, for good reason, considered the world center of culture. The greatest and most important art exhibitions were organized in Paris. As I went frequently to the Louvre, I joined the society *Les Amis du Louvre*. Among the most novel exhibitions was "The Masterpieces of Italian Painting from Italian Museums." It was the first time that so many great paintings had traveled from Italy to another country.

On Sunday afternoons in the spring, I would go to Saint Leu-la-Forêt, about one hour north of Paris, to attend recitals by Wanda Landowska and join enthusiasts and supporters of "early music." Landowska was at that time already known for rediscovering the harpsichord and reestablishing many baroque works in the repertory. She struck me at first as a homely, frail-looking woman but I soon found out that she was actually tough as a steel cord. Students from all over the world went to Saint Leu-la-Forêt to learn the harpsichord from her, and she terrified many of them. Once, a student asked her how she managed to play a passage. She gave him a withering look and said, "Do you think I can tell you in one moment what has taken me thirty years to learn?" Another time, a student, a Dutch girl, started a promising relationship with another student, a Dutch boy. For some strange reason, their mentor encouraged other female students to flirt with him. But it was in her efforts to rediscover forgotten music that her toughness really showed.

At the turn of the century, Landowska was already a piano prodigy playing romantic music when she became fascinated with keyboard music from the time of Handel, Bach, and Rameau. She had already made a tour of Russia and played for Tolstoy, who showed great interest in her ideas about "old music." She was living in Paris and researching the archives for baroque keyboard pieces when she became convinced that since the music was originally written for the harpsichord, she should play them on this instrument. She was met with almost universal derision when she told other musicians of her wish to revive the harpsichord. A Frenchman, Louis Diemer, had already tried to revive the harpsichord and it proved disastrous. The instrument was called "bloodless," a "tin pan." A friend of Landowska's, the choral conductor Charles Bordes, tried to discourage her, writing, "enough of this cage of flies which reduces large-scale works to the size of its tiny, spindly legs."

One problem was that surviving harpsichords at that time were indeed feeble-toned. Another problem was that the technique of producing dynamic fluctuations in harpsichord playing was lost. Landowska was not discouraged. She commissioned the piano builder Pleyel to construct a harpsichord for her that would have the same vigor as the ones available to Bach, Handel and Couperin. It took several years, with Landowska and a Pleyel engineer going from museum to museum, before Pleyel could construct the harpsichord. In Landowska's own words, "The harpsichord ... people knew only as a museum piece, adorned with rich carvings, decorated with faded colors and dim gold, they appeared like phantoms, formerly magnificent, now forever mute." Landowska reestablished the harpsichord, and her determination paid off, perhaps even beyond her expectations. Now there are harpsichord virtuosos on compact discs, and it has become standard to see the instrument in productions of operas and music from the baroque period.

I heard Landowska play the "Goldberg Variations" in public for the first time at Saint Leu-la-Forêt in 1933. Bach had written it in 1741 for Count Keyserling, the Russian Ambassador to Dresden, but it was never heard in a public performance until Landowska played it. One major reason was the difficulty of the hand-crossing passages, since Bach had written it for a harpsichord with two keyboards. Landowska's performance caused a sensation. The "Goldberg Variations" are of course now one of Bach's most popular works.

Oftentimes, when I get stuck or lose my way in my experiments and scientific writings, I remember the willpower and tenacity of artists like Landowska, and their faith in serendipity, and I draw strength from their example.

Landowska was by no means the only one making Paris the world's most adventurous place for music. I never had time to read the newspapers, but I subscribed to an inexpensive weekly periodical that announced the concerts. The finest performers made Paris the venue of their premieres. Among them were the violinists Bronislav Huberman and Jascha Heifetz; the pianists Walter Gieseking, Arthur Rubinstein, and Vladimir Horowitz; the tenors Benianimo Gigli and Lauritz Melchior; the conductors Bruno Walter, Wilhelm Furtwängler, and Arturo Toscanini; the bass Feodor Chaliapin; the Ballets Russes; the Capet and Lener Quartets; and the sopranos Kirsten Flagstad, Elisabeth Schwarzkopf, Germaine Lubin, Lotte Lehman, and Elisabeth Schumann.

At the Palais Garnier, there was the yearly Wagner Festival, with the performers arriving from Munich and Bayreuth. I went to the festival every year, more for the spectacle and the musicianship than the music itself. It was true that Wagner was a genius and that his music was original and astounding. But somehow, the effect it had on me was similar to that of an asthma attack.

I already knew only too well, by then, what real asthma felt like, having recently suffered a series of asthmatic attacks.

At that time, medical students about to graduate were permitted to temporarily replace physicians. Through my friends, I had been recommended to a physician, a so-called *docteur du quartier* (approximately, neighborhood family physician), who wanted to go on vacation in the south of France for the Easter break.

The physician for whom I substituted had a large clientele, and my job was to go and see the patients in their homes in the mornings and late afternoons, a practice still common at that time. From 2 to 4 PM, patients would come to the office, which was located in his apartment in the north of Paris.

This physician had two superb Siamese cats in the apartment. He and especially his wife were very fond of these cats.

The apartment was huge. One of the rooms had more than fifty bronze statuettes from the late nineteenth and early twentieth centuries. The physician referred to this room as his "sculpture room."

Before leaving for vacation, he took me to his "sculpture room" and showed me the statuettes. "I call them my *bronze d'art*," he told me. They were mostly kitsch versions of popular subjects such as nymphs, peasants, horses, angels, and dogs; and miniature imitations of famous statues like the Winged Victory and the Venus de Milo.

"These are all gifts from my wealthiest patients," he said.

"Very nice of them," I ventured.

Each statuette had a small chain with a name tag. "Look here, these are the names of the donors," he said. "You should study these names and remember them."

I examined the name tags with curiosity.

"Now listen," he said. "If any one of these patients makes an appointment, you must get the *bronze d'art* with the right name on the tag and put it on the desk of the consultation room. Without the tag, of course. And after the visit, please put it back in the sculpture room."

My substitution satisfied the physician and he asked me to fill in for him again for Whit Sunday (forty days after Easter). I was not one hour back in the apartment when I got a severe attack of asthma. I felt I was inside a locked closet. My chest felt blown up but I could not exhale despite all my effort. I finally found relief by injecting a solution of adrenaline into my thigh. This, however, resulted in alarming palpitations. Still, I found this better than the feeling of utter helplessness I had just gone through.

I soon realized that I had developed an allergy to cats during my first sojourn in the apartment. My case had the interest that the sensitization period, i.e. the time between the first contact and the actual attack of asthma, was well documented.

A good friend of mine, Andrée Hugo (wife of a grandson of the writer Victor Hugo) was then working with the foremost professor and specialist in allergy in France. Andrée persuaded me to see her *patron,* as a case like mine, where the sensitization period was so well documented, would be of great interest to him.

Andrée's professor was the sole grandson of Louis Pasteur. He was himself a famous professor at the University of Paris and headed a medical department in one of the major hospitals in Paris. He was so proud of his grandfather that he insisted that everyone always refer to him by his full name—Professor Louis-Pasteur Pasteur Vallery Radot, redundancy and all, or at least as Professor Pasteur Vallery Radot. Some got around this long-winded requirement by just calling him *"mon cher ami."*

The day before I went to see Professor Pasteur Vallery Radot, I dropped one cat's hair into a tube containing 5 milliliters of 0.1% sodium hydroxide. This hair weighed less than one-thousandth of a milligram. The extract from this hair would in turn be one thousand times less than the hair in weight, a remarkably minimal amount.

The next morning, I went to Professor Pasteur Vallery Radot's office and found Andrée waiting for me. We took out the cat's hair from the tube. The hair had apparently not been modified at all. Then we neutralized the remaining solution in the tube by mixing it with 5 milliliters of 0.1% hydrochloric acid.

Andrée made a scratch about 3 millimeters long on my left forearm with a sterile scalpel. She put on the scratch one drop of the neutralized hair extract, this being an infinitesimally small amount of cat hair protein. For control, we used a similar scratch on my forearm, where we put one drop of a similar mixture but without the cat's hair.

In less than ten minutes, an itchy redness began to take shape around the first scratch. Then an irregular papule with several lateral extensions grew in the middle of this redness. This was the typical triple response formulated by Lewis that was characteristic of histamine liberation, proof that I was allergic to cat's hair.

Professor Pasteur Vallery Radot found our experiment very interesting. It demonstrated how minimal was the amount needed to provoke an allergic reaction. And it showed that I had developed antibodies against the cat protein in forty days or less, i.e. the period between Easter and Whit Sunday. Until this time, scientists had no information on how long it took humans to develop allergy. The only data we had then was from experimental animals such as the rabbits Professor Pasteur Valery Radot had been working on.

It happened that two days after my consultation, I met Pasteur Valery Radot at the opera, where Debussy's *Pelléas et Mélisande* was being performed. He told me he knew Debussy personally and had seen this opera at its premiere in 1902. He recalled the furor it caused.

Before its premiere, the opera was already controversial. Maeterlinck, the author of the drama on which the opera was based, originally supported the adaptation but later published scathing attacks against it. One of the major reasons was that Maeterlinck wanted his mistress, Georgette Leblanc, for the lead role. However, Debussy and his producer had chosen Mary Garden, an American soprano, who could not pronounce the French words correctly, much less understand them. Outside the Opéra-Comique, partisans of Maeterlinck jeered and booed during rehearsals and at opening night.

In fact, it was only Mary Garden who came out of the furor unscathed. She sang beautifully, everyone forgot her American accent, and the papers showered her with raves. Debussy, however, was vehemently attacked by the critics, some calling his music decadent. Just the opposite, it was in fact an original. It was the first contemporary opera that did not sound like Wagner or Verdi. By the time I saw it with Professor Pasteur Vallery Radot in the early 1930's, it was already part of the repertory.

Like many eminent Frenchmen before the Second World War, Pasteur Vallery Radot was remarkably cultured and knowledgeable about the world, but spoke French only.

Victor Hugo upheld this same tradition at the time he went into exile on the English islands of Jersey and Guernsey in the 1850's. In nineteen years of living on those rocky islands, he never learned to speak English properly. "When England wants to speak to me," he would say, "she will learn to speak French."

Pasteur Vallery Radot strayed a bit from this tradition, some thirty years after we first met, when he visited the Johns Hopkins University in Baltimore in the late 1950's. I was by then working as a researcher and professor at the university, and I eagerly went to his lecture. Pasteur Vallery Radot delivered a talk in superb English, though barely looking up from his script. Afterwards, he showed me the script. The English was written phonetically.

He asked me to write immediately to Andrée Hugo, who had translated his lecture for him, to tell her how well his English went.

· VII ·

ambassadress cerruti

IN THE MID-THIRTIES, Italy sent a new ambassador to
Paris, Vittorio Cerruti. He formerly held the post in Peking,
Berlin, and Moscow, and was one of the most outstanding
ambassadors Italy ever had. His wife, Elisabetta de Paulay,
who came from a Hungarian noble family, was a long-time
family friend of ours, going back before the First World
War.

Soon after her arrival in Paris, Ambassadress Cerruti began making the Italian embassy on the rue de Varennes a
major center for artists and musicians. She organized many
major and impromptu art exhibitions, concerts and theatrical
shows. She invited me regularly to these events and I always
looked forward to their replenishing powers after a tiring
day at work.

Ambassadress Cerruti's father, Ede de Paulay, had been
Director of the Hungarian Academy of Acting, Hungary's
equivalent of the *Comédie Française*. Before de Paulay's time,
acting was not considered a respectable profession in
Hungary. Paulay elevated the level of both the profession
and the Hungarian Academy. He became known as the
renovator of Hungarian theater, and the city of Budapest
honored him after his death by naming a street after him.

His daughter Elisabetta studied acting in the Hungarian
Academy and became one of Hungary's leading actresses.
She appeared in many Shakespeare, Ibsen and Strindberg
productions as well as plays by Hungarian writers. Besotted
critics variously called her the Hungarian Duse or the

Hungarian Sarah Bernhardt. After World War I, she met Vittorio Cerruti, then a plenipotentiary minister stationed in Budapest, and decided to give up acting for a diplomatic life.

It is not often that the wife of an ambassador becomes noted for any active policy role. The Hungarian-born Princess Metternich, daughter-in-law of the famous Austrian statesman, performed such a role as the Austrian ambassadress in the court of Napoleon III. The Ambassadress Cerruti played a similar part. It was said that once, when Mussolini sent Ambassador Cerruti to a new post, he remarked, "With Cerruti, Italy pays one ambassador, but actually, we are sending two, as Mrs. Cerruti's intelligence and judgment of people are extraordinary."

This was the time, in the early thirties, when Mussolini was still extremely popular among the Italians and recognized for his strong stand against Hitler. There was wide support for him when in 1935, at the Stresa Conference, he led the creation of an anti-Hitler front to defend Austria. Many ordinary Italians still say that if Mussolini had the good luck to die before 1939, he would now be considered one of Italy's great statesmen. He still gets credit for such diverse achievements as eradicating malaria in Italy and prohibiting the exportation of national works of art, a first in the world, then hemorrhaging out of Italy at a deadly rate. Many Italians supported him for saving Italy from social chaos, at least for a while, until he himself became a source of this chaos. In 1939, he committed the mortal sin of entering into the so-called Pact of Steel with Hitler that soon dragged Italy into the war and its atrocities. The rest is history.

In the early thirties, soon after Ambassadress Cerruti took up her post in Paris, she became known for her lively luncheons and dinners for government officials and social leaders. It was here that she excelled in making policy suggestions and drawing out commitments that her husband could never have brought up in a more formal setting.

In her book *Ambassador's Wife,* she recounted her life in the theater and as an ambassadress. The book was a success in its Italian, French and English editions. (The English edition—not translation, as she wrote the manuscript in English—was published by the Macmillan Company in 1953.)

She had, like other ambassador's wives, her less serious duties. Once, Mussolini instructed Ambassador Cerruti to investigate the debts that the Italian poet and patriot D'Annunzio made when he was living in Paris. Mussolini said he wanted to pay the debts from his own private funds, as he admired D'Annunzio tremendously.

Ambassador Cerruti told his wife that there was one debt of D'Annunzio's that should be seen to by her, as it was something of a feminine nature: the debt to the perfumer Coty. Ambassadress Cerruti called up the shop and it was agreed that the next morning she would go there to settle the debt.

When she arrived at the shop, located on the Place Vendôme, footmen were waiting for her. A red carpet had been laid out especially for her outside the door of the shop.

"Really, Monsieur Coty," she exclaimed. "It's exaggerated to make such a fuss about the debt of a private person!"

Coty responded, *"Mais, il est important!"* He did not, however, specify if it was the debt that was important or the person who had incurred it.

Coty showed the Ambassadress around the shop and, after the tour, she finally asked Coty, "Now, please tell me, how much is the debt?"

Coty showed her the bills. She was taken aback. It was more than she had expected. Hundreds of times more.

She asked Coty, "Now, tell me, how come it is so much? Did D'Annunzio take baths in perfume?"

"No, Madame," answered Coty, "but as you might know,

the great man was very fond of *midinettes* (young women who made a living usually as apprentices in haute couture *ateliers* in Paris). You see, he often came to the shop with one of them and would say only one word: '*Choisissez*'. Well," Coty added, "they certainly chose!"

Not too long ago, I attended some performances of the great Kirov Ballet at the Lincoln Center, and this brought back to mind an amusing anecdote the Ambassadress told me. (Like the incident with Coty, this story is not found in her book.) When she moved as ambassadress to Paris, she happened to meet the Russian Grand Duke Andrei Vladimirovich. The Grand Duke, a cousin of the last Czar, was then living in exile in Monte Carlo. Of all the Russian imperial family, he was known to be one of the two most interested in ballet. The other one was the Grand Duke Sergei.

Grand Duke Andrei was then married to Mathilda Ksessinskaya, the famous *prima ballerina assoluta* before the Russian Revolution of the Maryinsky Ballet (the Kirov's original name). Her "protector" for many years happened to have been her husband's cousin, the Grand Duke Sergei.

This state of affairs produced Ksessinskaya's well-known riposte to Sergei Diaghilev when he congratulated her for having not one, but two Grand Dukes at her feet.

"But Sergei Pavlovich," she exclaimed, "you forget that I have two legs!"

The Grand Duke Andrei, knowing that Ambassadress Cerruti had just been in the Russia to which he could never return, was eager to hear her impressions of the country and of the ballet troupe in St. Petersburg that he had once sponsored. There was one question he wanted to ask: "Who is the current prima ballerina there and what do you think about her?"

The Ambassadress replied, "Oh, there are still absolutely superb dancers. But there are no more prima ballerinas," she said. "There are no prima ballerinas where there are no Grand Dukes!"

In her will, Ambassadress Cerruti left me some letters that Bela Bartok wrote to her in the thirties after his concert tour in Russia. During the sixties, an official from the Hungarian Communist government approached me about these letters, as the government was particularly eager to obtain them. These letters happened to be the only known surviving documents in which Bartok expressed his feeling about politics, and wrote of his deep revulsion of Communism. I thought that the Communist government could very well bury the letters in some inaccessible archive or even destroy them. I refused their offer and instead published the letters in a musical journal.

I had been fortunate to have Ambassadress Cerruti as a friend in Paris. I didn't know then how helpful she would be much later when we would meet again, in Rome.

· VIII ·

back to transylvania

Having obtained a degree in paris, I could practice medicine in France. However, I had always wanted to work eventually in Kolozsvar, its name by then changed to Cluj by the Romanian authorities. So in the early thirties, I went back and passed the Romanian examination to validate my medical diploma, then went back to Paris to resume work at the Pasteur Institute.

In 1940, the northern portion of Transylvania, which included Kolozsvar, was given back to Hungary at the Arbitrage of Vienna. I became a Hungarian citizen again. This was how I got my third citizenship even though I officially remained resident of the same city.

In order to practice in Kolozsvar, I now had to pass examinations again to validate my diploma for medical practice in Hungary.

Then I got my fourth citizenship. In 1947, after the armistice of World War Two, northern Transylvania was given back to Romania. Suddenly, I became a Romanian citizen again.

Anyone forced to go through these irrational mutations soon learns to place the highest value on common sense.

I soon lost my Romanian citizenship because I chose not to go back to Romania. I became a stateless person, a so-called "apolide," and got a Nansen passport. This became my fifth citizenship or rather citizenship status.

In 1952, I got an Italian citizenship, another story for later. This became my sixth citizenship. Finally, in 1962, I obtained citizenship in the United States, my seventh citizenship.

◆§§◆

In the fall of 1939, I was working back in Paris when I received an official letter from Romania. The army required that every few years, young men had to undergo a period of military service. This was a routine draft and was not due to the war that had already begun elsewhere in Europe. I loved my work at the Pasteur Institute and was reluctant to leave. But I had to say goodbye to my friends and take the train at the Gare de l'Est. As soon as I arrived in Transylvania, the army sent me for my military service to Bessarabia. My unit's duty was to fight and prevent typhus.

As a former student of Charles Nicolle, who won the Nobel Prize for discovering that typhus was spread by lice carrying the microorganism *Rickettsia prowazekii*, I had learned a lot about the disease through classroom and laboratory lessons. But it was something else to see patients actually suffering from this often fatal illness.

Not long after I arrived in Bessarabia, I was called to see a young man convulsing with chills and delirium. I examined him and saw dark-reddish eruptions on his skin. No question about it, this was a case of typhus, the first I had ever seen in person.

I immediately took steps to eliminate all lice from his body and clothes. I shaved him from head to toe. It was not easy, as he was shaking all over. I had all his clothes and all the household linen boiled. We immediately transported him to a nearby hospital. I just hoped that with the help of antipyretics and hydration, the only therapies then available against typhus, the young man could weather the illness.

I ordered that everyone in the village should change underwear and that all dirty underwear be boiled. DDT, a compound that would soon prove effective in eliminating lice, had not yet been invented. (The Swiss scientist Paul Herman Müller would get the Nobel Prize in 1948 for this invention.) I had all the men shave their heads. Many of the vainer ones did so only with the greatest reluctance. There was one precaution we decided not to carry through, that of having the women shave their heads. For them to cut off their long hair was considered a sacred disgrace. Besides, we conceded, the women were not as promiscuous as the men. So I just went around explaining to the women that they should bathe with soap and wash their hair vigorously every day for eight days. No other cases of typhus appeared in the village.

I was soon traveling from village to village, speaking from the pulpits of the Orthodox churches about the dangers of typhus and what the villagers must do to save themselves.

On one occasion, an old man raised his hand.

"I would like to ask your permission that I may ask a question," he said.

"Of course, yes," I replied.

He stood up and, cap in hand, asked, "Tell me, does every louse spread typhus?"

"No," I replied, "only the contaminated ones."

"Then I would like to know why we should kill all of them if only some are contaminated. This is not fair!"

I could not fault his sense of justice. So, I just said, "Unfortunately, we are unable to separate the infected from the non-infected lice. Therefore, we must eliminate all of them!"

"You do differently from the command of Jesus, who said that we must not kill the weed before the harvest, for doing thus, we might kill the good wheat too."

I remembered having been told about this story when I was a boy taking religious lessons at the Piarist gymnasium. I glanced around at the people sitting in the pews and standing in the aisles, waiting anxiously for a reply.

"Yes, you are right," I said. "But we have to remember,

nowhere in the Bible does Jesus say that wheat and lice are the same!" This answer satisfied the old man and the other people in the church.

On one of my church visits, I saw an old Bessarabian carpet woven in the kilim technique, with plants and flowers in shades of beige, pale green, and rose. "This is a lovely carpet," I remarked to the priest.

"But it's such an old carpet!" he exclaimed. "Unfortunately, we don't have money to replace it." Like people in most carpet-making societies, who used carpets everywhere, as bags, protection from heat and cold, animal saddles, infant hammocks, even covering for the dead, the priest must have looked at carpets as part of the natural cycles of life, not as objects for detached admiration.

"Well, " I told the priest, "if you like, I could buy you a new carpet if you give me this one."

He turned to his assistant and switched to the local dialect he mistakenly thought I would not understand. "This fool wants to get the old rag and give us a new one. Let's take advantage of him."

This was how I bought the lovely carpet and gave the church a new one of their choice. I later gave the old carpet to my sister as a gift. Almost half a century later, I inherited it back from her. It is now in my living room in New York, a reminder of my days preaching from pulpit to pulpit in Bessarabia.

In 1940, when Kolozsvar became Hungarian again, the Romanian army discharged me and sent me back to Kolozsvar. I had a standing offer to go back to work at the Pasteur Institute in Paris, but this was out of the question as Paris was already under German occupation. At that time, the war elsewhere in Europe had not yet reached Kolozsvar. People went on living with the expectation or hope that the conflict would be resolved and the country spared.

As soon as I got back to Kolozsvar, I set up an office in

our house on Monostori Avenue and started a private practice as an internist. The illnesses I treated were mostly the
same ones still common today such as flu, colds, indigestion,
diabetes, and rheumatism. However, treating them was very
different then. Immunization was still in its infancy, a long
infancy I must say. While Jenner had already discovered
smallpox immunization in the late 1700's, and Pasteur the
prevention of anthrax in the mid-nineteenth century, there
were no other major developments in disease prevention by
vaccines until Jonas Salk discovered the polio vaccine in the
1950's. Sulfonamides, compounds that could kill specific
bacteria without being poisonous to human beings, had been
invented in the 1930's, but their action was still extremely
limited. Penicillin was still in the laboratories and not available to the public.

The doctor was useful for diagnosis, i.e. for determining
that the patient was suffering from this ailment and not that
one, or that the illness was not an imaginary one. After the
diagnosis, there was not much medication available. Pharmacies at that time looked more like the apothecary's shop,
familiar since the middle ages, with their curious jars, rather
than the drugstores of today with their bewildering array of
packaged medicines. As treatment for most diseases was
nonexistent, the few medications available in Paris were the
same in Kolozsvar—aspirin (first synthesized in 1897) for
fevers and colds, quinine for malaria and flus, tincture of
iodine for wounds.

My first patient was my godmother, the Baroness Karola
Bornemissza. Then in her sixties, she was of such healthy
constitution that I ended up giving her nothing but regular
checkups. The clinical examinations and laboratory tests always showed everything was in order. In fact, she was one
of those rare persons who never even suffered colds, when
most others around her were sneezing and coughing or
taking to bed with fever. It was good to be able to say to a

patient, "You are in perfect condition," especially if the patient was your godmother.

She lived in a simple and healthful way, always a good night's sleep and a diet without excess. She took a walk of about an hour every day in the company of my mother, going up the hill on Majalis Street in the southwest and coming back on Trefort Street in the southeast. My mother loved these walks and on the few occasions my godmother could not join her, my mother would go alone.

As before, my godmother came to our house every night for literary discussions and dinner. My sister Magda, whom we all called Baba, had moved to Italy by then, after marrying an Italian diplomat. Otherwise, the seating arrangement for dinner was the same as always, my mother at one end of the table, my godmother at the place of honor to her right, my father at the other end, I to his left. It was a memory I would cherish through all the troubles ahead, all these wonderful people I held most dear, finding so much joy in each other's company over a simple dinner.

❧

As was the practice then, I went to the homes of my patients to diagnose and treat them. Among my earlier patients was a young woman who was working in the household of a good friend of the family. She complained about the enlargement of her neck and a feeling of fatigue when, in the past years, she had always been full of energy. I examined her and found a slightly enlarged thyroid gland and, something extremely rare, palpable nodules in her thyroid. No one knew then how to cure this condition. In fact, no one does even now, which shows that however far we have come, we are still at the beginning of treating illnesses.

My patient stared at me with a sad face. I did not know

what to do, but she was desperate that I should give her a prescription, anything. Knowing the importance of iodine for the thyroid, I asked her to try a very simple treatment. One drop of iodine tincture diluted in one glass of water daily for a week, then after a week's interval, another week of the iodine treatment. I was sure it was not toxic, but I had no idea whether it would work or not.

When I visited her three weeks later, she came out bustling with energy, a large smile on her face. I felt her thyroid gland. It was back to normal size. Moreover, the nodules were all gone! It was nothing short of a miracle for me. For my patient, it was an absolutely natural result, as she had believed in the cure right from the start. I was astonished more by her determination to get cured rather than my treatment. Or was it just the spontaneous evolution of a mysterious illness? I still don't know, and medical science has not given me an answer after all these years.

At that time, medicine had made no inroads at all in treating cancer. One of my patients was a close family friend, the widow of a bank employee. Her surgeon referred her to me after diagnosing her illness as inoperable cancer. Though she bore her suffering with grace, hers was one of my difficult cases, as I could give only temporary relief and nothing else. It was not easy to go two or three times a week to this nice and dear lady, to provide her some sedatives for alleviating her suffering and to try to comfort her as best I could. Today, we have made major advances in the treatment of cancer and other illnesses. But all doctors still come to a point when all we can do is listen with all our feelings as we hold the patient's hand.

Among the many anxieties of my patients at that time was the war advancing through Europe and the rest of the world. Through most of the war, the Hungarian government under the Regent Nicholas Horthy was walking a tightrope in trying to placate the Axis powers and simultaneously negotiating a separate peace with the Western powers. Hitler was very unhappy with Horthy's secret dealings with the Allies and his refusal to deport the Jews to Germany. The war finally came crashing into Hungary when the Germans occupied the country in the spring of 1944 and set up a puppet government.

A week later, I got draft orders from the Hungarian army to go to a field hospital at the Russian front in Worochta, Ukraine. Refusing the draft meant being killed on the spot as a deserter, without any investigation. I sadly said goodbye to my family and my patients in Kolozsvar.

At the front, I was assigned to a field hospital or "Feldspital" hastily improvised by the Hungarian army in an evacuated school. The common ailments then, as now, did not choose war or peace. The majority of people I treated came complaining of colds, fevers, and indigestion. As an internist, I was not charged with treating wounds, but I helped the surgeons whenever I could.

Due to my military service in Bessarabia, I was more familiar with epidemic typhus than anyone else in the Feldspital. DDT was still unavailable to the Hungarian army. There were several outbreaks of typhus at the front, and we did all we could through sanitation to stop them from spreading.

The commandant of the Feldspital was a nephew of the top Hungarian army physician. Soon after I arrived, the commandant summoned me for a private talk. He told me he knew all about my family, how "pro-Western" my family was, and that I had worked in Paris.

Then he told me that the Germans had already lost the war and that he did not want to become a prisoner of the Russians, but instead preferred to be captured by the Americans. His frankness amazed me.

Actually, I could not disagree with him. Neither of us believed in the official Hungarian or German radio, as they never spoke about any defeat or any retreat. It was always "strategic displacement of the victorious German army."

The commandant then gave me a small radio and asked me to listen to the BBC transmission and translate and report the news to him daily. He could always ask his uncle to order the Feldspital to move west, to the zone of American interests. I reminded him that to listen to the English radio was punishable by death. Of course he knew this, but he told me he trusted me. My instinct told me he was sincere.

A few days before the war ended, we were near Pilsen in Czechoslovakia when an old German general showed up and spoke to our commandant. He said that as Hungary had now been completely occupied by the Russians, we should give our oath to Hitler. I told our commandant in Hungarian that the American army was very close and that, if nothing else, it would be foolish in the extreme to do as the German general asked.

Our commandant then told the German general that we had already given our oath to the Hungarian Governor and we could not give it to anyone else without word from the Governor.

It so happened that the general was of the old-fashioned German officer type. He told us that we were considered prisoners of war and that we must give our arms to him. Because of the difficult physical situation, he had no way of imprisoning us. However, he trusted our word and the commandant's signature.

I quickly told our commandant to ask for a signed document of all the German general had declared. The general did as we asked.

Two days later, the Americans captured our Feldspital. We presented the German general's document to them.

The American general looked over the document. Then he told us, "You are not prisoners of war. You are displaced persons."

Food was very scarce at the camp of displaced persons. When the American army hospital at the camp began recruiting ward boys, I signed up. Since physicians were not allowed to volunteer, I had to hide my MD. The American army hospital already had enough MD's and they did not want to give menial jobs to professionals. They took me as a ward boy, so I began working in the American hospital, where the food was much better.

A few days later, an American soldier convulsing with fever and chills was admitted and put in a small isolation ward. I immediately diagnosed his malady as typhus.

Unlike many American doctors, I had a lot of personal experience with typhus. I immediately went to work, putting DDT, the anti-louse compound, on the patient and everywhere, to prevent contagion. I found some antipyretic medication and, with a lot of drinking water, gave it to the soldier. His trembling subsided.

In the afternoon, there was a big consultation with many physicians, including one with the rank of colonel. It happened that I had been assigned to the ward. There were lengthy discussions that led everywhere and nowhere. I could not restrain myself and raised my voice.

"Forgive me, your patient has typhus. Make an agglutination with his serum and Proteus X_{19}. The titer will be very high, but don't be afraid, I put DDT everywhere."

A dreadful silence followed. What was this ward boy talking about!?

Finally, the colonel spoke and asked me how I could know anything about all I was saying.

I confessed that I was a physician and former student of Charles Nicolle in Paris who got the Nobel Prize for his work on typhus.

A few days later, the Americans began asking for proof of our whereabouts on the day that they declared war. Those who could provide proof would be given the choice to go back to the city where they happened to reside at the declaration of war.

By chance, I found a useless store bill from Paris that, for no particular reason, I had never cleaned out of my wallet. The bill was dated two days after the declaration of war. The American authorities, perhaps mindful of the typhus incident, accepted it as proof, and so allowed me to go back to Paris.

india ink

FROM PARIS, I DID NOT GO BACK to Transylvania but
went to Rome, to be with my sister Magda. She was then
living in Rome where her diplomat-husband Umberto
Natali was working at the Italian Foreign Ministry in the
Palazzo Chigi.

To earn my living in Rome, I wanted to practice internal
medicine. However, this was impossible without an Italian
medical diploma.

My brother-in-law turned to one of his friends, an eminent law professor at the University of Cagliari. The professor
arranged that the university would accept my medical diplomas and grant me a medical doctorate, in the process giving
me my fourth medical diploma.

I had no idea that it was not enough to have a valid diploma from an Italian university in order to practice medicine. It was also necessary for me to be a member of the
Albo degli Medici, the Italian medical association. However,
only Italian citizens could be elected members of the *Albo
degli Medici*. To make the prospects even more difficult, Italy
after the war was overcrowded, had unmanageable problems
with immigrants, and was not accepting applications for
citizenship.

By this time, Ambassador and Ambassadress Cerruti had
moved back to Rome. When the Ambassadress learned of
my predicament, she insisted that I should begin practicing
medicine in Rome. She told me that she sensed I had inher-

ited something from my maternal grandfather and that I would be a great doctor like him.

I mentioned that as I could not be a member of the *Albo*, I could never get permission to practice in Italy.

"Nonsense!" she exclaimed, and went directly to the telephone. She rang up the Ministry of the Interior and told them, "I am Ambassadress Cerruti and I want to speak to Scelba personally and not to a secretary."

To my surprise, the Interior Minister Scelba picked up the phone immediately.

Ambassadress Cerruti told him, "My dear Scelba, I am sending a very dear friend of mine to you now and please do what he asks of you!"

The Ambassadress turned to me. "Take a taxi and go speak to Scelba." So I went. To my amazement, Minister Scelba received me right away. I told him I was afraid it was not possible to do what the Ambassadress was asking, that I be allowed to practice medicine in Rome, not being an Italian citizen.

Minister Scelba said, "*Sì! Sì! Ma bisogna contentare l'Ambasciatrice!* (I know! I know! But we must make the Ambassadress happy!)"

Then he came up with an idea. "Rome is the capital of Italy, and it is the capital of Catholicism. Therefore it has two diplomatic corps. If your patients are diplomats, you have the privilege of extraterritoriality," he said. "So be the physician of diplomats."

Scelba, an eminent lawyer before he became Interior Minister, had found a way to legally circumvent the law he was supposed to uphold. When I went back to Ambassadress Cerruti with the advice of Minister Scelba, she exclaimed, "Wonderful! I shall call up my friends and let them know!" This was how my private practice began and why it was at first limited to high-ranking diplomats.

Ambassadress Cerruti tried hard to get an Italian citizenship for me. She would always go to the top. But Minister Scelba himself could find no legal way to grant me citizenship. So the Ambassadress went to Pope Pius XII (Pacelli). However, the laws were so strict that even the Pope could not do anything.

I still have a letter written to Ambassadress Cerruti by the Secretary of Pope Pacelli, Monsignor Montini, who would later become Pope Paul VI. The letter regretted, on behalf of the Pope, the impossibility of getting Italian citizenship for Dr. Zoltan Ovary. I framed the letter and hung it on the wall behind my bed. A friend asked once why it was hanging up there. I joked, "If it falls on me while I'm sleeping, I shall take it as a double Papal blessing."

I was not satisfied with just having a private practice. I also wanted to continue working as a medical researcher, as I had done at the Pasteur Institute. The Chairman of Internal Medicine at the University of Rome was Cesare Frugoni, then considered the best diagnostician in internal medicine in Europe. Frugoni happened to know one of my cousins, a professor of internal medicine at Szeged University in Hungary. I asked my cousin to write Professor Frugoni a reference letter on my behalf. Frugoni accepted me as a volunteer without salary at the university's Clinica Medica.

At that time, when Italy was just trying to recover from the war, most of the physicians at the Clinica Medica worked without salary. So famous was Professor Frugoni, doctors offered their services *gratis* just to have the chance to learn from him and perhaps add his prestige to their resumés. For the ten physicians on payroll, there were 104 working for free. I became the 105th volunteer and the only non-Italian-citizen.

Among the volunteers was a young physician, Guido Biozzi, who had been studying the release of histamine in asthma. I proposed to Biozzi that we do some experiments together, as I had a new technique for studying histamine release *in vivo* (i.e., in a living animal or human, as opposed to *in vitro*, in a test tube). I had learned this technique from the pharmacologist Nicholas Jancso on one of my visits back to Kolozsvar from Paris.

Jancso's father, Nicolas senior, had been my grandfather's successor as Chairman of Internal Medicine at the University of Kolozsvar. When the Romanians took over the university in 1918, Hungary created a new one in the city of Szeged as the successor of the University of Kolozsvar. Nicolas senior moved his family to Szeged and took the position of Chairman of Internal Medicine at the new university.

At that time, relationships between the professors' families and those of their student-successors were close, and so we were good friends with the Jancsos.

Nicolas Jancso junior went to study in Germany and became the last and most brilliant student of Ludwig Aschoff, the greatest pathologist in Europe in the first half of the century. He then took a position as professor of pharmacology at the University of Szeged, where he made sensational discoveries concerning the reticulo-endothelial system (RES).

I liked visiting him for a week or so every time I went back home for summer vacation. It was from him that I learned the use of India Ink in experiments, a technique he had developed in his study of the RES. On one of my visits in the early 1940's, Jancso took me to his lab and said he wanted to show me a new technique. He injected a rabbit intravenously (into the vein) with India ink. Immediately after, he injected the rabbit intradermally (into the skin) in one spot with a compound that released histamine, in another spot with histamine itself, and in a third spot with physiological saline as a control for no release of histamine. We waited, and in a few minutes, two similar black spots appeared on the two sites that involved histamine.

It was a very interesting experiment, but at that time neither Jancso nor I thought of using it in any study of allergy.

It remained in my memory, and only later in Rome in the late 1940's did I have the chance to do something with it. I thought that the Jancso technique could be very useful in investigating histamine in allergic reactions. After all, it had been discovered as early as the 1930's that histamine is the cause of the most important symptoms of allergy.

Before studying the role of histamine in allergic reactions, it was necessary to experimentally demonstrate histamine liberation in the living organism. So I said to Guido Biozzi, "There are all these substances known to liberate histamine. Why don't we use this technique to study them?"

He agreed, and we experimented with different compounds, injecting them into albino rats, which were the cheapest and most available laboratory animals. With the Jancso technique, we were able to dispense for the first time with the older, more complicated methods for showing histamine liberation. We got very interesting results, verifying in the laboratory earlier theories on histamine release and identifying new histamine-liberating substances.

Guido and I developed such close personal bonds through our experiments that he asked me to be his best man when he married Liliana, a lovely and talented amateur painter from Naples.

Being only a volunteer scientist, I could get no funding for our research, neither from the university nor anywhere else. I was happy that finally I could do research and discover new things. But everything had to be paid for by one person, namely myself.

· X ·

the day of saint anna

A T THAT TIME, a physician needed two things to be successful: (1) the ability to observe the patient very carefully in order to make the correct diagnosis; and above all (2) a good bedside manner.

Having patients in the diplomatic corps permitted me to finance my research. The money I earned from my wealthy and faithful patients I turned into albino rats and guinea pigs. And to save money, I often did preparation work on the experiments at home.

There was a time when I needed a constant supply of ovalbumin for the laboratory. Nowadays, one can easily order crystallized ovalbumin, a constituent of egg white, from the big pharmaceutical firms, but at that time it was not yet so readily available.

To obtain ovalbumin, I had to crystallize it myself from crude egg white, a lengthy process. Fortunately, my sister and brother-in-law had already taken their ambassadorial post in Damascus, leaving their house in Rome to me, so I was free to turn the kitchen into an extension of the laboratory and do all the crystallizing of ovalbumin at home. I needed the egg white, not the yolk. This meant that for weeks I had *crème caramel* every day, as its principal constituent was egg yolk. Our cook Lina became an accomplished accomplice, not just with the *crème caramel* but with the research, in her capacity as chief ovalbumin crystallizer.

At the time I started my private practice, Ambassadress

Cerruti gave me this advice: "You must ask the same fee as the high-ranking university professors, since you should consider yourself equivalent to them. Besides, if you ask less, people will think that you're not as good. Don't forget, people think that a cheap doctor cannot be a good one."

She also warned me that I should not accept cocktail invitations, because if I did, the Romans would think that I was a fashionable, not a serious doctor.

"Cocktails, no. Dinners, yes, but not too many," was her recommendation.

One day during the course of my practice, I was called on the telephone by Ambassador Dunn, the American ambassador to Italy. So I went to his residence at the Villa Taverna, a private palace complete with a huge garden right in the middle of Rome.

The Ambassadress was not feeling well. I checked her and assured her it was only a cold and it was nothing to worry about.

Ambassador Dunn thanked me and escorted me out of the room. Just before I left, he asked why I seemed less cheerful than usual.

I told him that, really, I did not want to speak about what was worrying me, but since he was asking, I would tell him. Just that morning, I got a letter from the Interior Ministry that my request for Italian citizenship had been rejected.

Ambassador Dunn just looked at me and said, "Oh!"

I went home after the visit, and while I was preparing to go to the laboratory at the Clinica Medica, our cook Lina told me that two policemen were waiting for me. I went downstairs, wondering why. They informed me that they were there to personally deliver an urgent letter from the Ministry of the Interior.

I opened the envelope with curiosity. It was a special decree from the ministry that my request for Italian citizenship had been granted. Along with it was a private note from one

of the secretaries whom I happened to know. It said that at
the intervention of the Ambassador of the United States,
the Minister had personally granted my request.

I found out only later that just at that time, there was a
big loan in question from the United States to Italy. When
Ambassador Dunn asked to speak to the Minister of Foreign Affairs, it was thought that something had gone wrong
with the loan. So the Minister asked the Ambassador if the
call was about the loan.

"Oh, no, the loan is going very well," the Ambassador
replied. "I'm calling about a private request. I am asking that
Zoltan Ovary's application for Italian citizenship be granted,
if possible."

There was great relief at the Foreign Ministry.

I was able to expand my clientele, many of my new patients referred by Ambassadress Cerruti, when I became an
Italian citizen. Among them was Marchesa Anna, widow of
Marchese Casati. She was American-born and never lost her
strong American accent when speaking Italian, although she
had been living in Rome for some thirty years. She occupied
the entire top floor of the Palazzo Barberini, one of the
most magnificent baroque palaces in Rome. Half the palace
had been created by Bernini, the other by his bitter rival
Borromini, the only instance when they worked on the same
building. Marchesa Anna had a collection of important old
master paintings in her apartment, the most marvelous of
these being a Madonna by Lorenzo di Credi.

She always invited me for the big dinner given every
summer on her name day, Saint Anna. No one who got an
invitation to this dinner ever turned it down. The number
of guests always corresponded to her age (then in the sixties), so that each year, there would be one additional guest.
She held the feast in the huge dining hall, its walls full of
old master paintings, and chandeliers swooping down from
the high ceiling. The tables gleamed with antique silver and

candelabra on linen tablecloths. The French food came in exquisite waves, each escorted by carefully chosen wines. But what made the dinner unique was the service.

Behind every chair was a valet. The Marchesa was well known for her generosity, which began with her household staff. She helped all her valets and other members of her household get good jobs after they finished working for her. She had, however, one condition: on the day of Saint Anna, they should come back to help her serve the dinner. I had never seen valets more happy and proud to perform their duties.

At that time, the Ambassadress Cerruti had also recommended me as physician to the Count Cecil and Countess Mimi Pecci-Blunt. They lived at the Piazza Aracoeli just below the steps of the Campidoglio in a late renaissance palazzo built originally for the Malatestas of Rimini. Their salon was always open to artists, musicians, writers, and archaeologists, who often called on them. The Pecci-Blunts had a special fondness for French culture, something they acquired when they were living in Paris before the war, where they held famous seasonal balls in their mansion in the Faubourg St Germain. Though I never met the Pecci-Blunts themselves before they became my patients in Rome, I happened to be familiar with a number of the same artists and doctors they had known in Paris, and this made them regard me readily not only as a physician but also a friend.

Count Cecil came from the Blumenthals of Paris and New York, a family well known for their generosity. In Paris, Cecil's uncle George Blumenthal, with his wife, founded many charitable foundations, like the *Goutte de Lait*, which ensured that needy children and sick people would get a free bottle of milk each day. In Marly-le-Roi, a town between Paris and Versailles, they established a free convalescent home for the needy, named Valfleury, the word being the French translation of the family name. In 1944, soon after I had returned to Paris, I happened to find work as temporary replacement for a doctor at Valfleury and became its physician-in-charge for a few months.

George Blumenthal's nephew Cecil married Mimi, the highly cultured and intelligent niece of Pope Pecci (Leo X). The Pope ennobled him and the new count took the name of Pecci-Blunt.

Countess Mimi often asked me to come over when she invited French musicians and writers, especially those I had already met in Paris, such as the musicians Hugues Cuenod, Darius Milhaud, and Francis Poulenc; and writers like Jacques de Lacretelle and Marguerite Yourcenar, then the only woman ever to get elected to the *Académie Française.*

Milhaud and Poulenc were both members of the new wave of French composers known as *Les Six* (the others being Honneger, Auric, Durey and Mme. Taillefer). They had all worked on a ballet by Jean Cocteau, *Les Mariés de la Tour Eiffel.* Cocteau was then making the pronouncement that modern French composers should revolt against Wagnerianism and French Impressionism, and should take their inspiration from the down-to-earth and witty worlds of the circus and the music hall. A journalist came up with the name *Les Six* for the composers working on the ballet, and they were forever lumped together under this name. In fact, they never worked together again, and their styles and goals were completely different from each other; for example, Auric was more interested in composing film scores and Honneger, opera.

Milhaud had the habit of writing his compositions anywhere and everywhere—in trains, automobiles, cafés, anterooms—as he believed that creativity should be as natural a part of life as breathing. He was famous for being the first composer to incorporate South American and black American rhythms and tunes into classical music. He came out with his jazz-filled *La Création du Monde* two years before Gershwin's *Rhapsody in Blue*. His inclination toward these musical forms came about as a result of two stints in the new world. The first was when his friend the writer and ambassador Paul Claudel employed him as an attaché at the French Embassy in Rio de Janeiro, just before the First World War. The next was during the Second World War, when Milhaud, a Jew born in Provence, fled to the United States, where he taught music at Mills College in California and made excursions to the jazz clubs in New Orleans.

Milhaud became celebrated after coming back to Paris from Brazil soon after the First World War, when a fantasia, *Le Bœuf sur le Toit (The Cow on the Roof)*, which he had based on Brazilian street music, was turned into a ballet by Cocteau. A new night club took the name of Milhaud's composition and it soon became one of the most fashionable night spots in Paris. Cocteau's avant garde surrealist ballet sought to amuse and shock at the same time. Among other touches, it called for a Parisian *gendarme* to be decapitated by a ceiling fan. Overnight, Milhaud became known as the brilliant clown of French composers. He told me he could not understand this, as he had been deeply touched by Brazilian street music and had thought all along that he had composed a serious work.

Francis Poulenc, for most of his life, was not considered a serious musician because he composed a lot of light-hearted parodies and also because, unlike the other *les Six* musicians, he came from a wealthy family and never had financial worries. I remember, when I was working in Paris between the wars, I was riding in a cab on the Champs Élysées when I noticed a man frantically waving his umbrella and calling out my name. I asked the driver to slow down, and saw that it was Francis Poulenc, whom I had met at the salon of a friend.

"Which way are you going?" he asked.

"To work. At the Pasteur Institute," I replied.

"Ahhh! We're going the same direction and I'm in a hurry. May I hitch a ride with you?"

"Of course, by all means," I told him.

He settled himself in the cab. "I always take the tram and the metro. I never take a cab," he said, "I am VERY rich, so I know the value of money."

Despite his lifelong reputation for flippancy, Poulenc turned out to be one of the great French composers, and even the most important French religious musician of this century, as could be seen in his poignant *Gloria* and *Stabat Mater*. His *Dialogue des Carmélites*, about a group of nuns who choose death to the dissolution of their order, is one of just a dozen or so operas composed in this century that remain in the regular repertory.

Marguerite Yourcenar, another friend of the Pecci-Blunts, had just published her masterpiece, *Mémoires d'Hadrien*, when she came to Rome for a visit in the early fifties. The Countess Pecci-Blunt invited me for a luncheon she was giving for the authoress. Mme. Yourcenar was gratified that the Countess had noted no anachronisms in her new novel set in ancient Rome, as the Countess was known to be an expert amateur archaeologist.

Mme. Yourcenar wanted very much to inspect some Roman road markers in a restricted area of the Terme di Diocleziano, one of Rome's great museums of Roman and Greek antiquities. Countess Pecci-Blunt happened to know that my sister and I were good friends with the director of the museum's lapidary section, Enrico Paribeni. She asked if I could arrange that Mme. Yourcenar see the road markers. I made the arrangements with Paribeni and it was agreed that I would pick up Mme. Yourcenar and accompany her the next day to the Terme di Diocleziano.

I was taking my breakfast early the next morning when

I got a phone call from Mme. Yourcenar. "Please tell me, should I wear white gloves or gray gloves?"

Off the top of my head, I answered, "Gray gloves."

I heard a huge sigh of relief.

At the museum, we went to the restricted section that contained various stone fragments including the road markers, squarish stone blocks with Latin inscriptions that would hold no interest for the casual observer. Mme. Yourcenar said she had always wanted to inspect these road markers. She took off a gray glove and with her fingers ecstatically traced the Latin inscriptions placed there by an unknown Roman many centuries ago.

The Countess Pecci-Blunt loved the modern art that was being made in Paris. She bought so many paintings, drawings, and prints that the Count had to have special cabinets made where the art works hung side by side, like coats. He complained to her that she was throwing away large sums for things that couldn't even be sold for pennies.

"I agree," she told him, "almost all of these works have no commercial value. But, you see, some could now be sold for ten times the whole amount I paid for the collection." She was referring to the dozens of works by Braque, Picasso, Leger, and Matisse in the cabinets. "And don't forget, we are helping all these artists, especially the ones whose works we could never sell."

One time, I went to see the Countess, who was nursing a slight fever. I found her in the study, struggling with an enormous pile of mail. "This is just today's. These are all invitations I have to decline as there is just no time. I realize it's not the biggest problem in the world, but I can tell you, it's so stressful and embarrassing to call and give my regrets all the time," she said. "But you know what would be worse? If these invitations stopped arriving!"

One day, I got an urgent phone call from another of my

patients, the Countess Consuelo Crespi, an Irish-American lady *née* O'Connor, who had married an Italian-Brazilian count. She was requesting that I rush to the Excelsior Hotel to see her friend, the Princess Gourielli.

I went right away and examined the Princess Gourielli. My diagnosis was pneumonia. The Princess was about ninety years old. (No one except the Princess herself knew her real age, and she was not about to give it away.) For anyone so old, pneumonia was an alarming illness.

I told her English secretary, Mr. O'Higgins, that I wanted to give the Princess an injection of the new drug penicillin as soon as possible. As was the usual practice when treating a critical illness, I wanted to get a second opinion and I suggested Professor Frugoni of the Clinica Medica. We tried to get hold of Professor Frugoni. He was out of town, and was coming back only the next morning.

I decided to give my patient not 200,000 units of penicillin, the recommended dosage then, but two million units. I just hoped for the best. In any case, it was understood that Professor Frugoni would come from the train station directly to the Excelsior at 7:30 AM. It was only after I left the Excelsior that I learned that the Princess Gourielli's maiden name was Helena Rubinstein, known throughout the world for her facial creams, lipsticks, and perfumes.

Early the next morning, I returned to the Excelsior. To my immense relief, my patient was without fever, reading the papers and taking breakfast. Professor Frugoni arrived a few minutes later. After examining the patient, he congratulated me for giving an unusually large dose of penicillin and doing it without delay. (Another account of this incident can be found in the Helena Rubinstein biography *Madame*, written by her secretary Patrick O'Higgins).

A few days later, I recommended a two-week vacation and suggested the island of Ischia opposite Capri. The island had a very good hotel. More importantly, telephone communications in Italy outside of Rome were very bad. I was certain the patient would have a good rest.

Two weeks later, the secretary, Mr. O'Higgins, paid me a visit and said that Madame Rubinstein was giving a cocktail at the Excelsior and wanted to invite me. I remembered Ambassadress Cerruti's admonition about never accepting any cocktail invitations, as a serious physician, so I politely declined.

Mr. O'Higgins insisted that Madame would really like me to come. Could I consider this a medical visit and they would pay me for it? Not getting an immediate reply, he pleaded, "We will pay double fee, but please come!" I found it so amusing to be paid for attending a cocktail, and double fee at that, I accepted, but of course did not take the fee.

In 1954, after I moved to work at the Johns Hopkins University in Baltimore, I got a telephone call from the Prince Gourielli. He said his wife was not well and could I come to see her in New York.

I told the Prince that I could not see private patients in the United States, as I had decided to concentrate on medical research and therefore had not bothered getting a license for clinical practice. The Prince was insistent. I said that if he and the Princess really wanted, I could go as a consultant, but her physician or physicians should be present, and I could participate in a consultation. So it was decided I would go to New York on Saturday morning.

It became clear to me that Madame Rubinstein was in the best hands, and everything was being done as it should. After the consultation, she asked what my fee was. I declined to get paid. She then asked if I would accept to have luncheon with her and her husband in the apartment. I accepted and said that though I didn't want monetary reimbursement, could she consent to pay me by showing her collection of paintings and by answering two of my questions.

Question 1: "Why did you want a consultation with me, when you obviously have the best medical care by the best physicians?"

Answer: "Because I trust you."

Question 2: "Princess, not long ago, I read in the papers that a man came to deliver roses to you, but he turned out to be a robber. What made you resist this obviously dangerous man?"

Answer: "You don't understand this because you are a man. When the robber asked for money and my jewels, I said, *No! I have lived long enough. Kill me! I don't give anything.* You see, at my age, to have the feeling that I still have power over a young man, it was worth all the risk!"

(The would-be robber was so flabbergasted he ran out of the apartment, leaving the hundred white roses behind.)

After luncheon, Prince Gourielli showed me the collection of paintings. They were mostly modern and most of them not to my taste. Among them were high-priced Picassos of women with three noses and such. In the place of honor, on top of the fireplace, hung a painting by Salvador Dali. It was a portrait of Madame Rubinstein holding up the world with two giant lipsticks.

· XI ·

the blue spot

At the time I first encountered Madame Rubinstein I was continuing my medical research at the Clinica Medica in Rome with my collaborator Guido Biozzi. One day, he got a fellowship to work for one year with Bernard Halpern, then one of the greatest authorities in experimental pharmacology, especially histamine. Dr. Halpern's laboratory was in Paris at the Broussais Hospital, which was directed by Professor Pasteur Vallery Radot. I had become a friend of Pasteur Vallery Radot's when we made our experiments on allergy before the war, so I volunteered to go to Paris to recommend Guido to him.

After I paid my respects to Pasteur Vallery Radot, he introduced me to Bernard Halpern, who headed the experimental section in Pasteur Vallery Radot's service. Another visitor dropped by a few minutes later. His name was Baruj Benacerraf. He was a young physician who had come to do research with Halpern. He was American but was born in Caracas. He spoke not only flawless English and Spanish but also a beautiful literary French. It turned out he had gone to the best schools in Paris as a teenager, then went on to get his baccalaureate at the *Lycée Condorcet*.

I learned later that his grandfather had emigrated from Algeria to Caracas and prospered in the clothing business. When his grandson Baruj was born, he decided that Baruj should get the best education, and so sent his son and the whole family to Paris.

Baruj and I immediately became friends. I asked him to

help Guido Biozzi, who was coming soon to the same laboratory, as Guido was unfamiliar with Paris and did not speak French.

In France at that time, medicine was still in large part a patriarchal profession. The service of Pasteur Vallery Radot was the most coveted by those who wanted to learn clinical medicine. On the same day I arrived to recommend Guido Biozzi, another visitor came and Pasteur Vallery Radot asked all his collaborators to come to his office so he could introduce them. Pasteur Vallery Radot began, "Dr. Richet is the grandson of Charles Richet who got the Nobel Prize for anaphylaxis," and so on. Everybody was the descendant of some illustrious medical person. At the end, he presented Halpern. "And Dr. Halpern ... uhm ... he is the son of nobody. And by Jove, he works wonders!"

As soon as Halpern met Guido Biozzi, he asked him to demonstrate the fixation of India ink into the site of injected histamine. It did not work! In Rome, Guido and I had used the best available product, the German Gunther-Wagner India ink. It was not available in France, as the French were quite chauvinistic, especially just after the end of the war. Biozzi was desperate. He sent me a cable: "Help! India ink does not work!" So I sent him some Gunther-Wagner ink and then everything worked all right.

As the commercial Gunther-Wagner India ink contained phenol, it was toxic for long-term experiments. Biozzi and his collaborator Benacerraf drove to Hanover in Germany to explain to the manufacturers what they needed. The result was that the non-toxic brand of India ink, C.11/1431a, was soon placed on sale to the public.

Biozzi enjoyed such success at the Pasteur Institute that the French never let him go back to Rome. It helped that Professor Pasteur Vallery Radot was the personal physician of President de Gaulle. The French parliament legislated the "Biozzi Law," permitting Biozzi, an Italian subject, to be officially and permanently employed by the French. Biozzi and Benacerraf became close collaborators in Halpern's laboratory, where they produced a series of classic works, chief of which were their study of the phagocytic activity of the liver's Kupffer cells and their quantitation of the function of the reticulo-endothelial system.

In Rome, I continued working on the experiments Biozzi and I had begun. The most important discovery we had made was the Passive Cutaneous Anaphylaxis, or PCA, Reaction. When we first described the PCA Reaction, we did not realize that it would become a basic part of countless scientific experiments in the following decades.

I am sometimes asked by laymen what Passive Cutaneous Anaphylaxis means, and why we had chosen these words. We used the word "Passive" because the antibody in this case is produced by another organism and is injected. "Cutaneous" because it is a reaction of the skin (from the Latin word *cutis* for "skin"). "Anaphylaxis" because it is a reaction of the same nature as that observed by Paul Portier and Charles Richet at the turn of the century. Richet created this term from the Greek *ana*, meaning the contrary of something, and *phylaxis*, meaning protection. He coined this word to designate the phenomenon of an antibody producing an adverse and harmful reaction, instead of protecting the organism, as it usually does.

(Richet got the Nobel Prize for this work on anaphylaxis. Why only Richet got honored and not Portier is a mystery to which only the Nobel Committee knows the answer. This circumstance, by the way, is not unusual. Portier, who was my teacher at the Sorbonne, was a gracious man, and he never showed any resentment for the oversight.)

Later, while working on the PCA reaction, I wanted to quantitatively study the production of antibodies, specifically in allergic reactions. At that time, allergic reactions and most other biological phenomena were only observed but not quantified.

Quantitation is essential for scientific research, but it is also the basis of many activities even in everyday life. For example, in a farmer's market, we buy a certain quantity of onions or eggs and we give a defined quantity of money for it. To build or renovate a house, we need exact measurements. Without quantitation, everyday life, as most of us know it, would not be the same. Without it, science is not science at all.

Friends outside medical research have sometimes asked me how the PCA reaction works. Before I could answer this, I should define a few concepts.

First, there are the different ways one may get injected. Intradermally, i.e. in the skin. Subcutaneously, under the skin. And intravenously, into a vein.

Of course, for many people, there is no difference: an injection is an injection!

I should also define, if only in the most simple terms, the words "antibody" and "antigen."

An antibody is a product of an organism when this organism comes into contact with an invading foreign substance —the antigen. (The mechanism is infinitely more complex than this! However, I am not writing a scientific paper.) The term antibody was coined in the 1880's by German and French scientists studying immunization against tetanus and diphtheria. They found out that organisms naturally secreted these protein molecules to neutralize invading substances.

Interestingly, the term antigen was invented long after its twin term, antibody. It was created by a Hungarian scientist, Laszlo Detre, who worked in Paris at the Pasteur Institute at the turn of the century. Back in Budapest for a summer vacation, he went for coffee one night to the Abazia Coffee House. This coffee house was known as the place where scientists came together for discussions after dinner. It was in the Abazia that Detre used the word antigen for the first time, to describe the substance which, when injected into a living organism, provoked the formation of a specific antibody against it.

I knew the Abazia Coffee House well, as it was on the Oktogon Square, just opposite the home of my grandmother. In 1990, when I attended the Congress of the Hungarian Association of Immunologists near Budapest, I wanted to propose placing a commemorative plaque on the Abazia. So I looked it up and was saddened to learn that it had been destroyed during the Second World War and no longer existed.

◆ᴐ§ᴐ◆

The PCA reaction consists of the intradermal injection of an antibody, diluted in a saline solution, into a guinea pig or other experimental animal. This is followed, after a sensitization period, by the intravenous injection of an antigen mixed with a suitable dye like Evans Blue.

In our first experiments, Biozzi and I had mixed the antigen with India ink instead of Evans Blue. I began using Evans blue for two reasons. First, I was able to get it gratis from the Geigy factory, a big help as I had no funding. Second, it was less toxic and easier to use than India ink.

During the sensitization period, the antibody gets fixed to antibody receptors on mast cells, a variety of white blood cells present in many tissues. These cells contain a lot of granules and store many important substances. One of these is histamine, the substance that produces the symptoms of such allergic reactions as hives, runny nose, and shortness of breath. The most serious symptom is lack of breath due to muscular contraction of the muscles in the small bronchial tubes. As many know, this could at times cause death by asphyxiation.

During the PCA reaction, the antigen injected intravenously reacts with the cell-fixed antibody. This leads to the bridging of the receptors and starts a chain of reactions leading to the liberation of histamine from the cells.

This liberated histamine increases the permeability of the small veins in the neighborhood. Since the antigen is mixed with a dye, this dye is able to leak out of the now more permeable veins. This causes the dye to color the skin.

When Biozzi and I started working on these experiments, nothing or nearly nothing was known of what I have just described. After Biozzi left Rome for Paris, the work continued to intrigue me and I often stayed in the laboratory late into the night, unaware of time passing.

I will never forget the excitement when, for the first time, I saw at the site of the injection a pale spot emerge within the first few minutes. Then within a few seconds, it increased in intensity and became a bright blue spot. The experiment fascinated me even though I did not immediately realize what an essential role this blue spot would come to play in countless experiments around the world.

⟡

Blood is a very complex mixture of all kinds of white cells, red cells, and platelets, suspended in a fluid called plasma. When we take blood from the veins, it coagulates rapidly if precautions are not taken. This coagulated blood is in turn made up of two principal elements, the coagulum and the fluid portion called serum.

In the following weeks, I increasingly diluted the serum of immunized animals and injected the different dilutions into the skin of unimmunized animals. I wanted to find out up to what dilution I could still get a blue spot.

In this manner I discovered that I had found a way to quantify nanogram (one-billionth of a gram) amounts of antibody. Before this, the main method used in detecting antibodies was the Quantitative Microprecipitin Reaction of Heidelberger. It was a precise reaction, but it could not detect less than 50 micrograms of antibody (less than one-fiftieth of an ounce). Though less precise, the PCA reaction was much more sensitive, able to detect less than 0.01 micrograms of antibody. With the PCA reaction, it became possible for the first time to design and carry out experiments using 10,000 times less antibody than before.

Since quantitation is so basic in science, the possibilities opened up by such a discovery were indeed promising. Still, I wondered if I had made an error somewhere, since the greatest immunochemist of the century, Michael Heidelberger, had shown that the least amount of antibody detectable was 50 micrograms.

I therefore asked my friend Pierre Grabar at the Pasteur Institute if I could go to his laboratory in Paris to perform the experiment under his supervision. So I took the train to Paris and had him give me sera with antibody content that only he knew. Our experiment confirmed my earlier findings.

At the time that we were conducting the experiment in Grabar's laboratory, two other scientists happened to be in Paris as well. One was Michael Heidelberger, no less; the other was Otto Bier, the leading immunologist in Brazil. So Grabar arranged a meeting where I was to demonstrate the PCA reaction for them.

Heidelberger thought that the PCA reaction was simple, sensitive, and easy to perform, and that it deserved to be known. He recommended me to one of his most eminent students, Manfred Mayer, at the Johns Hopkins Medical School in Baltimore.

As for Professor Bier, he invited me to work for a few

months in his laboratory in São Paulo. I accepted and booked a seat on the Scandinavian carrier SAS from Rome. It was the only connection possible at that time (1950). There were no first—or business or coach—classes, only one cabin class. SAS sent a limousine to the house to drive me to the airport. Things were certainly different then!

On the way to São Paulo, we had to stop first at Dakar for refueling. The heat at the airport tarmac hit me like a blast from hell. I found it impossible to breathe. Never did I experience such heat, before or after.

We dragged ourselves to the air-conditioned restaurant where the passengers ate courtesy of SAS. There was only one dish on the menu: camel meat. I was starving, but the food smelled to me like dung, which left me no choice but to remain starving.

In the dining room there were some local vendors, and I bought a small wooden sculpture, the bust of an African woman with the contemplative expression of a Boddhisatva. I regarded it as a masterly work of primitive art; or art, period. When I later brought it back to Rome, my sister dubbed it my fiancée, and quickly incorporated it into a still-life she was painting.

We had a little bit of time before the plane left Dakar, but no one dared step out of the terminal until it was time to get fried again while crawling back to the plane for its next destination.

The only place in Brazil with an international airport was Rio de Janeiro, so before I could get to São Paulo, it was necessary for me to go to Rio first. I took the opportunity to see for myself the famous bay with its strangely-shaped islands and mountains. One only needed to look at the postcards to see that Rio had one of the most spectacular settings for a city, but it was different being right there. In the other splendid bays ringed by mountains that I had seen—for example Naples, Gaeta, and Amalfi—dawn and sunset hap-

pened gently and gradually. Rio was different, especially at
sunset. The colors on the mountain and the bay changed
from one minute to another. I was dazzled as I watched sun-
light, shadow, and reflection trounce each other in shades of
red, yellow, green, and blue.

One could only imagine how Rio must have appeared to
the first Portuguese explorer who came upon the bay on
January 1, 1502, the strip of land between water, rising forest,
and ghostly mountains still in a pristine state, uninhabited
except by a tribe of Indians. It was this Portuguese explorer
who started the misnomer by which Rio is known. He
thought the deep bay was the mouth of a river, so he named
the place Rio de Janeiro (River of January).

It made me wistful to see that many of the old buildings
in Rio had been supplanted by ungainly modern buildings.
What seemed from afar to be colorful colonial villages cling-
ing on the mountainsides were the *favelas*, shanty towns
without sanitation, well-known breeding grounds of hope-
lessness and crime. Everywhere I went, people would tell me
that I should by no means go near the *favelas*, or ride any
trams or buses that went there, "especially if you don't speak
Portuguese!" It made me sad to hear this kindly reminder in
a place of such splendor.

I took a small local plane from Rio to São Paulo. I went
straight from the airport to the *Istituto Biologico* where Otto
Bier was waiting for me. He took me to his apartment where
his wife had prepared dinner. He then drove me to a nearby
apartment occupied by a Brazilian family, where he had reserved a room for me.

I was surprised to find São Paulo such a modern city.
Despite the lack of an international airport, it was already
the largest, wealthiest, and fastest-growing city in Latin
America, with the greatest number of skyscrapers, the longest freeway, and the tallest building. The headlong drive to
modernity came at the expense of the beautiful old buildings

that were being torn down everywhere to make way for sky-scrapers. There was a grand boulevard, the Avenida Paulista, full of old mansions surrounded by elaborate iron grills and gardens. When I came back a few years later for a confer-ence, all the gardens had disappeared. In their place were skyscrapers; and it was impossible to see if the graceful man-sions were still there.

Otto Bier and I immediately went to work in his labora-tory. We collaborated on a number of studies on allergy that were later published in American journals. It so happened that Bier had also invited Anne Marie Staub, a colleague of mine at the Pasteur Institute in the 1930's. I had admired her then but we were always too busy with our own work to become more than just colleagues. It was at Professor Bier's laboratory that we became warm friends. After work, we would go to the attractions that São Paulo offered in seem-ing compensation for its reckless modernizing. It had the continent's largest park, greatest number of art galleries, and best museum of old European master paintings. It also had the world's largest snake farm. The farm was then already a world center in the research and production of antidotes against venomous animals as well as tetanus and rabies. It had more than 70,000 snakes, many of them penned in the open air. I had always been fascinated by snakes for their elegant malevolence, their silent yet spectacular comings and goings; and seeing so many of them slithering on top of each other seemed straight out of a surrealist's hallucination.

Sometimes, I would make expeditions to Santos, the port city that connected São Paulo to the ocean. There was a beach near Santos that changed completely between high tide and low tide. It was a sight I had never seen elsewhere. The beach would stretch out some two miles wide at low tide, piled with starfish, scallops, seaweed, conches, drift-wood, and sea horses. High tide would suddenly gobble up this bounty only to disgorge it six hours later.

There was a market I visited in Santos that sold all kinds of tropical hats, pots, beads, hammocks, etc. I stopped by a stall selling tropical birds, with a baby monkey thrown into the inventory. The monkey spotted me. It followed my every move with its big eyes. I went to pat it, and soon it was climbing all over my arms and shoulders and hugging me. I almost took it home; but at the last moment, I thought it would be cruel to keep a baby monkey in the little room I rented in the middle of rampantly modernizing São Paulo.

· XII ·

the beating heart

I WENT BACK TO ROME after six months working in São Paulo with Anne Marie Staub and Otto Bier. We were happy to have a reunion a year later in Rome at the 6th International Congress of Microbiology. Professor Bier had been named president of the immunology section and he had asked me to be the section secretary.

Part of my duties as secretary was to compile and publish abstracts submitted by the participants. At that time, all submissions were accepted for publication. Two abstracts I received made me push for the stricter guidelines that were adopted in later congresses.

One abstract was entitled "The Influence of Mind on the Growth of Bacteria." The article described experiments involving the cultivation of two identical sets of the microbe *Staphylococcus aureus,* each set grown on ten soft-agar plates. The only difference was that on one set of microbes, the author, before cultivation, repeated 30 times: "You are sterile. No growth. No growth."

The article claimed that a lesser number of microbes developed on the plates which the author had concentrated on, and moreover that the result was statistically significant. I had sympathies for the author's metaphysical aspirations, but as far his experiment was concerned, it was not well-designed to say the least. I had no mandate, however, to reject any submission, and as the author did not wish to withdraw the article, I had to publish it.

The congress organizers had requested that if possible,

abstracts should be no longer than one page, including the bibliography. However, I received one that was 32 pages long and contained some 2,000 references that included both Aesculapius and Hippocrates, from whom no written remains exist—especially Aesculapius, a mythological figure, a god!

I wrote about my problem to the congress president, Sir Alexander Fleming, who some years earlier had won the Nobel Prize for his discovery of penicillin. Sir Alexander's response was concise: "Rubbish!"

Still, I was hampered by the absence of any mandate to reject submissions. The author could not be persuaded to withdraw the paper, even by an enumeration of the glaring fallacies in his article. Finally, I found a diplomatic way around the problem. I persuaded the author that he would be better off publishing his masterpiece somewhere else, as the number of people reading the Congress extracts was limited to the participants only.

As compensation for all these problems, there were a good number of participants who came with solid work and whose feet were on the ground.

There was Anne Marie Staub, whom I had invited to stay at our house in Rome during the congress. She was working on the bacillus of typhoid fever, particularly on the chemical composition of its polysaccharide. A great discovery in polysaccharide chemistry had just been made at that time in Germany by Otto Westphal and his student and collaborator Otto Luderitz, and Luderitz was due to present their yet unpublished data at the congress.

Luderitz had written to me that he would like to contact Anne Marie Staub in the congress, as Staub was then the leading name in polysaccharide chemistry. I soon found out that arranging this meeting would not be easy.

Anne Marie was an intense French nationalist. The German occupation of Paris during the war was very much on her mind. Never would she consent to sit down with a German. It was only after much persuasion that she agreed to meet Luderitz—not publicly, but in our house. And not for dinner, only for tea.

A few years later, after ground-breaking articles jointly signed by Anne Marie Staub, Otto Luderitz, and Otto Westphal, Anne Marie appeared as guest speaker, in fact the sole speaker, at the opening of the new Otto Westphal Institute in Germany.

Apart from science, Westphal and Anne Marie had something else in common: music. Anne Marie loved singing Bach cantatas. Westphal was an ardent flutist, as I learned many years later when I heard him play in New York at the home of Baruj Benacerraf, another immunologist with a passion for music.

At the time of the Rome congress, very little was known about the blood and its components. For example, all we had learned about the lymphocytes was that they were small mononuclear white cells in the circulating blood. There prevailed a great confusion about lymphocytes, as they all looked the same under the microscope. Virtually nothing was known about their functions. What a change in less than fifty years!

Now we have found out that lymphocytes, even if they all look the same, are really a heterogeneous population divided into B, T and NK cells, which are further subdivided into different cell types. Today, a huge portion of the public is aware that different types of T cells exist, due to the many articles about the AIDS epidemic and about the destruction by the HIV virus of one variety of lymphocytes, the CD4 T cells.

At the time of the Rome congress, there was still a raging dispute and confusion on whether antibodies were produced by lymphocytes or plasmacytes. Astrid Fragreus from Stockholm was the first to advocate that it was the plasmacytes that produced antibodies. To underline her contention, she came to the closing banquet in a white silk gown embroidered with purple granules representing the plasma cells. The inventiveness of her dressmaker did not stretch to depicting antibodies. Astrid was more than happy to make up for her dressmaker's shortcoming, with tireless explanations of her gown as it related to her scientific position.

Today, we know that plasma cells are *the* antibody-producing cells. It's not as simple as this, however, for all plasma cells start their lives as B lymphocytes. Of all the varieties of lymphocytes, it is only the B type that produces antibodies. While young, these cells produce but don't secrete antibodies. When they get older, they secrete antibodies but in negligible amounts only. At the end of their lives, they turn themselves into plasma cells. It is these plasma cells that secrete the significant amounts of antibodies. So all in all, Astrid, dancing gaily that night in Rome in her white and purple gown, turned out to be right.

⚜

After the congress, I went to Damascus, where my brother-in-law had been posted as Italian ambassador to Syria. He and my sister showed me the splendid mosques and other Islamic monuments in the capital and brought me to the out-of-the-way places in Syria and Lebanon, most importantly the Roman ruins of Baalbek. We went to visit Jerusalem and Bethlehem, then still under Syrian administration. I later went back to these cities several times on my own, to give lectures or attend scientific meetings. They had become Israeli by then.

I met some interesting persons during my first Syrian sojourn. Among them was an elderly gentleman who was a friend of my brother-in-law. He had a fabulous collection of old coins, mainly gold, used by the crusaders and the ancient Greeks. He was impressed that I knew something about antique coins. I explained to him that I also had a collection once, when I was a boy, mainly Roman, Greek and medieval coins, though not in gold but in copper and bronze and some in silver. It had remained in Kolozsvar and was now lost.

He felt sorry for me and gave me two gold coins, one from 13th century Egypt and the other from 16th century Venice. I hesitated to accept them but he told me that in Syria, to refuse a gift was a serious offense. So I happily realized I had no choice.

The gentleman told me that he was Catholic and came from an old Venetian family. Even though his family had lived in Damascus for generations, they had kept their Italian citizenship. His name was Marco Polo. As I found out at the Italian embassy, he was a direct descendant of the medieval explorer.

Back in Rome, other kinds of explorers were being feted. There was a huge exhibition of Picasso's work at the Museum of Modern Art. After the Picasso retrospective, denizens of the art world wanted to organize another exhibition by another famous Spanish artist, Salvador Dali. I knew some members of the organizing committee, like Irene Brin, who told me the following story.

When the committee met with Dali, he asked how many paintings had been displayed at the Picasso exhibition. When he got his answer, he declared he would expose twice as many.

This would be too many for the funds set for the exhibition. Therefore the committee members came up with the idea of telling Dali that one painting by him would be better than all the paintings together exposed by Picasso. This mollified Dali.

Dali was also very concerned about the exhibition space.

He wanted a better place than the Modern Art museum. The committee asked the Princess Pallavicini if she would lend the Casino Rospigliosi-Pallavicini at her palace complex in Rome. This was the grand pavilion where Guido Reni had painted his celebrated fresco, the *Aurora,* and for which Bernini created a fountain. This would certainly be more prestigious than the Modern Art museum building. Princess Pallavicini accepted. Dali was satisfied.

Ambassadress Cerruti had recommended me to the Princess Pallavicini, who became not only a patient but also a friend. From the beginning, I admired her knowledge of art, which rivaled that of the greatest scholars. She was, moreover, a lady who was extremely mindful, in an old-fashioned way, of her obligations and commitments. I continue to admire her. She radiates joy and concern for other people even when she herself struggles with a chronic, paralyzing illness. Her immense fortitude and sense of duty sometimes make me recall her predecessors, like Isabella d'Este, the renaissance patron of the arts, and Caterina Sforza, the duchess who defended her city from Cesare Borgia.

Before the opening of the Dali exhibition, I got a telephone call from Princess Pallavicini asking me to have luncheon at her palace with the artist himself. Princess Pallavicini told me later that she thought I would be a better person to ask than Federico Zeri, the leading art connoisseur, who was known as the "Berenson of Rome." I had met Zeri at the Palazzo Pallavicini several times while he worked on the illustrated catalog of the collection of the Princess. I knew Zeri as the passionate, outspoken advocate of Art with a capital A, quick to get into a brawl over any opinion he perceived to be foolish or ignorant.

During the luncheon, Dali announced he had just finished his "Christ on the Cross." He said he had finally found the exact place for it. "But," he stated, "of course the

Moses of Michelangelo must be moved." I understood then why the Princess did not want Zeri and Dali together.

A good friend of mine, the linguist Andrew Sihler, gave a postscript to this incident many years later when he wrote to me that perhaps Dali was not an egotist after all. In Andrew's eyes, Dali was, instead of being an egotist, "a mountebank, a showman. He seemed to have recognized that without theater—mostly in the form of outrageous personal behavior on his part—his art wouldn't go anywhere, once people got over marveling at the technique."

At Princess Pallavicini's invitation, I went to the *vernissage* of the Dali exposition. The actual opening was at 7 PM, with a pre-exhibition reception at 5 PM given by the Princess at her palace. The palace was packed. When afterwards someone asked me who was there, I answered with only a touch of hyperbole, "Everybody but everybody, alive and half-alive. Some even crept out of their sarcophagus to get there!"

Princess Pallavicini held the reception at the red salon that contained the thirteen Rubens paintings. There were two main groups of people. One around the Princess, a crowd of well-wishers and flatterers. The other around Salvador Dali, who was surrounded by so many admirers and curiosity-seekers that only the ends of his moustache pointing to the ceiling could be seen.

At 7 PM the *Aurora* pavilion opened. We all went from the palace through one of the side portals and made our way through the suspended garden to the grand pavilion. In the main hall and two adjacent ones hung the paintings, dreams or nightmares depending on how one took Dali's art. Another hall held Dali's jewelry, including some mechanical pieces like the famous beating heart in diamonds and rubies.

I was standing in one of the halls, speaking to one of my patients, the French Ambassador to the Vatican, Vladimir d'Ormesson. It so happened that the Ambassador did not like Dali's paintings. Suddenly Dali entered the room and, seeing the Ambassador, went directly to him.

The Ambassador exclaimed with wide open arms, "Maestro, this is remarkable!" It was a lesson in how to say something complimentary without committing oneself.

america

IN 1954, UPON THE RECOMMENDATION of Michael Heidelberger, Manfred Mayer invited me to join his Department of Bacteriology at the Johns Hopkins University in Baltimore on a Fulbright fellowship.

The fellowship stipulated that I go by ship. I chose the steamliner Queen Elizabeth II and traveled to London for embarkation. By coincidence, my friend Paul Kallos, a Hungarian who moved to Stockholm after the war, had invited me to an allergy conference then being held in London. Kallos' specialty was allergy, and he founded a society of scientists interested in allergy, naming it "Collegium Allergologicum Internationale." I believe he chose a Latin name not only because Latin was an international language, but also because it had remained a living language for physicians in Hungary as late as the 1940's, when autopsies were still being written in Latin.

The first gathering of the Collegium Allergologicum was held on a Sunday afternoon at a reception at the Ciba House, the London headquarters of the Swiss pharmaceutical company. Soon after I entered the ballroom, a small, elderly gentleman approached me, looked at my name tag, shook my hand, and introduced himself as Dr. Giles. "I like your blue spots on the guinea pig," he said.

I was pleased that somebody had read my publication and said, "It is only the application of the Prausnitz-Kuestner reaction." In 1921, Karl Prausnitz, in Hamburg, showed that human allergies could be transferred. He made this famous discovery after injecting his own skin with the serum of his colleague Kuestner, who was allergic to fish, and then re-injecting the same site with fish extract.

Dr. Giles laughed and said, "Oh, this Prausnitz is really nobody," and went off to get a cup of tea.

I was surprised by the man's statement and went to Daniel Bovet and asked, "Who is this Dr. Giles? His ignorance is appalling!"

"But he *is* Karl Prausnitz," answered Bovet. It turned out Prausnitz hated Hitler so much, he had emigrated from Hamburg to the Isle of Wight, and taken his mother's maiden name.

Prausnitz and I remained in contact after our first meeting. I was later invited to give the Karl Prausnitz lecture at another of the biennial conferences of the Collegium Allergologicum when I published the story about our first encounter, along with a cordial letter he sent me not long after.

After the conference, I embarked on the Queen Elizabeth II for the five-day voyage to the United States. At that time, making the trip by air was considered a great luxury. Travel on the grand liners was the habitual, cheaper way. How things have changed!

The Fulbright Fellowship authorized me to take cabin class, somewhere between luxury and steerage. I spent most of my time on the liner reviewing scientific journals and writing papers. The ship had a small cabin with a typewriter reserved for the passengers. I often went there to write my papers. One day, the door of the cabin opened and a striking lady came in. It was the Queen Mother of England. The captain was showing her and her escort around the ship. I stood up and made a bow.

The Queen Mother smiled at me and said, "Please sit down."

I said, "But how can I continue typing when Her Majesty is in the same room?"

She nodded graciously at me. Her genuine smile and simple behavior made me sense why the Queen Mother was so popular with her people.

Her appearance also reminded me of a chance meeting I had with her hat maker some three years before. At that time, she was still the Queen, as King George VI was still alive.

I was flying from London, where I had attended a conference, back to Rome with a stopover in Paris to see some friends. A gentleman was seated beside me. He was shaking and twitching all over and kept muttering, "Oh my God! When will this flight be over? Oh my God!"

I asked him if he was all right. He said no, as he was in mortal fear of flying and always knew that every time he flew, the plane would crash.

I assured him that plane flights were no longer so extraordinary and he shouldn't be so afraid. Nothing I said could assuage his fear, so I asked him why he didn't take the train and ferry instead.

"Unfortunately," he replied, "I have to fly back and forth all the time from London to Paris as I have no time to spare, with all the shows in both places."

It turned out that he owned the most successful millinery house in London and among his duties was making the Queen's hats. As she was eager to keep up with the fashion in Paris, he always had to fly to Paris for the hat shows.

"After enduring these horrible flights, I go to the palace to show the Queen my latest designs," he said. "She always likes them very much, but the trouble is she always has to call the King for his approval. And when he comes, he also likes the hats a lot, but objects that the Queen must be seen by the people. So he asks me to turn up the front a little, and make the brim a little narrower. I do as he asks and then he goes on to make other suggestions." With an exasperated sigh, he said, "And so we always end up with very much the same hat the Queen always wears!"

I looked at the Queen Mother's hat as she dutifully bore the onus of following the captain showing her the typewriters in the room. She was wearing a small, nondescript hat with a narrow, upturned brim. The Queen Mother smiled and nodded goodbye to me and then they left the room.

With the distraction of the Queen Mother's hat gone, I sat down and continued my musings on allergy at the typewriter.

It wasn't long before the QE2 began her approach to New York harbor. Suddenly, everyone was rushing to the deck, eager to catch the first glimpse of the Statue of Liberty. I myself was more concerned about the formalities of the debarkation, my mind filled with images of endless streams of tired immigrants herded into draughty halls at Ellis Island. My own arrival didn't quite measure up to the myth, as the disembarkation went faster and less dramatically than I had imagined. I took a taxi to the hotel where my friend, the Hungarian writer Sandor Marai, had made a reservation for me. From the windows of the taxi, I watched the passersby. It seemed to me a different world, with the people dressed more casually and moving more informally than in the cities of Europe I had lived in.

The fabled skyscrapers of New York impressed me, of course. But I was not struck by any beauty. For sure, New York was different from any other city I had seen before, but that was it. The city, as I would learn, had attractions other than massive buildings.

Early the next day, I called my friends from Kolozsvar, Ella Farkas and Paul Savet. They were now both living in New York. Much had happened to them, especially to Ella, since the time that all three of us were studying in Paris in the twenties and Ella chose to marry Joseph Kory over Paul Savet.

As it turned out, Ella's marriage to Joseph Kory did not work out and Ella wanted a divorce. Her father Mozsi came to my father and told him, "Elemer, try to persuade Ella not to divorce. I know that Jozsi is a difficult man. But what can you expect? He's an artist! And besides, I have learned to like him."

However, Ella and Joseph did divorce. As Joseph continued coming to my mother's salon every night, Ella stayed home with her new husband. But I remained friendly with her and the husband, a charming man, Miklos Sebestyen. His father David was one of the most prominent Jews in Kolozsvar, the founder and patron of Kolozsvar's Jewish Hospital, and knighted by Ferencz Jozsef.

Hitler's invasion of Hungary in 1944 was so swift most Hungarians were caught unprepared. When the deportations began, Augusta Kemeny, the wife of Janos Kemeny and the lady of the Marosvecs castle (where the writer's group Helicon of Marosvecs met regularly), offered to shelter Ella and her family either in the castle or in one of the empty hunting lodges in their forest. Augusta was among the numerous Hungarians who offered shelter to the Jews. It was only after the war that most people learned of the gas chambers and extermination camps of Auschwitz and Dachau. Even those who listened to the BBC, a crime punishable by death, never heard a word about the death camps. Many Jews thought of the deportations as yet another episode in their long history of persecution that they could nevertheless survive. So it was not surprising that Ella declined Augusta Kemeny's offer. She and her husband were deported to Auschwitz. Ella's husband died in the camp. Ella herself barely survived. She was no more than skin and bones when the war ended.

She returned to Kolozsvar. Paul Savet, who had stayed on in Paris and escaped the deportation of Jews from France by emigrating to the United States, heard about Ella. He had always loved her from the first time he saw her, when he was only ten years old. He went back to Kolozsvar. He proposed to marry her and raise her son Laci as his own. Ella accepted.

Ella and Paul now live in Long Island, New York. We are all now in our nineties and late eighties, and we still see each other regularly. We usually get together in their house or my apartment or in French restaurants in Manhattan. We don't speak about our tragedies from the past, as we want to spare each other all of these painful memories. But sometimes we revisit the days when we were students in Paris in the 1920's and went out together for dinners in the little restaurants on the Left Bank. Who would have known that three quarters of a century later, we would still be sitting together in another French restaurant, and another world away?

The first time I arrived in the United States I also saw another Hungarian friend, the writer Sandor Marai, who had left Hungary for Italy and then emigrated to the United States. He and his family were living on the upper East Side of Manhattan. To visit them, I took the New York subway for the first time. The ride was a crowded, disorienting experience. It was therefore a relief to get out of the noisy tunnels and find the familiar face of Sandor. To start life in another continent is never easy. I was thankful that my old friends from the old country were there in the New World to welcome me.

◆◦§◦◆

I could not stay long in New York as I had to take the train to Baltimore for my new appointment. Soon after I arrived,

Manfred Mayer and his staff asked me to demonstrate the PCA reaction. Mayer, whom I would get to know as a superb investigator and a warm-hearted director, did everything from the start to make my new job in the United States a rewarding one.

I started doing research with Abe Osler in Mayer's laboratory. We soon discovered that the old puzzle from before the First World War, i.e. the liberation of poisonous substances during anaphylaxis, the so-called anaphylatoxins, was really not a mystery at all. We established that it was nothing but the breakdown of important constituents of body fluids, called complement. It had been for the discovery of this complement that Jules Bordet, one of my teachers at the Pasteur Institute, got the Nobel Prize forty years before, and it was he who first made me realize the importance of complement in medical research.

Apart from laboratory work, I worked as a teacher at the Johns Hopkins medical school. I also received numerous invitations to lecture on the PCA reaction, thereby getting the opportunity to travel around the United States. Among the institutions that invited me was the Walter Reed Army Hospital. After my lecture at Walter Reed, the hospital director sent a thank-you letter. I stuck the letter inside my attaché case and then completely forgot about it. It would later reappear unexpectedly from its hidden corner when I needed it most.

At that time, I had also started collaborating with John Fahey of the National Institutes of Health in Bethesda, Maryland, on classes of human antibody able to sensitize mice. One day, he asked me to give a seminar of two lectures at the National Institutes of Health, one on the PCA reaction and the other on the subject of my choice.

"Are you sure that I can speak on any subject I want?" I asked him.

"Definitely," he replied.

I went home and thought about it. Then I wrote to him that the subject of the second talk would be "The Evolution of the Doric Capital in the Temples of Paestum, with slide illustrations." He thought it was a joke but I assured him I was serious. He reckoned the subject was too unorthodox for the National Institutes of Health, but he let me go ahead.

As it turned out, the second lecture was as well attended as the one on the PCA reaction. I told the seminar participants all about Paestum, a place that gave me much inspiration in life and work. It lay some two hours by train from Naples, south beyond the ruins of Pompeii and Herculaneum. It had three Greek temples from the fourth and fifth centuries BC, all with Doric columns, standing in a silent plain between the mountains and the sea. The temples had miraculously survived the ravages of time and neglect. Studying these temples built in different periods, one could see how each group of artisans had built on the innovations of earlier ones. It always left me marveling how the labor of these unknown workers could still reach out and inspire through the distance of millennia. People approached me afterwards to thank me for a refreshing lecture. Fahey was relieved and delighted at the response to such an unusual talk at the National Institutes of Health.

Soon after I began my fellowship at Johns Hopkins, the chairman of the Department of Bacteriology, Thomas Turner, offered me a permanent research and teaching job. It was necessary for me to change my visa before I could formally accept the offer. This meant having to go back to Italy to apply and wait for the visa.

Permanent-immigrant visas to the United States were at that time granted only at the American consulate in Naples. After several months, I decided not to wait any longer for the summons from the consulate and went down to Naples with my papers. There were huge crowds of applicants and as the hours went by, more people kept squeezing into the choking consulate. Finally, I reached an officer, who began looking over my papers. He told me I should have no problems about my application. However, I would have to wait a long time, possibly years, as there were so many applicants ahead of me. I felt downhearted and distracted. When I got up, my briefcase fell and my papers scattered on the floor. I knelt down to gather them. The officer came over to help me. He was picking up some papers when he stopped and asked, "What is this?" He was holding the thank-you letter from the Walter Reed Army Hospital.

"Oh, it's nothing, it's only a letter of thanks for one of my lectures," I said.

"You gave a lecture at Walter Reed?" The officer looked over the letter more closely. Then he said, "Your visa is granted." Once again, I found out what an important role chance played in my life.

Finally, I could go back to Baltimore and work again in Manfred Mayer's laboratory.

· XIV ·

hypersensitivity

PHILADELPHIA WAS JUST OVER AN HOUR away from Baltimore, and it was there that the eminent immunologist Fred Karush worked. He was then working with rabbit antibodies against hapten molecules. We had met at the International Congress of Bacteriology in Rome in 1952. I contacted him as I wanted to try out the PCA reaction with antibodies against haptens.

The word "hapten" had been coined by Karl Landsteiner from the Greek word meaning to hold or to grasp. A hapten is generally a small molecule capable of reacting with a specific antibody. But the hapten is unable to provoke the formation of an antibody if it is not coupled to a larger protein molecule. Landsteiner therefore called this protein molecule the "carrier." He demonstrated these findings after he emigrated from Vienna and began working at the Rockefeller Institute in New York. When Landsteiner got the Nobel Prize for his work on blood groups, he exclaimed, "They gave it for the wrong thing! My work on haptens is more important." Working with Fred Karush, I soon confirmed that the PCA reaction also works well in quantifying antibodies against haptens.

In the 1930's, Michael Heidelberger had already shown that antibodies are not a "property" of the serum, but real substances that can be weighed. His research solidly put an end to many more or less fantastic theories on antibodies.

Heidelberger's student Elvin Kabat, working with the

Nobel Prize laureate Theodor Svedberg in Stockholm, then showed that antibodies are gamma globulin molecules. As scientists knew, gamma globulins are proteins with a high molecular weight of 150,000 daltons. It was no surprise that they faced daunting problems in trying to analyze such a huge and elaborate molecule.

In 1959, the English immunochemist Rodney Porter published his first investigation on the nature of gamma globulin. Porter had the idea to reduce the size of gamma globulins, first by digestion and later by dissociation of their amino-acid chains.

He used the enzyme papain, obtainable from such sources as the papaya fruit, to digest the gamma globulin molecule. He obtained two types of fragment, each fragment reduced to less than half of the original molecule.

One fragment could still combine with the antigen. Therefore he called it Fab (fragment antigen binding). The other could no longer bind with the antigen but became crystallizable. He therefore called it Fc.

It was curious that nobody thought at that time that if the fragment was crystallizable, it must be the same in every antibody. After all, if two crystals from two different samples are the same, then the two samples must also be the same.

In any case, my friend Fred Karush had been studying rabbit gamma globulins specific for sugars. He repeated Porter's experiments a few days after Porter's report came out in the journal *Nature*. Instead of using non-specific gamma globulin as Porter did, Karush used gamma globulins specific for well-defined sugars. These sugars were hapten molecules that he coupled to carrier molecules to make complete antigens.

I went to Karush's laboratory in Philadelphia to do our first collaborative experiment.

We injected different antibodies made against specific antigens into the skin of guinea pigs. (As a reminder, antigen is a substance, generally a foreign one, against which an organism makes an antibody.)

Then we injected different antigens dissolved in physiological saline and Evans blue dye into the veins of the animals.

A blue spot would appear in about thirty seconds at the sites where we had injected the antibody earlier, but only under certain conditions.

1) We did not get a reaction (blue spot) at the sites where we had injected the control (physiological saline solution);

2) We got a reaction only when the antigen was specific to the antibody;

3) We got a reaction only when we injected the antigen several hours after the injection of the antibody.

Fred and I became convinced that with the PCA reaction, we could investigate many problems regarding antibodies. Our collaboration is an example of how two scientists with different interests can complement each other, thereby producing unexpected results. Fred was especially interested in the structure of antibodies, and I in their biological activity, such as the hypersensitivity reaction produced by antibodies.

Through our experiments, Fred and I discovered that the Fc (crystallizable fragment) of an antibody carries its biological properties. This finding opened a new field in the study of antibodies. Each antibody has what is called specificity, i.e. it recognizes and reacts only with one specific antigen. For example, an antibody specific for pollen will react only with pollen but not with the polio or HIV virus, etc. With our finding, scientists could now study the specificity of the antibody separately from its biological activities such as neutralization, complement fixation, and detoxification.

Afterwards, I made an interesting observation. I found that to provoke hypersensitivity reactions, two molecules of an antibody must first get fixed to some receptors on the mast cell and then get bridged. This bridging of two cell-fixed molecules is the first step for a great number of biological phenomena. It was the first time that this step had been defined.

I wanted to quietly investigate the line of research that this discovery had opened up. At the same time, I wanted to publish it in order to establish priority. I asked my friend Daniel Bovet what I should do. He replied that if I published in the *Comptes Rendus* of the French Academy of Sciences, I would get the priority and not the publicity. Though much respected by researchers in my field, it was not read widely. And he was right. I established priority and even today, now that the bridging hypothesis has become an accepted fact, most scientists have not learned where this idea first appeared.

⊷⟩§⟨⊶

In 1958, I received a letter from Hugues Cuenod, whom I had met in Paris in 1936 when we began rehearsing Bach's *Christmas Oratorio*. He wanted to let me know that he would be singing the role of Apollo in Claudio Monteverdi's opera *Orfeo* in Annapolis. As Baltimore was so near, he was enclosing a ticket as an invitation.

I went to hear him and ended up transfixed by the music written more than three hundred years before. At that time, most people, even in musical circles, had not heard Monteverdi's music. As I listened to the opera, I could not believe how such timeless music, so acclaimed during Monteverdi's time in Mantua and Venice, could end up completely forgotten for centuries.

After the concert, Hugues took me to a party that was being given for the musicians. It was here that I met the pioneer of the early music movement, Albert Fuller. He was the harpsichordist who played the continuo at the production. I became not only an admirer of his musicianship but also a close friend. He later established the ground-breaking musical foundations, Aston Magna and the Helicon, devoted to researching and performing music with authentic period instruments. I happily accepted when he asked me to become a founding board member of the Helicon.

It was my friendship with Hugues Cuenod that made it possible for me to go for several years to the musical performances at the annual Glyndebourne opera festival near London. Generally, it is impossible to get a seat, as all are taken by subscribers from the previous years. However, they always made an exception for Hugues.

It was at Glyndebourne that I heard for the first time one of the greatest operatic works, Claudio Monteverdi's *Incoronazione di Poppea*. Like Monteverdi himself, it was completely forgotten until Monteverdi was rediscovered in this century as one of the timeless masters.

The production, conducted by Raymond Leppard, was the highlight of the season. Cuenod sang the role of Nero's drunken friend with comic aplomb. As for the leading role of Poppea, it so happened that a cousin of mine, Magda Laszlo, was playing the part.

Magda came from the Armenian side of my family, which produced some excellent singers. My paternal grandmother Polyxena Vikol was one, though she never performed anywhere except the church on the main square, where she sang as soprano soloist on holidays. Her cousin Rosa Vikol, the mezzo soprano, sang regularly at the Opera in Vienna. Another cousin of mine, Elizabeth Torok, performed major soprano parts throughout Hungary.

Magda Laszlo gave a commanding performance as Poppea, who would stop at nothing to become Nero's wife and empress of Rome. Magda rounded her portrayal with touches of dignity and unguarded innocence. I was happy and proud of her achievement.

Monteverdi's opera ends happily for Poppea. Nero sends the conspirators Ottone and Drusilla to exile, repudiates his wife Octavia and orders her to be cast adrift in a boat, then crowns his lover Poppea empress. Of course we know that the real story did not end as happily, for Nero later kicked the pregnant Poppea to death.

Aside from Glyndebourne, I had the privilege of seeing Cuenod whenever he visited New York, about once a year in the seventies and the eighties. Once he was in New York when singers from the Paris Opera were performing at the Metropolitan Opera. A friend of mine, Fred Koch, who was a benefactor of the Morgan Library, called me up, inviting me to a reception he was giving for the Paris Opera singers.

I told Fred Koch that I would like to bring a friend to the reception. "I'm sorry," he said. "Only persons who know the artists are invited, and nobody else."

I brought Hugues Cuenod anyhow. Fred Koch was visibly shocked when I came in with someone he did not know. Suddenly, the French singers exploded: "What a wonderful surprise! Hugues is here! You never told us! How pleased we are!" Fred soon recovered from his shock and thanked Hugues Cuenod for making his reception a success.

When I first met Hugues in 1936 for our performance of the *Christmas Oratorio* in Paris, he was in his mid-thirties. He was 56 years old when he sang the role of Apollo in Annapolis. He wrote to me, "I was asked to sing this role, at my age! But I accepted it after all."

Well, it turned out that many years later, he would be asked to sing the role of the Emperor in the premiere of Franco Zeffirelli's production of *Turandot* at the Metropolitan Opera in New York, and became the only person to make his debut at the Metropolitan Opera after the age of

80. (He was 84, to be exact.) His was in fact the oldest documented debut ever in a major opera house.

Hugues more than held his own with the other cast members that included Placido Domingo and Eva Marton. The *New York Times* review called his debut "a special triumph," citing his "firmly and expressively sung Emperor" (3/14/87). Another *New York Times* writer noted simply that Cuenod remained the best Emperor he had ever heard (John Rockwell, 4/12/87). Hugues Cuenod is now in his mid-nineties and he still continues to sing professionally, among his latest performances being the comic Monsieur Triquet in a production of Tchaikovsky's *Eugen Onegin* in Lausanne.

Recently, I decided to visit him in his ancestral chateau in Lully in Switzerland on my annual European trip. He was already committed to give master classes at the Alde-burgh music festival in England on the first date I proposed, so I advanced my arrival by a few days. He met me at the train station and since I was allergic to cats he kindly hosted me in a hotel room overlooking Lake Geneva and the Alps. We spent the afternoon on the grounds of his chateau, a stone's throw away from the late Audrey Hepburn's, and we spoke of old times and old friends as we leafed through his guest books. Guests had written haphazardly on the pages, so it was not unusual to find a thank-you note from the 80's, followed by another from the 60's, then another from just a few weeks ago. I stumbled upon an entry by my cousin Eva, the one who wrote that letter to Queen Mary; Hugues point-ed out another, by our harpsichordist friend Albert Fuller. We looked for nesting swallows in his barn, in the garden drank wine bottled in his chateau, and under an overcast sky picked peaches from his orchard. So much had changed in the world since we met in the 1930's, but between us, it seemed not much had changed after all.

· XV ·

experiments

IN 1959, WHILE I WAS STILL WORKING at Johns Hopkins, I received an invitation to give a lecture at New York University. It was made upon the recommendation of Baruj Benacerraf, who was now professor of Pathology at NYU. Immediately after the seminar, Chandler Stetson, head of the Department of Pathology, offered me a permanent position at NYU.

Stetson had just succeeded Lewis Thomas as department head. Thomas, who had gone on to become dean of the medical school, was a brilliant scientist and an equally brilliant writer. He would become celebrated outside the medical field for such popular bestsellers as *The Medusa and the Snail,* and *Lives of a Cell,* which won the National Book Award. Stetson had been the student of Thomas and, as new head of the department, he prudently carried on the progressive policies of his predecessor.

My work in Baltimore had been very rewarding, but a permanent position at NYU could not be turned down. Moreover, New York had so much to offer. Even while residing in Baltimore, I would often commute to New York to catch its exciting exhibitions and musical events. So I moved to NYU and, the very day I arrived, sold my car, as New York was one of the few places in the United States where having a car was not only unnecessary but was in fact a burden.

I had no grant when I started working at NYU, so Baruj Benacerraf supported my work with his. Thankfully, I was soon able to get my own grant from the National Institutes of Health. In the fifties it was not yet so difficult for a scientist to do this, unlike today, with the vastly increased number of applicants and government cutbacks on basic research. With the grant I received, I was able to start my own projects and continue collaborating with other scientists, principally Baruj.

I found a small room across the street from the medical school, in a corner apartment building ten blocks from the Empire State Building, then still the world's tallest building. Soon, construction started in a huge empty space in front of the school. I learned that the architect I.M. Pei (the Louvre pyramid not yet a glimmer in his eye) was building a twenty-one-story apartment complex complete with its own ten-acre park, an absolute rarity in Manhattan. The area had originally been a bay called Kips Bay before some developers filled the bay in. Pei's apartment complex was to be called Kips Bay, a reminder of the fishermen and sailboats seen here in the past. I submitted an application to the apartment board for a lease and was the first person to move onto the floor as soon as the building was finished. I am still living in the same apartment forty years later.

Not long after I moved to New York, I got a call from a friend, the Transylvanian violinist Johanna Martzy. I had met her in Budapest and saw her often in Kolozsvar whenever she came to perform. She was among the best violinists of her time, performing and recording as soloist with such conductors as Wolfgang Sawallisch, Paul Kletzki, Hans Schmidt-Isserstedt, and Walter Susskind.

Johanna told me that she was in transit at the airport on the way to Chicago to play in a concert with George Szell. In two weeks, she would be back in New York and would love to have a good goulash with me. I said I would ask around for the best Hungarian restaurant in New York.

"Oh no," she said. "You will cook it."

"But I have never cooked anything in my life except scrambled eggs!" I told her.

"Well," she said, "I've heard you make pretty complicated experiments. Now, tell me, what is more difficult? To do one of your experiments or to cook a goulash?"

"Well, no doubt the experiments," I replied.

"So!" was all she said, and put down the receiver.

I was in a quandary. I had not the slightest idea about cooking and now I must cook a goulash! I called up the few Hungarians I knew in New York. A friend of my sister happened to be working as a nurse at the Roosevelt Hospital in Manhattan. She said she had an excellent recipe. It had been given to her long ago by my sister.

I thought about whom I should ask for dinner. There were the Benacerrafs. Baruj was an amateur flutist and his wife, Annette, an amateur pianist. Then perhaps I could ask Albert Fuller, the harpsichordist I met in Baltimore through Hugues Cuenod. Albert was glad to accept. As it turned out, he and Johanna had played together in Amsterdam not so long before.

Just before dinner, Baruj called to say that something had come up and he was sorry he could not make it. Could he instead send one of his young medical students with Annette? The student happened to be Lloyd Old, a brilliant scientist as well as the best amateur violinist I would ever meet. My friendship with Lloyd Old started at this dinner and during all these years grew stronger, if that is possible for one that began with such rapport.

To my relief, the dinner was a success. For the first time in my life, I got interested in cooking. At the advice of Annette, I bought a book of classical French cooking that had just come out, the first by Julia Child. (It is one of the more negligible mysteries that people always misspell her name as Julia Childs.)

Soon after, I invited Albert for a meal based on the new book. After the dinner, Albert asked me, "Why did you cook it for 35 minutes at 450 degrees when the recipe says 40 minutes at 400 degrees?"

I gaped at him and asked, "How did you know?"

"I tasted it," Albert said. It was then I found out that Albert was an excellent cook in addition to being an accomplished musician.

Years later, when Harvard University offered a position to Baruj, the Benacerrafs moved to Boston. One of Baruj's new collaborators had been living in Boston, and his wife offered to show Annette the best places to buy food.

They went to a butcher shop and she told Annette it was the one that Julia Child used. The butcher, overhearing the conversation, announced, "And Julia Child is the lady just behind you."

They turned around and Annette introduced herself. Julia Child remained glacial. Then Annette told her they had a mutual friend who had insisted that she ring Julia Child.

"Oh!" Julia Child exclaimed. Suddenly she turned nice and warm like a soufflé melting on the palate.

A few months later, Annette rang me from Boston, inviting me for dinner. I said perhaps it would be more practical if I invited them instead on one of their frequent visits to New York. I knew that Annette had always wanted, but feared, to invite Julia Child for dinner. So I added, "Except of course if that were the dinner for Julia Child. In which case I would take the next plane!"

"Well precisely, she has accepted to come!" Annette exclaimed. "And I need advice on whatever I should cook for her."

"Boiled potatoes," I volunteered. "Everything is described in her books except boiled potatoes."

"You are dreadful!" Annette exclaimed. "Baruj is also dreadful. He suggested porridge."

In the end, she settled on an elaborate couscous she had learned from Baruj's ancestral Algeria. The dinner met the approval of Julia Child, who turned out to know as much about literature and painting as she did about *haute cuisine*. This deep background surely played a part in how her books read better than most other cookbooks, and why she has become one of the publishing phenomena of our times.

· XVI ·

music for a while

A FEW MONTHS after my arrival at NYU, Dean Lewis Thomas called and asked if I could come to his office for a "friendly chat." I had met Thomas a few years earlier at a small immunological meeting in Gif sur Yvette, near Paris. I was struck by his brilliance right from the start. At that time, he had yet to publish his popular bestsellers such as *Lives of a Cell* and *Medusa and the Snail.* But he had already made a discovery that would be even more popular: the nature of the enzyme papain.

The research by Lewis Thomas is one of many examples of the unexpected results of basic medical research. Thomas was professor of Pathology at NYU when he made his studies on papain, the substance commonly found in unripe papaya. He discovered that intravenous injection of this substance has predictable effects on certain tissues. He would demonstrate his findings by intravenously injecting a rabbit with papain. The injections would invariably result in the rabbits' ears drooping like wilted leaves. His studies on papain spurred other studies by scientists on the biological effects of papain. Thomas' investigations led directly to the mass production of papain a few years later in the form of commercial meat tenderizer. Though Thomas did not make a penny from his discovery, others have made fortunes out of it. As for me, whenever I prepare food by rubbing tenderizer on it, I remember my friend Lewis Thomas.

The morning I went to his office, I wondered why the Dean wanted to see me.

"I would like to ask your thoughts on the education of medical students," he said.

I told him that though memorizing volumes played an important part in medical education, it was also necessary to give the students the freedom to explore, to question the dogmas.

"We should always remember that learning is an adventure," I said.

"Something we should never forget," he said.

I went on to say that we should also never forget the humanities, because the future doctor would be in intimate contact with other human beings.

"I agree with you completely," Thomas said. "Tell me, how do you think we could implement this approach?"

"Well, for a start, one could do it through music," I replied. "It's often said that music is the most direct of all languages. And besides," I added, "it is usually easier to organize a chamber music recital than to put on a play or mount an exhibition."

"You're right," Thomas said. "However, there is one obstacle. The usual one. Unfortunately, there are no funds available, even for such recitals."

A few months later, Albert Fuller told me he had two harpsichord programs: one, sonatas by Domenico Scarlatti and the other, various pieces by Rameau. He would like to try them out before giving them in a public recital. He was looking for a recital hall, free if possible, as transporting the harpsichord was already so expensive. Since he was a harpsichordist, he was, by definition, not rich. I went to Dean Thomas and told him he could have two free concerts for the students.

We held the recitals in the school auditorium. For the first recital we managed to fill only about half the hall. Most of those who showed up had never heard a harpsichord before. The hall for Albert's second performance was full.

Albert had also invited some of his friends to the recitals, among them a lady, Miss Alice Tully.

Some time later, I attended another concert at the Metropolitan Museum, where Albert Fuller was performing with the Musica Aeterna orchestra under Fritz Waldman's direction. Miss Tully was giving an after-concert dinner in her apartment and Albert asked her if he could take me along.

And so we went up to Miss Tully's apartment in the Hampshire House on Central Park South. After Albert introduced me to Miss Tully, a tall and graceful lady, she told me she had attended the two recitals Albert gave not too long ago at NYU. She said she knew I was working there and was instrumental in the production of these concerts.

"It is a great honor for me that you could attend," I told her.

Detecting my foreign accent, she said, "May I ask where you studied medicine?"

"In Paris, where I also worked, after finishing my studies," I replied.

"And when were you there?"

"From 1924 to 1939."

"Oh, I was living in Paris at the same time, also as a student," she said.

It turned out that we had gone to the same concerts and recitals in Paris. She asked me what performances I remembered the most.

"Elisabeth Schumann singing *Exultate, Jubilate* was one of them," I replied.

"Yes, at the Salle Gaveau. I was also there. It was splendid!"

And that was how our friendship started.

A few weeks after Albert Fuller's harpsichord recitals at NYU, Hugues Cuenod wrote that he had been asked to sing in Boston and was planning to stop a few days in New

York. I called up Albert and wondered about the possibility of holding a concert in New York with Hugues as a singer. Albert thought about it and said he would work on it.

Next day, he called me back. He said he had a friend named Gregory Smith who had been at Albert's previous recital at NYU. Gregory Smith, the son of one of the founders of General Motors, was willing to pay for Hugues' recital if we could find a concert hall. Albert said he himself could play the accompaniment.

I went to Dean Thomas, who eagerly accepted my offer. Thomas, as it happened, had a real passion for music. In one of his essays, he wrote that if we wanted to communicate with any possible extraterrestrials, the best way would be to send out a stream of Bach cantatas. I asked my students to help me advertise the concert and we posted signs everywhere. Hugues and Albert presented a program of baroque songs. Among them was Monteverdi's *Lettera Amorosa*, one of the great masterpieces written for voice, but at that time rarely sung.

The song, really a miniature opera for one voice, was first performed in Venice in 1619. For centuries, singing had been governed by the unbending rhythms of medieval polyphony. Monteverdi did something revolutionary by writing, in the volume of madrigals containing the *Lettera Amorosa*, that they should be performed *senza battuta*, without a regular beat. He directed the singer to slow down or hasten his delivery according to the meaning of the text. This new style took Europe by storm and became the basis of the invention of opera. However, *Lettera Amorosa* and other compositions by Monteverdi were soon buried in the Venetian mania for novelty. It was only at the beginning of this century, with work by musicians like Hugues Cuenod and his teacher Nadia Boulanger, that the *Lettera Amorosa* was rediscovered.

At the end of the recital, the students wanted more.

Hugues and Albert gave in with encores. Sitting in the audience was Miss Tully. After the concert, she asked to speak to me.

"It was such a privilege to hear the recital," she said to me. "Thank you for making it possible."

I recounted my conversation with Dean Thomas about opening up the world of music to the students.

"What a wonderful idea!" Miss Tully said. "Tell me, what will the next concert be and when?"

"I really don't know if there will be a next one," I said, "as we don't have any money. The cost of this one was shouldered by Gregory Smith."

Then she looked straight into my eyes and told me, "If you would not tell anybody and if you would keep it a deep secret, I will be glad to sponsor your project of bringing music to the students." Her proposal took me completely by surprise.

Next day, I rang Dean Thomas and said I would like to speak to him about something that would please him. He was intrigued and asked me to come to his office right away. I told him that a very nice person who had been at the concert yesterday offered to sponsor our music project, and that we were now in business.

This was how the NYU Medical School concert series began. It took place every month for fifteen years from the sixties to the seventies. Organizing and publicizing the concerts, on top of my already hectic load of teaching and laboratory work, took a lot of time and energy, but it gave me much fulfillment.

Dean Thomas, who had met Albert Fuller at his first recital at NYU, came up with the idea of nominating him Musician-in-Residence (without salary). It was an amusing gimmick, I thought, but it worked out well.

At the beginning of my "career" as concert organizer, I

met with one of the agents of the artists to discuss fees. I pointed out that the concerts were given free and that NYU was a nonprofit institute.

The agent interrupted me and exclaimed, "But dear Dr. Ovary, these starving artists who make chamber music, they are also nonprofit!" I could not dispute this, and there went my bargaining strategy.

The concert series became known beyond the school, and music lovers outside NYU started to attend them regularly. I found many outstanding artists for our concerts, including the New York Chamber Soloists, the pianists Gina Bachauer and Christoph Eschenbach, the singers Elaine Bonazzi and Betty Allen, and the violinist Jaap Schroder, who later went on to record as first violinist the complete Mozart symphonies with Christopher Hogwood. A wind ensemble organized by Melvin Kaplan performed Giovanni Gabrieli's music, with half the group on stage and the other half responding from the balcony. This was how singers originally performed the music in 16th century Venice but for New York in the 1960's, it was a daring innovation.

It gave me pride to present the Vegh Quartet, whose recording of the complete Beethoven quartets remains unsurpassed. The group's founder, Sandor Vegh, was a childhood friend of mine. We first met when he was five and I was ten, and we grew up in the same street in Kolozsvar. People in our street were already calling him a violin prodigy then.

The pianist Michael Rogers was another of the artists I was happy to present. Dean Thomas himself had recommended Rogers, who was giving piano lessons to one of his daughters. Michael and I became good friends. With him, I published Bartok's letters that Ambassadrss Cerruti had left me. These were the letters that Bartok sent to her in 1929, expressing abhorrence of the Communist system. We published the letters with commentary in the musical journal

Notes (3/73). As I was not a professional musician, I felt it would help to co-sign the commentary with somebody who was in the field.

The tenor Robert White was among the most popular performers in the concert series. His appeal was no doubt due to his superb command of different musical styles—baroque cantatas, Schubert lieder, Broadway tunes, cabaret songs, and Irish airs. Bobby began his professional career at the age of five, performing in radio and TV shows in New York. He has sung for the Popes, the royal families of Monaco and England, and at the White House for five Presidents. The BBC featured him for years in the weekly broadcast "Robert White Sings." Among the most beautiful recordings made are his collections of Handel arias and Schubert songs.

One day, my sister Magda called from Rome to say that she was coming to New York quite unexpectedly. Marisa, her best friend's only daughter, was stopping by New York on the way to Florida and had insisted that my sister should come along. My brother-in-law raised no objections as the trip would take only a few days.

Marisa and my sister flew in one of the personal jets owned by Marisa's father, who had made a fortune from petroleum. I went to see my sister and her friend at Marisa's family apartment on the top floor of the Olympic Tower, beside St. Patrick's Cathedral. They were staying in New York for just a day, then flying on to Boca Raton, where Marisa had just bought a house.

"This is for you!" Marisa said, handing me a huge package when I came in. I opened it and found four pounds of the best caviar.

Marisa told me that on the way to New York, they had stopped at a duty-free market in Newfoundland and she found herself buying all this caviar being sold at bargain prices. She then asked my sister, "Now what shall we do with all this? I really don't *like* caviar. But you know I could never resist a bargain!" They thought about it and Marisa said, "Well, let's give it to your brother!"

This happened two days before an NYU concert. Christoph Eschenbach was performing a piano recital. So I asked him and Miss Tully to come up to the apartment for supper. I took out the fine Italian linen I kept for special occasions and served them Veuve Cliquot *brut* and the caviar. Miss Tully was delighted. I thought it was one of the few things I could do to thank her for the NYU concert series.

At that time, part of my job at NYU was to give lectures in the school's Pathology program. One of the subjects I had to teach first-year students was complement. There were two main reasons I was given this job. (1) I had just worked for five years at the Johns Hopkins University with Manfred Mayer, then the world's number one authority on complement; and (2) I had studied in Paris in the 1930's under Jules Bordet, who in 1919 got the Nobel Prize for his discovery of complement.

In very much simplified terms, complement is a mixture of proteins that, as the name suggests, complements the action of antibody in killing microbes. The antibody is the specific, the complement the non-specific, portion of the mixture. Whereas antibody is secreted by the B cells, complement is secreted by a variety of other cells in the body. Without complement, the antibody could not kill. The antibody could fix to the microbe but the microbe would just laugh at it (so to speak).

At the time I was asked to give the lecture on complement in the Pathology department, another one was being given on the same subject in the Microbiology department. I thought it was a good idea for such an important topic to be presented in two departments by two teachers who could discuss it from different perspectives.

The lecture in the Microbiology program was scheduled

about two weeks before mine, so I went to hear it. To my horror, I found out that the lecturer was not at all acquainted with the latest important discoveries on the subject and was giving an inadequate treatment with some serious mistakes.

After the session, I went to see the lecturer, a friend of mine, to point out his errors. Instead of getting offended, he was relieved to hear my criticisms. He admitted that he really didn't know much about the subject. It was forced on him by his chief, and when he protested that he really didn't want to teach it, his chief prevailed on him to just do extra research. Thankfully, he said, it was his last year at NYU, as he was due to move to the Albert Einstein Medical School, where he would not have to teach complement. He would be happy, he told me, if I were to tell his chief about his errors.

The same medical students were hearing both our presentations, so I had to clear up the disparities. As the other professor was a friend of mine, I tried to be subtle about my criticisms of his lecture. I would say, for example, that in the other lecture, the latest findings were not reflected, and so on.

I also brought a song for the students, as a little joke and a sort of musical coda to the lecture. I had asked my friends Robert White and Annette Benacerraf, an amateur pianist, to record the song. It was based on one of Schubert's most exquisite creations, *An Silvia* ("Who Is Silvia?"), with lyrics by Shakespeare from a passage in *Two Gentlemen of Verona*.

Schubert's piece had three stanzas. I had Robert White sing the whole composition, except I played around a bit with the lyrics. The first stanza was from the German version. For our second stanza, I used the first stanza of the English version. I made up the third stanza to allude to the two contradictory lectures the students had heard on complement. Instead of "Who is Silvia?" and on to an enumera-

tion of her attributes, ours went like this: "What is complement?" and on to the contradictions.

So at the end of my talk, I complimented my students for
listening to such a difficult subject as complement. As a little
treat, I said, I wanted to give them a song. Their faces lit up
when we reached the third stanza and they started getting
the jokes. They were smiling and clapping by the end of the
song. After the lecture, one of my students approached me.
He said the session got him very interested not only in complement but in Schubert as well.

· XVII ·

addictive but not habit forming

At this time, I had taken a subscription for the concerts of the Musica Aeterna at the Metropolitan Museum. I sat regularly in the second row of the balcony, just behind Alida Waldman, the wife of the conductor. My friend Janie Schang, widow and daughter-in-law of eminent music impresarios, often went and sat with me. Miss Tully always sat in the orchestra section. Many years later, I learned that Miss Tully was also the anonymous patron of these concerts.

Miss Tully, who was an heir to the Corning Glass fortune, would always invite me to the after-concert dinners she gave in her apartment at the Hampshire House. Later when the Hampshire House restaurant changed its policy and would no longer serve dinner in the apartments on Saturdays, Miss Tully would take us all to a French restaurant, the Poulailler. After a few invitations, Miss Tully told me she would no longer invite me as I was always invited.

Through our friendship, I learned to admire Miss Tully's genuine generosity and modesty. Apart from her formal charities for needy people and artists, she often gave personal donations, gifts, meals, theater passes, and what she didn't have much of, time, to people around her. She was a naturally shy person, and whenever possible, she would give donations through a third person or a fund she had established, the Maya Foundation, in order to remain anonymous. Nothing gave her more pleasure than going to a concert or recital she had sponsored, watch the audience respond, and see that the time they were spending there was making a real difference in their lives.

She was a musician herself. She had studied voice in the 1920's with Jean Perier in Paris and made her operatic debut as a soprano in 1927. For the next fourteen years, she worked as a singer in Europe and the United States, at one time performing on an ocean liner on the same program with Josephine Baker. The war came and she volunteered as a pilot and nurse for the army. After the war, her voice had lost its bloom. She went to Milan to consult with voice specialists but to no avail. She decided to get over her sadness by helping out other singers and musicians.

She supported the smaller musical groups such as the Helicon, Aston Magna, New York Chamber Soloists, Clarion, and New York Chamber Music Society, as well as the huge institutions such as the Metropolitan Opera and the Juilliard School. She helped out established artists such as her old friend Martha Graham, as well as the many more who unfortunately could not make a living out of their talents and dreams.

Her help was vital at the beginning of many musical careers. On one occasion, Miss Tully sat as a member of the jury of a singing contest. The next day, she was talking on the phone to a friend who told her about a young girl who had a remarkable voice but did not have the means to support herself if she were to develop her talent.

Miss Tully told her, "I was a member of a jury yesterday and I too heard a girl whom I admire very much."

"I wonder if we're talking about the same girl," her friend said.

"If so, we should do everything to help her," Miss Tully said.

As it happened, they were in fact talking about the same girl: Jessye Norman.

"Please find out what I can do for her and how much she needs," Miss Tully asked the friend. "But I have one condition. She should not know that I have given her anything." It was only many years later, after Ms. Norman had become a star, that she found out who her patron had been.

The President of the Metropolitan Museum in the mid-fifties was Arthur Houghton, a cousin and friend of Miss Tully. One day, she went to her cousin and suggested that it would be a good idea for the museum to give concerts and recitals as part of its program. Houghton liked her idea but called her attention to the most serious obstacle—money. She proposed regular performances by the Musica Aeterna, the orchestra she had formed, and offered to assume the charges anonymously. When she told her mother about the project, her mother exclaimed, "Darling, it is your money. If you want to pay for an orchestra or if you want to throw your money out the window, it's your business!"

The Musica Aeterna became one of the most adventurous musical groups in New York. While it did not neglect the established repertory, it sought out rarely heard works by the famous masters such as Handel, Haydn and Vivaldi, presenting, for example, the first modern performance of Handel's *L'Allegro ed il Penseroso*. Those were the days before the "Handel boom," when most people hadn't heard of Handel's operas and thought that he wrote only one oratorio. Now of course we know that Handel wrote more than fifty operas and oratorios, one more beautiful than the other.

The Musica Aeterna concerts introduced numerous people to then-obscure masters such as Monteverdi, Couperin, Corelli, Schütz, and Rameau. Many famous artists performed with the group, such as the pianists Claudio Arrau, Clifford Curzon, and Gina Bachauer; the violinists Itzhak Perlman and Pinchas Zukerman; the cellists Yo Yo Ma and Lynn Harell; and the singers Hermann Prey, Kiri Te Kanawa, and Janet Baker.

One day, I got an invitation from Douglas Dillon, the successor of Arthur Houghton as museum president, for a reception and dinner in honor of Miss Tully. It was to be given at the museum's Blumenthal Patio.

The patio, a two-story renaissance courtyard in marble, had been built in the early sixteenth century for the Spanish castle in Velez of Don Pedro Fajardo y Chacon, a relative of the Spanish king, and his wife Doña Mencia de la Cueva Mendoza de la Vega y Toledo. The couple had imported master architects and sculptors from Lombardy, one of the great centers of renaissance sculpture, to create their court-yard.

At the end of the last century, the Spanish castle began to fall apart. The American businessman George Blumenthal bought its central courtyard and rebuilt it in his New York townhouse on Fifth Avenue. He later bequeathed it to the Metropolitan Museum, with enough funds to install it in the museum. It is now one of the great *cinquecento* Spanish, or rather Italian, masterworks of the museum.

It was the same Blumenthal who had founded Valfleury near Paris, the convalescent home for needy and elderly people, where I worked soon after the Second World War. A nephew of this Blumenthal, Count Cecil Pecci-Blunt and the nephew's wife, Mimi, were my patients in Rome in the 1950's. My mind toyed idly with these haphazard connections when I received the invitation for the reception in Miss Tully's honor at the Blumenthal patio.

The reception had come about almost accidentally, and I learned the story from Miss Tully some time later. One day, the new museum president Douglas Dillon asked if he could come and speak to her. She was curious as to Mr. Dillon's intent and invited him for tea. It was simple. He wanted to know if she would consider becoming a bene-factor of the Metropolitan Museum.

She told him, "What a pity that you don't love music."

Dillon was taken aback and asked her what made her say this.

She replied, "Because if you did, you would know that I am the person who keeps the Musica Aeterna concerts going."

Dillon made up for this oversight by organizing the candlelit dinner in the Blumenthal patio.

❦

As a friend of Miss Tully's, I became familiar with the magnificent trove of paintings, sculptures, and furniture in her apartment. To get to it, one had to take the elevator to the 27th floor of the Hampshire House, on Central Park South. The apartment occupied the entire floor and was in fact originally five separate ones, including two that were the former residence of Greta Garbo.

One entered through a small vestibule where some small renaissance paintings hung. On open shelves stood pre-Columbian terracotta sculptures, Mayan jade ear spools, and a pair of fifteenth century German wooden sculptures of the Madonna.

From the vestibule, one entered the oak room, so-called because the panels of the room were made of solid oak. Miss Tully often received her visitors here by a bar that had access to a small kitchen. On the bar stood two renaissance bronzes depicting Saint John and a baby Hercules. Tucked in the fireplace were some more renaissance pieces, an iron coat of arms from Florence and gilded lion andirons from Venice. There were niches in the wall on both sides of the fireplace. They contained an Egyptian bronze statuette of a falcon from the Third Intermediate Period (10th to 7th century BC), small Greek jars from the 5th to the 3rd century BC, and a pair of Italian renaissance bronze male heads. Chairs from the period of Louis XV and XVI stood around the room. On the walls hung a view of a valley by Courbet, four waterscapes by Boudin, a rare early glimpse of Paris and the Seine among four landscapes by Corot, and Magritte's apple filling up a room with a view of the sea. Several small bronze animals by Antoine Louis Barye and François Pompon clustered on the broad window shelves. Two bigger bronze figures stood out on the window shelves, a pensive man by Daumier and a ballerina, the *Préparation à la danse* by Degas. The windows opened out to a view of Central Park.

A door gave way to an anteroom. This contained two singular pieces from the renaissance, a drawing of the "Betrothal of Eleanor of Portugal and the Holy Roman Emperor" by Raphael, and a fifteenth century marble relief of a woman who was most probably Isabella d'Este.

The foyer led to the music room where Miss Tully often hosted recitals before dinners. By the opposite wall stood a Steinway piano that Miss Tully valued, as she said that it had the best tone of all the Steinways she had ever heard. An open eighteenth century armoire in blue-green and cream stood in a corner. An eighteenth-century giltwood angel, holding a flaming heart, perched on top of the armoire. The shelves held a golden Hittite bull and seventeenth century giltwood sculptures of saints and angels from Italy and Spain. A pair of renaissance bronze angels, by the Florentine master Antonio Susini, each with a foot and an arm raised back, looked as if they had just landed on the mantelpiece.

The theme of angels lingered on through a couple of paintings in the music room: "The Dream of Alessandro Farnese" by Tintoretto, showing the young Duke of Parma held up by angels; and "Saint Peter Martyr" with hovering angels painted by Titian and his students. A large fragment from the studio of Veronese showed two women and a young child. This fragment was one of the most gorgeous paintings in the apartment, and only lack of tight documentation could make anyone doubt that it is by Veronese himself. The other paintings in the music room were renaissance portraits, including that of the Burgundian ruler Phillip the Good, attributed to Rogier van der Weyden; a Saxon elector by Lucas Cranach the Elder; a Byzantine emperor by Gentile Bellini; and the humanist Erasmus of Rotterdam, painted by Erasmus' contemporary Hans Holbein the Younger. Miss Tully was particularly fond of this last painting. On nights she could not sleep and was feeling sad, she would often contemplate the portrait of Erasmus, whom she considered a friend. She found comfort in the wise humor of Erasmus, who made the remark, "I think, therefore I am helpless."

One side of the room opened to a small balcony overlooking Central Park. Another side led to a small salon containing a seascape by Winslow Homer, street scenes by Childe Hassam and Alfred Sisley, and a woman reading a book, by Renoir. Musicians often used this salon as a backstage room during recitals.

A door from the salon led to the red room, painted cream and filled with red accents. Miss Tully used the room as a library, but its profusion of graceful eighteenth century French furniture arranged in small groups made it look more like a salon. Unlike the music room, it was free of paintings except for two flower pieces by Odilon Redon.

The room contained a mix of chairs from the periods of Louis XV, with their curving, playful, asymmetrical forms; and Louis XVI, with their more sober, neoclassic, and symmetrical design. In Miss Tully's apartment, I was able to sharpen my appreciation of all the different ways the eighteenth-century French turned the humble chair into an art object, at that flashpoint when art informed every aspect of life, not just painting, music, and architecture, but also furniture and other everyday objects, when even a teaspoon was made to give an esthetic experience. They gave each kind of chair a name, like the *canapé* (a cushioned chair for four people), *bergères à oreilles* (featuring a backrest with earlike projections), *bergère à la reine* (straight-backed with detachable cushion), *fauteuil de bureau* (chair with a bowed, padded back), *fauteuil à la reine* (flat-back armchairs), *marquise* (deep, cushioned armchairs for two), and *fauteuil en cabriolet* (round-backed armchair). Miss Tully had developed her passion for chairs while she was studying in Paris in the 1920's. This was how she ended up collecting chairs signed by the greatest furniture makers of the eighteenth century.

From the red room, a door led to the blue room, painted cream and decorated with blue accents. Miss Tully normally used it as a salon, but when she had too many guests she would use it as an extension of the dining room. The blue room also contained exquisite Louis XV and XVI chairs and tables. Two display shelves held old Sèvres and Meissen porcelain. On the walls hung small portraits, already famous in the eighteenth century, of Louis XVI and Marie Antoinette, by Wertmüller; a Venetian scene by Boudin; and seascapes by van Goyen and Turner.

A door led to the last main public room, the dining room. Curiously for such a huge apartment, Miss Tully's kitchen was tiny, and far from the dining room. Actually, the kitchen was hardly ever used except for making tea; all the food for meals was brought up from the French restaurant on the first floor of the Hampshire House.

Louis XVI commodes and consoles stood ready to hold the food in the dining room. A suite of fourteen Louis XVI chairs gathered around a huge table topped with green marble. Tall windows and doors surrounded the room, and on the remaining wall space hung two flower paintings by Fantin-Latour and Renoir, and two seascapes by Boudin.

Beyond these rooms were others that most guests never entered. Because she considered me a close friend and she knew that I appreciated their contents, Miss Tully gave me the privilege to visit the other rooms whenever I wished.

One could gain access from the dining room to a suite of three smaller salons that Miss Tully did not use much. Like the rest of the apartment, these rooms contained furnishings from eighteenth century France, as well as neoclassic and rococo pieces from eighteenth and nineteenth century Italy. Three of the most magnificent paintings in the apartment hung in these inner salons: Salomon van Ruysdael's river-scape with fishing boat, windmill, cows, and church; Francesco Guardi's view of Venice's Giudecca Canal; and Canaletto's view of San Giorgio Maggiore, the Grand Canal, and the waterfront of San Marco.

From the last of these salons, one went to a corridor that led either to two guest bedrooms, furnished with rococo furniture; or to Miss Tully's study room. A gilt Louis XVI writing table in ebony served as Miss Tully's study table. The study room reflected her love of Venice. It contained Canaletto's *capriccio* of a bridge leading to the lagoon, Francesco Guardi's view of the island of Santo Spirito and its monastery, and forty more views of Venice by Guardi's nephew Giacomo. I was particularly interested in Francesco Guardi's Santo Spirito monastery, because a cousin of my forefather Simon (the one who had 32 children) became head of this monastery after he left Hungary for Italy.

The study led to Miss Tully's bedroom, which was pre-dominantly colored mauve, Miss Tully's favorite color. This room contained a faded Watteau drawing of a lute player; two extravagantly detailed Dutch bouquets from the six-teenth century, by Ambrosius Bosschaert and Andries Daniels; and a round painting of *nymphéas* by Monet.

Once, I was scheduled to attend a scientific conference in Paris when Miss Tully asked me go to a big Monet retro-spective being held at the Grand Palais. She had lent her *nymphéas* for the retrospective but could not go herself, so she asked me to tell her how the painting was exposed. Miss

Tully told me that in the 1950's, a friend informed her that the French actress Lana Marconi, widow of the prodigious dramatist-filmmaker Sacha Guitry, wanted to sell the painting. Guitry, a friend of Monet's, had bought it from the artist himself in 1914. Miss Tully paid Madame Marconi $45,000 and thought it was not cheap. Some thirty years later, the organizers of the Grand Palais retrospective insured it for $4.5 million. "It was the best investment I ever made," Alice told me.

The *nymphéas* was one of the more unique works in the retrospective, being the only round painting (tondo) on display, and one of only four tondos Monet ever painted. Monet created the three other tondos within a year of this one, all of them *nymphéas*. Miss Tully's was the only tondo left in private hands, the three others being in the Dallas museum and in two municipal museums in France. Miss Tully's *nymphéas* hung all by itself on a wall at the Grand Palais, with a label saying it had been lent anonymously. The painting showed white, red, and rose water lilies, all bathing in light and floating on water reflecting a mauve-tinged sky. It communicated a feeling of ecstasy. Monet had painted it soon after he distraughtly destroyed thirty canvasses.

To reciprocate Miss Tully's hospitality, I sometimes took her to shows she would likely have missed. One evening, I brought her to a performance by a troupe that her friend Dame Joan Sutherland had been urging her to see, the Gran Scena Opera. The troupe consisted of males impersonating opera divas. They had rented a tiny hall in the Village, all they could afford at that time. The performers kept the audience laughing with their sendups of great divas in familiar scenes from Verdi, Wagner, and Puccini. It was fascinating to watch the infinite ways divas could devise to upstage each other, be it higher notes, longer death scenes, or bigger hair. "They make such funny parodies," Miss Tully enthused. "But there's something else that impressed me. They're real artists in their own right. They understand music and sing beautifully!"

At the end of the 1950's, when the three principal performance halls of the Lincoln Center were finished, officials of the center approached Miss Tully for help in building an additional theater where musicians could perform chamber music.

Miss Tully's contributions eventually amounted to $4.5 million. Her only condition was that no one outside the board would know of it. When the building was almost finished, the board decided to name the hall after her. They thought it would be the only right thing to do for someone who had done so much for musicians.

Miss Tully turned down the offer immediately. She wanted her anonymity more than anything else. The board persisted. Several months later, at a big dinner at the Caravelle restaurant, Miss Tully gave in. However, she had one condition.

She already knew the board would spare nothing to get the best acoustics. However, she disagreed with them on one thing. Legroom. She had had enough of concert halls where the experience was ruined by uncomfortable, tightly-packed seating. The board was determined to squeeze as many seats into the hall as possible. Miss Tully had to put up a sustained fight, until she prevailed on the board to give up a few rows of seats so that everyone could get enough legroom. Just to make sure, she had her friend and companion, the heldentenor Edward Graefe, who was a six-footer, sit down while the builders took measurements. This was how the Alice Tully Hall became the most comfortable hall in New York, and how Miss Tully finally gave up her anonymity.

❧

Once, when Alice was already in her eighties and frail, she told me that she was traveling to Paris alone and that she was going on the Concorde. It happened that I was going to Paris at the same time. So I went and booked a ticket on the same flight. Knowing that Alice always sat in the front row, I asked for a seat next to hers.

I also booked a room, the cheapest they had, at the Bristol, as I knew she always stayed there. Thus I could look after her bags and anticipate her needs through the journey.

Flying on the Concorde was well above my means. But, I thought, why not, if it was to please and help somebody I loved?

I went out to Kennedy airport well ahead of time. When Alice got there, she was surprised to see me, and even more so on learning that I was going to Paris seated next to her. "Dearest Zoltan," she said, "with you I have learned to expect the unexpected!"

The flight took a mere three hours. We were served a luncheon of classic French cuisine catered by Maxim's, and soon after we finished dessert we were already landing in Paris. It was like going to a restaurant in New York and coming out in Paris. It brought back those medieval stories of bilocation, with a person found in two places at the same time.

It was quite an experience, supersonic flight; but with its equally supersonic bill, I could sum up in one phrase my impression of flying on the Concorde: addictive but not habit-forming.

It happened once that I was attending an international immunological conference in Venice at the same time that Alice was in Venice. She asked me to accompany her to see the *regatta* from the palazzo of Miss Peggy Guggenheim, on the Grand Canal. The palazzo was an interesting one. It had been left unfinished in the mid-eighteenth century by the original owners, the Venier family, as influential neighbors had objected that such a large palazzo would block their views. The unfinished portion ended up becoming a terrace, the only one on the Grand Canal. It was from this accidental terrace that we had the chance to see the *regatta*, Venice's traditional fluvial procession and boat race complete with renaissance pomp and ceremony. It was possible, with a bit of effort, to forget the other tourists and to imagine oneself back in the time when Veronese, Tintoretto, and Titian were still traversing this same canal.

After the *regatta*, Miss Guggenheim graciously took us on a tour of her famous collection of modern art that she planned to leave as a gift to the city of Venice. She showed us a life-size metal sculpture of a naked horseman made of separate pieces and assembled with exposed joints. Miss Guggenheim complained that just a few days ago somebody had stolen a portion of the statue, and she pointed out the horseman's missing genitalia.

In New York, I often went to the Metropolitan Museum with Alice, either for special exhibitions or to revisit the permanent collections. The museum permitted her to go on Mondays when it was closed. In the beginning, we would walk through the galleries; but later, when she reached her mid-eighties, she preferred to sit in a wheelchair. I would push the wheelchair through the silent galleries and she would ask me to stop in front of a favorite painting where, every now and then, we would lose all sense of time.

⟨◦⟩

One September evening, I went to Alice's house for her birthday party. Among the well-wishers were her friends Martha Graham, Fritz and Alida Waldman, and the director of the Pierpont Morgan Library, Charles Ryskamp.

Miss Tully was a great benefactor of the Morgan Library through her Maya Foundation. She was the sponsor of its concert series and had given the library many important works, including an extremely rare *quattrocento* Book of Prayers illuminated with a veritable garden of medieval flowers by Michelino da Besozzo. Alice loved the Morgan's collection of autograph music manuscripts, one of the world's greatest. It includes Mozart's "Haffner" Symphony, Beethoven's "Ghost" Trio, Brahms' First Symphony, Schubert's "Death and the Maiden," Liszt's Piano Sonata in B Minor, and major Bach cantatas.

One day, the Morgan allowed her to hold Schubert's autograph manuscripts of *Die Winterreise,* of which the Morgan has two, the final version and a work in progress written in two shades of ink, pale brown for tentative ideas and black for final passages. "I was so moved," she later told me, "my eyes began to well with tears. Then suddenly, I was seized by the terror that my tears would fall and ruin the manuscript!"

Before the birthday party, I had asked myself, What on earth could I give to someone who had everything? Then I thought, perhaps something really special could be the letters of Bartok.

When I handed her the envelope, she asked, "What is this?"

"These are the letters of Bartok left to me by Ambassadress Cerruti," I answered. Alice knew about them, as I had previously given her a copy of my published commentary on the letters.

"No," she told me. "You should give them to the Morgan Library." She immediately asked Charles Ryskamp if the Morgan Library had letters of Bartok.

"Unfortunately not," he answered. "They are very rare and difficult to get."

"Well, now you can get them," Alice told Ryskamp. "Zoltan will donate them to the library." She asked me on the spot to give the envelope to Ryskamp. This was how, soon after, I found myself elected Fellow of the Morgan Library.

As a Fellow, I got invitations for the musical performances in the concert hall on the second floor. At that time, during the early sixties, almost all the Fellows were elderly persons. It was only later that Charles Ryskamp started actively recruiting younger Fellows.

At one of the first concerts I attended, I was sitting next to the viola player Inez Lynch and her husband Melvin Kaplan, the oboist, both of whom had appeared in the NYU concert series.

I could see from the rapt faces of the audience that they loved the performance. However, at the curtain call, there was only the faintest applause. I asked Inez, "But why aren't they clapping more?"

"But Zoltan," she answered, "don't you see? They are too old to clap!"

◆)§ 2(◆

On one occasion, the library got an offer for a celebrated drawing by Raphael. The drawing's value lay not only in its virtuosity but also in its history, locating Raphael in Siena as a student of the renaissance master Pinturicchio in the early 1500's.

There is in Siena's Libreria Piccolomini a fresco by Pinturicchio of the same subject and design as the Raphael drawing. Cardinal Francesco Piccolomini had attached the library to the Siena Cathedral in 1495, housing there the manuscripts and collection of books of his famous uncle, the writer and humanist Aeneas Silvius, who had become Pope Pius II in 1458.

In 1501, Cardinal Francesco Piccolomini himself became Pope, as Pius III, but he died before a month was over. He had, however, the opportunity before his death to commission Pinturicchio to paint a fresco cycle in the Libreria Piccolomini to commemorate the life of his uncle. The fifth fresco in the cycle would depict the betrothal in Siena in 1452 of Eleanor of Portugal to the Holy Roman Emperor Frederico, in the presence of scores of courtiers and the bishop of the city, Aeneas Silvius Piccolomini, not even cardinal yet.

Pinturicchio asked his young student Raphael to make the drawing for this fresco. When it came time to paint the fresco, Pinturicchio closely followed Raphael's detailed drawing, adding only a Sienese landscape. The fresco can still be seen in the Libreria in Siena.

Raphael's drawing turned up in New York in the early 1970's when an American businessman and art collector offered it to the Morgan Library. He was selling it for a sum in six figures, a bargain for a work that could easily fetch millions in the market.

(A few years later, a perfectly preserved Raphael drawing of the hand and head of a Disciple was bought at auction for $4.5 million by Barbara Piasecka-Johnson, the Polish immigrant to the United States who experienced a spectacular change in fortune when she got work as a kitchen maid in the household staff of J. Seward Johnson, the pharmaceutical magnate, and ended up marrying him. Before the auction, I went to see the drawing at Christie's. A friend of mine who worked there showed me the drawing and said, "Quick! Hold it in your hands! This could be the first and last time you shall see this masterpiece!")

The Morgan Library wanted very much to obtain Raphael's betrothal drawing but could not afford it and so they called to ask Miss Tully for help. She offered to buy it for the public collection with the condition that she would display it in her apartment while she was alive, after which it would pass on to the Morgan Library. This was in consonance with instructions that almost her entire property should be auctioned so that her charities and patronage would continue indefinitely. The Raphael is now one of the great treasures of the library.

· XVIII ·

fountain of chance

IN THE SUMMER OF 1975, I went to the Sloan Kettering Institute to discuss some scientific questions with my friend Lloyd Old. He was then working at the world's leading cancer research institute, where his fundamental research would lead to his discovery of the Tumor Necrosis Factor, an important defense mechanism naturally produced by the body against cancer tumors.

I had just left Lloyd's office when I met the director of the institute in the corridor, the famous researcher Robert Good, who was the first American to invite Chinese scientists to work in his laboratory, after Nixon's historic trip to China. Good had just come back from a visit to China, having been the first scientist from the United States to be invited to China as a private person since the end of the Second World War.

"How did you find China?" I asked him.

He replied with a question, "Well, why don't you go see for yourself?"

"I would certainly like to do this," I said. "However, I am no Robert Good!"

"Well," he said, "in China, I was asked to recommend somebody who could come and lecture in Beijing and Shanghai on experimental allergy. And I actually thought of you." He added, "You should not forget to ask for a chauffeured car and an interpreter."

I thought no more about this, but two weeks later, I got an official invitation to lecture in Beijing and Shanghai.

Would I accept, the letter asked, even if they could not pay me even for expenses?

I wrote back saying I was accepting the invitation and requesting that they book me in the best hotels and arrange for a chauffeured car and private interpreter. I added that I would like to visit the Forbidden City, the Great Wall, and the tombs of the emperors in Taiyuan.

I soon got an answer with regrets about what the visit would cost. For the best hotels, food, chauffeured car, and interpreter, the ten-day visit would cost a lot of money, namely $450. But if I would accept to shoulder this sum, they would immediately send the necessary documents for me to obtain a visa. Well, for all I was asking for, $450 even in 1975 was nothing! This was how I became the second scientist from the United States invited as a private person to China after the last world war.

The Chinese officials gave me a special welcome. A gentleman was waiting when my plane arrived. He escorted me out of the line of passengers and took care of all the formalities. Then he introduced me to my interpreter, a charming lady who spoke perfect English. We drove to the hotel in strangely light traffic. There were hardly any other cars in the streets. All the cars I did see were, according to my interpreter, government vehicles. Everybody but everybody in the streets wore black trousers beneath black jackets or sweaters. There was not the slightest appearance of feminine (or masculine) coquetry.

The Chinese Communists I encountered in Beijing were certainly a different breed from the old-time Russian Communists I met in Paris in the 1930's. When I was working at the Pasteur Institute, many Russians were being assigned there for a spell of a few years. This was an old tradition, dating back to the turn of the century when Pasteur invited the great Russian biologist Elie Metchnikoff.

I remember that when one of the Russian scientists, an

accomplished lady bacteriologist, went back to Russia, she took away many cultures in sealed flasks. Among these were two flasks, duly labeled just like the others, but containing perfumes by Coty.

In Beijing, they had reserved a room for me in the city's best hotel. The hotel was not luxurious but my room had a good view. I looked for the key but couldn't find any, so I went down to ask for one.

"For what?!" The concierge looked surprised. Then he explained matter-of-factly, "It is your room. Nobody will come in. Everything is safe. There is no need for a key."

Whenever I ventured out, people in the streets smiled warmly at me. But they were also reserved, and would never start a chat with a foreigner like me. Everyone traveled around on bicycles. People just left their bicycles on stands outside the buildings without locking them. My interpreter told me matter-of-factly, "Nobody will take it because they know it's not theirs."

Shanghai had a more European feel than Beijing. People in the streets were more informal. They would come up to me and we would try to exchange words in broken English or Chinese. A great part of Shanghai's landscape was made up of nondescript concrete boxes built during the Communist period. But along the waterfront boulevard, known as the Bund until 1949, the historic Victorian and Edwardian buildings were still standing. Originally built as international trading houses, consulates, and banks, the buildings were now mostly government offices. The fabled Cathay Hotel with its bronze-green roof still dominated the boulevard and was now called the Heping (Peace) Hotel. All along the boulevard, the Huangpu river teemed with ocean-going vessels swaying side by side with sampans, rusty ferries, and steamers from before the last world war, still miraculously afloat.

There was an outstanding collection of Chinese porcelain at the Shanghai Museum, fortunate survivors of the Cultural

Revolution. I went to see them with two immunologists from the Shanghai University. When we entered the first gallery, I exclaimed, "These are the most exquisite Kangxi porcelains!"

I particularly pointed out a vase in ox-blood glaze and a bowl in peach-bloom. "These are the most beautiful. I believe they were made in the late seventeenth or early eighteenth century."

My companions scrutinized the Chinese labels and exclaimed, "How do you know all this, and how do you know the period?!"

"I love Kangxi porcelain," I replied, "and my sister had some examples. That's why I know all about Emperor Kangxi's passion for porcelain, and how his reign was such a great age for porcelain."

At the medical institutes I visited in Shanghai and Beijing, I went to the laboratories of many investigators where we discussed their research and the methods they were using. They were always keen to present their work and to hear my comments. The equipment everywhere was antediluvian, but more important, everybody seemed eager to learn and improve their methods.

I also gave a series of formal lectures on experimental and clinical allergy. Invariably, the scientists would at first be too shy to ask anything. I had to inquire several times whether they understood this point or that and I had to coax them to express themselves. They would finally open up, and we would always end up exploring meaningful questions and engaging in fruitful discussions. As I soon learned, many of the scientists spoke good English and nearly all knew enough English to follow my lectures without the translation.

◆⋙⋘◆

Ever since the possibility of entering China came up, I had

looked forward to visiting the Forbidden City. It was a place that had always fascinated me since I was a child, when there was still a Chinese emperor in a place called the Forbidden City. Now that I finally reached it, I found the Forbidden City truly stunning even after it had been emptied of its contents, and all its pomp and ceremony reduced to nothing more than a memory. Through a procession of immense walls, towers, moat, gateways, courtyards and corridors, its builders made sure that the visitor was awed enough, or at least exhausted enough, by the time he found himself at the Hall of Supreme Harmony, the first of six palaces that towered one after another through a further procession of courtyards and gateways.

One of the few remaining objects was The Dragon Throne in the Hall of Supreme Harmony, a silent reminder of the absolute authority, almost unparalleled in history, that the Chinese emperor once held. The Chinese believed that as the Son of Heaven, the emperor ruled the whole world, even if the barbarians beyond the borders did not know this. From this throne, the emperor announced the dates and months of the new year that he, with the help of his astrologers, had the power to set; he gave the massive yearly audiences for princes and princesses, eunuchs, concubines, court officials, generals, merchants, soldiers, warlords, musicians, priests, ambassadors and civil servants; he read the yearly list of successful civil service candidates who were ready to carry out his every word with unquestioning obedience to the far corners of the empire. Near the throne stood a massive stone sculpture of a gargoyle, half-dragon and half-tortoise. The highest-scoring candidate gained the right to mount its tortoise back and stand cheering on its dragon head.

The Forbidden City gave an impression of having been there forever, but in fact it was only in the early fifteenth century that Yong Le, the third Ming emperor, built the palace complex after he decided to move the capital north from

Nanjing. Later, the complex was almost entirely rebuilt by the Ching emperor Qianlong, Kangxi's grandson and contemporary of Louis XV and XVI of France. (Compared to the Chinese emperor with his absolute authority and opportunities for tyranny, Louis XVI lost his head for being, as it were, a populist democrat.)

As the Son of Heaven, it was the Chinese emperor's duty to hold the universe together. So he would leave the Forbidden City at certain times of the year to perform ceremonies in China's most magnificent temple, the Temple of Heaven, which still stands in southeast Beijing. All windows and doors along the way were shuttered, all sounds were forbidden except the chants and music from the emperor's procession, and no one was allowed to be seen in the streets except the emperor's retinue of court officials, musicians, priests, eunuchs and soldiers. The Forbidden City, now almost an empty shell, still had the power to bring back these and many other haunted scenes, and to recall how the Chinese dynasties, unable to adapt to changing times and beliefs, failed to hold together and disappeared.

◆§◆

At my Beijing hotel, I was always the first guest to come down to the dining room. I soon found out how they prepared the fried eggs served with the European breakfast. They cooked all the eggs at 7 AM, so if you came down at 9 AM, your eggs would have been fried two hours before.

I asked the waiter why they didn't fry the eggs to order. He answered, "They are fried eggs. We don't say they were fried one minute or one hour ago, just fried eggs. And even if they were fried two hours ago, they are still fried eggs." I was unable to argue with his impeccable logic.

One of the curious coincidences that seem to happen only to me occurred in the hotel restaurant. On my second morning, a young Asian guest came into the dining room soon after me, and the waiter put him at the table next to mine. Judging from his well-tailored suit, I could guess he was a foreigner. We struck up a conversation and I found out that he was Japanese, a mathematician, and had been officially invited by the Chinese government.

He gave me his card bearing his name, Yoichi Motomashi. His specialty was "numbers theory." I told him I was an immunologist from New York and was originally from Hungary. He suddenly began to speak Hungarian. I could not believe my ears. A Japanese mathematician in Beijing speaking Hungarian?!

He then told me that the greatest scientists working in the field of numbers theory were Hungarians, and he had therefore gone to the University of Budapest to study with them. He started talking about two of his great idols from the past, the Hungarian mathematicians Lipot Fejer and Alfred Haar. I exclaimed that I actually knew both of them very well when I was a child. They were then both young professors at the University of Kolozsvar and both happened to be members of our guest family. This was how I met a new and lifelong friend.

❧

One time, I was flying to Sydney to attend the Third International Congress of Immunology. I had so much mileage that I could upgrade my flight, so I went first class. The plane stopped at the Fiji Islands and everyone went out for a little walk. I followed the crowd from the first class cabin. We were directed to a room at the airport building where a reception awaited us. We were all greeted warmly and festooned with garlands. We went to a table loaded with expensive food and drinks that included lobster, caviar, foie gras, pineapples, and Dom Perignon.

I was in the middle of eating out of my plate when I realized that the reception was being held in honor of the governor of Fiji and his suite. It so happened that they had all flown in the first class cabin. It was too late to back out without making an embarrassing scene. In any case, nobody seemed to have made out that I was not a member of the governor's suite. In fact, everybody was coming to talk to me of people and events of which I had not the slightest idea. So I just listened with a nice smile on my face and said, "Oh, how interesting!" or "Hmmm!" or something else non-engaging.

I was reminded of a story I heard when I visited Damascus. It supposedly happened to a very rich man who did not have any training in foreign service but got a job as a Syrian diplomat to Rome through connections. The man was not worried about his lack of foreign languages as he could afford to take an interpreter with him. However, the man loved going to receptions and wanted to attend even on those days his interpreter could not go. So he was instructed to learn phrases in French, at that time still the language of diplomacy. He should start with "How are you?" or "I'm fine, thank you," or some other pleasantries. Then he should move on to a safe subject, saying "The weather is beautiful (or not too good)." If the interlocutor pressed on, he should ask, "How is your wife?" And if he could not handle the conversation any more, he should just say, "*Qui sait? Qui sait?* (Who knows? Who knows?)" nod graciously and slip off to another group.

It so happened that one time, a cardinal tried to chat with him. After exhausting the usual pleasantries, the man asked, "How is your wife?"

The cardinal, taken aback, exclaimed, "But I have no wife! How can you say such a thing?!"

The man, who did not understand the cardinal, responded, "Who knows? Who knows?" then left the dumbstruck cardinal.

At the reception, I began to wonder why everyone was taking so much time and seemed to have forgotten all about the plane. Then I learned that everyone else in our group had Fiji as their final destination. I asked the waiter where the bathroom was, left my half-emptied plate on the table, and escaped just in time before the plane flew off.

Another time, I went on a safari organized by the American Academy of Allergy. It was held in Kenya after the association's conference in Tel Aviv. We traveled in a safari van, and all around was a primeval, fantastical world full of antelopes, wildebeests, lions, hyenas, water buffaloes, hippopotamuses, birds of all colors and sizes, and mammoth elephants. One concern kept intruding into this reverie, however: How come the elephants haven't overturned our van yet?

We reached the equator and stopped at a tiny settlement. There were some twenty small stands and huts where the natives sold hand-made baskets, carvings, ceramics, beads, etc. They were quite insistent, dragging us this way and that to see their merchandise.

One of them grabbed my left hand and was pulling me to his stand when he happened to see my watch. He exclaimed, "Timex! Cheap watch!" He let go of my hand and that was it. Nobody else came to ask me to buy anything.

This convinced me that the world was shrinking indeed!

In 1983, I was scheduled to attend the International Congress of Immunology in Kyoto. I had accumulated so much mileage on Pan American that I could make a free trans-Pacific trip in first class, and even take somebody with me gratis. I mentioned this to Tomio Tada, the organizer of the congress, who suggested that I take Albert Fuller, whom he had met in New York.

Needless to say, the idea thrilled Albert. However, a

trans-Pacific trip meant additional expenses, for hotels, food, etc. He told me that as a harpsichordist and as a professor at the Juilliard School of Music, his earnings were just sufficient for living expenses, not a trip like this.

There are very few professional instrumentalists who gain monetary success by concertizing. These are mostly the renowned piano or violin soloists. Earning money was even more difficult for the harpsichordist, especially at that time before the wide acceptance of authentic music performance and the invention of the compact disc. His instrument had a delicate range of sounds that limited the size of the hall, so he could play as a soloist only to small audiences.

I had a thought, but I did not tell this to anyone. The next time I saw Miss Tully, I told her that I was going to Kyoto for the immunology congress but that I was also going further, to the jungles of Borneo, which I had always wanted to visit. I said I had earned so much mileage I could take a friend free on the plane for the entire journey.

"Well, whom have you invited?" she asked.

"Albert Fuller. But he could not come, as I could offer him only the plane but not the hotel and living expenses, which are beyond his means."

"If you don't mind," Alice began (she was always so discreet and tactful), "I would like to contribute by paying the extras for Albert, so you and me, we can invite him." But she had one concern: "How could you do it so he doesn't know I am inviting him for the extras?"

I knew that Alice was very shy whenever she gave something. "Well, I don't want to lie," I said. "I think the best way is for me to tell him the truth but to ask him not to mention it to anyone, not even you!"

I called Tomio and told him I had found the money to invite Albert. This was how Albert Fuller, harpsichordist and musician-in-residence of NYU Medical School, got invited to the International Congress of Immunology.

Alice recommended that we stop in Singapore, as it was a gracious modern city full of gardens. She asked us to pass by the botanical garden and think of her when we looked at the orchids. It was a mission we were only too happy to carry out.

I had always wanted to visit the jungles of Borneo with its profusion of wild animals and primeval plants. Among its inhabitants, I was particularly interested to see the orangutans. I was not looking forward, however, to encountering the Bornean mosquitoes which were known to be extremely vicious and efficient. As Albert and I trekked through the jungles and witnessed, amidst the vines and orchids, people and animals covered from head to foot with mosquito bites and scabs, I began to covet the bottle of insect repellent in my bag and would not part with it even for a hundred bottles of cologne.

The orangutans had always fascinated me because of their proximity to the human species. I had seen them in zoos, but it was certainly not the same as encountering them in their native habitat. It was necessary to go with guides in Borneo to meet the orangutans, as it was forbidden to feed or touch them. Some of the friendlier orangutans approached us and touched us. They were apparently as curious of us as we were of them. I found orangutans in the wild who still made their beds each night by weaving branches together and covering them with leaves, a habit abandoned by many human city dwellers with no time or aptitude for making beds.

Our guide invited us to a local festivity and I went alone, as Albert was feeling tired. The entire village was built on wooden poles, some ten feet above the earth. Glimpsed afar through the leaves, the houses appeared to levitate. The feast on the ground below the houses was in full swing when we arrived. People were praying, swaying, and chanting. They were placing small offerings on a big dish. I had nothing but dollars and I put in a ten-dollar bill. Suddenly, people stopped what they were doing and stared at me. I began to worry that I must have done something wrong. Then the village elder rushed over and thanked me profusely. As I found out from the translator, I had put an unheard-of sum in the dish. The elder said he would like to give me a souvenir. He offered a carved, black arrow topped off with a kneeling spirit. He said that in the old days, these arrows were used to hunt game. However, nobody used them anymore, as there were better and more modern means, like buying cans in the store. I gratefully accepted the spirit-arrow.

In Kyoto, Albert wanted to stay in a *riokan*, one of those old Japanese guest houses where they still practiced the traditional arts of hospitality. Finding a *riokan* was not easy. As a rule, the owners accepted only Japanese clientele. But through Tomio's solicitation, Albert got a room in a *riokan* that stood, or seemingly floated, in the middle of a lake.

Next morning at 7 AM, Albert called me up, saying that I should come immediately and take him away to a modern hotel. I went over with a mix of curiosity and concern.

I found Albert in a nervous state. "They are so nice that I cannot make a move without somebody coming into my room and trying to help me," he said. He did not speak a word of Japanese and so communication had been difficult. "I sit up on the tatami and somebody comes in to help me. I look out the window and somebody comes in to help me. I turn right or left and somebody comes in to help me. No, this is too much!"

So he moved with his luggage out of the *riokan* to a hotel in the middle of Kyoto, a city that was not bad in the traditional arts either.

The ancient city of Kyoto and nearby Nara are both examples of how loss of status could be a blessing in disguise. Without this loss of status, much of what was artistic in these two cities would have disappeared a long time ago.

Nara was founded in 710 by the Japanese Emperor Kammu and became the imperial capital of Japan. As befitted a capital, many great palaces and temples rose in the city. The building material was always wood, abundantly available from Japan's vast forests.

In 784, the capital was transferred to Kyoto. Nara lost its political importance and as a result it was spared the battles that were to ravage Kyoto repeatedly in the following centuries when various armies clashed to capture the prized capital. It was only in the late sixteenth century that the civil wars ceased and Kyoto, then almost leveled to the ground, was rebuilt.

In the eighteenth century, the capital was again transferred, to Edo (now Tokyo). Kyoto lost its pride of place, to the displeasure of its citizenry. Then in World War II, most of Japan's major cities were bombed to the ground. Kyoto and Nara, cities of no political consequence, were left untouched. In particular, General MacArthur had wanted to spare Kyoto, and he encountered no difficulty convincing others, as Kyoto had no strategic value, political or military.

This was how Kyoto and Nara ended up the two most beautiful cities of Japan, filled with hundreds of elegant old inns, houses, temples, palaces, shrines, mansions, nunneries, and monasteries, instead of the anonymous, ugly buildings produced by much of modern architecture. Since practically all of Kyoto and Nara's ancient buildings were built of wood, it's amazing how many of them have survived in a country with a long history of earthquakes, fires and civil wars.

One temple, the Main Hall in the Horyu-ji temple complex near Nara, dates from 623 AD and has the distinction of being the oldest surviving wooden structure in the world. It is no rudimentary square box, as one might expect, but an intricate masterpiece, in two stories, of carved roof, eaves, columns, corridors, and balustrades.

Like many of Kyoto and Nara's old buildings, the Horyu-

ji Main Hall possesses the characteristics I have come to associate with classic art—grandeur, balance, and restraint—
whatever culture it is from, however small the work, such as
a classic Chinese bowl.

Many of the temples and monasteries in Kyoto and Nara
were once princely mansions that, upon the death of their
owners, were bequeathed to religious orders. One of them,
the Golden Pavilion (Kimkaku-ji) in Kyoto, was built in the
mid-fourteenth century by the Shogun Yashimitsu Ashikaga
to serve as his retirement villa and as a worthy place for receiving the emperor. He had the three-story mansion built
so that it seemed to be floating over a lake. He intended to
have the whole structure painted with gold leaf but saw this
done only on the third-story ceiling before he died, whence
the villa became a temple. In 1950, the temple burned to the
ground when a student-priest with metaphysical ambitions
set it on fire. Five years later, it was rebuilt exactly as it was
except that most of the temple was gilded in resplendent
gold leaf, finally fulfilling its builder's wishes from more than
six hundred years ago.

It was against this backdrop of survival and renewal that
the Kyoto International Congress of Immunology was held.

Soon after I registered for the congress, I learned that a
big hall had been reserved for a forum on AIDS. It was not
too long before, in 1980, that I got a phone call from my
colleague, Alvin Friedman-Kien, a dermatologist at NYU
Medical School. He wanted to tell me of a very curious coincidence. He had just seen two cases that same morning of
Kaposi sarcoma, both in young men. Till then, Kaposi sarcoma was an extremely rare disease observed only in elderly
people from the Mediterranean. It was described late in the
last century in Vienna by the Hungarian dermatologist
Kaposi. The morning that Friedman-Kien called, neither he
nor I knew that the strange coincidence actually signalled
the start of the AIDS epidemic.

Soon afterwards, when the Kyoto congress was being organized, I suggested to Tomio Tada, one of the chief planners, that the program should include a session on AIDS. I had no expertise, so I proposed my colleague at NYU, Suzy Zolla-Pazner, one of the first scientists to work on this problem, as chairperson of the session.

It was not easy for Tomio to convince his Japanese colleagues to hold a session on AIDS, as no cases had yet been observed in Japan at that time. However, he was finally able to get a consensus, and a small room was designated for this session. A year later, when the congress opened, interest was so great, they had to transfer the session from the small room to a huge hall.

Since then, of course, the pressing tragedy of AIDS has always been one of the most important, persistent concerns of international congresses of immunology, and it always commands the biggest halls. It will be a happy day when the subject of AIDS would again command no more than the smallest room, if any at all.

◀◦§◦▶

At the same congress in Kyoto, Bill Paul asked to speak to me. We had been friends from the years he worked at NYU with Baruj Benacerraf. At the time of the congress, Bill was working as Director of the Institute of Immunology and Allergy at the National Institutes of Health (and certainly had no foreknowledge that President Clinton would years later pick him to become the so-called "AIDS czar" as Director of AIDS Research at NIH).

Bill knew of my friendship with Tomio Tada and asked that I intercede so that his young collaborator Mark Davis would be allowed to present his work, even though Davis was not in the program. Bill said the work was very recent and of great interest: Mark had found a receptor for antigen on T cells.

It was already known by then that without T cells, no antibody production could take place. Mark Davis' discovery finally explained the mechanism by which the T cell recognizes the antigen and collaborates with the B cell to produce antibody. The implications of this discovery were enormous. From then on, scientists could design experiments to study and modify antibody production, leading to methods of increasing or decreasing antibody in order to help patients fight diseases.

I went to Tomio, who understood the importance of Davis' findings. He immediately included Davis as a special speaker in the congress.

At the closing congress banquet, Tomio placed Albert and me at a table with a Hungarian friend of mine, George Klein, a professor at the Karolinska Institutet in Stockholm. He asked me if the gentleman I had introduced to him was related to the harpsichordist Albert Fuller. "I have his records and often listen to them," he said.

"No, he is not related," I replied. "It is him." And I proudly added that he was the musician-in-residence of the NYU Medical School.

Another free journey for Albert occurred a few years later. Tomio wrote to me saying he had received a brochure from the Metropolitan Museum about a trip to Egypt that included a cruise along the Nile and visits to the great archeological sites. He was going with his wife Norie and asked if I would be interested as well. I had visited Egypt several years before. The place was so rich in antiquities that I managed to explore only a small portion of its marvels, and felt regretful when I left. I wrote to Tomio that I would gladly go.

Tomio wrote back, saying that his former student Masaru Taniguchi would like to join the trip and that Taniguchi would like to save money, if possible, by sharing a cabin with me. Taniguchi was a good friend of mine, so I had no hesitation agreeing.

A few days later, I was invited for the weekend to the country house of Alice, and the only other guest was Albert Fuller. During dinner the first evening, I mentioned that I was going to Egypt. Alice was fond of Egypt which she had visited several times. We discussed the Valley of the Kings, the antiquities in the Cairo Museum, the kingdoms and the dynasties, the disarming informality of the Egyptians we met. Albert joined the discussion and was extremely knowledgeable.

"When were you in Egypt?" Alice asked him.

"Never," was Albert's reply. "But I love it so much I have read a lot about it since I was young."

Then Alice asked him, "Why don't you go with them?"

"I would love to," Albert replied. "There is only one obstacle: I cannot afford it."

"So, then be my guest!" Alice said. "I would like to go as well. But really, at my age it would be too much." This was typical of Alice, inviting a friend *in absentia* to a trip.

Two days before our departure, I got a phone call from Masaru Taniguchi. His cousin was very ill and he had to cancel the trip. I called the Metropolitan Museum, but it was too late to get reimbursement. We were left with a vacant post all paid for.

I put down the phone and went to the other room in my laboratory, where I found my student Akira writing down the results of an experiment we had just finished.

"Akira," I said, "would you like to go to Egypt?" And I added, "It's for free!"

Akira blurted out "Yes!"

And that's how Akira Ueda, through the mysterious workings of chance, found himself exploring the ancient tombs and temples of the Nile.

· XIX ·

enthusiasts

THROUGH THE YEARS, I remained in touch with Michael Heidelberger, whom I first met in Paris when I verified the PCA reaction at Pierre Grabar's laboratory. I deeply appreciated the constant support this great scientist had given me from the moment we met.

Michael was one of the very first people I called when I moved from Baltimore to New York. Soon after, he invited me to his home for dinner and chamber music. Michael played the clarinet joyfully. He was accompanied by Charlotte Rosen, a professional violinist who owned and played the Stradivarius that had once belonged to one of the century's greatest violin players, Bronislav Huberman. Not long afterwards, Michael and Charlotte, both widowed for many years, got married.

One day, Michael told me that unfortunately he had had to retire from Columbia University, as they were very strict with the age limit. So he was now working at the Waksman Institute, the research laboratory in New Brunswick, New Jersey, established by Dr. Selman Waksman, who had won the Nobel Prize for his work on streptomycin.

I felt sorry for Michael having to travel so far every day, so I set up a little plan that I just hoped would work. When I moved to Kips Bay Towers, I asked Michael and his wife for dinner. I also invited our department head, Chandler Stetson. After dinner, Dr. Stetson learned that Michael was now working in New Brunswick. "Oh, I didn't know you've moved out of New York!" Stetson exclaimed.

"No, I commute," Michael said.

Stetson was shocked that such a great scientist had to undergo, at his advanced age, the strain of commuting to work for hours each day. Before the night was over, Stetson asked Michael if he would consider an Adjunct Professor position in our department.

This was how, through Chandler Stetson's kindly concern for his working conditions, Michael Heidelberger came to the Department of Pathology, to the glory of NYU. He continued working at NYU until his death in 1991 at the age of 103.

By the mid-sixties, NYU had become a mecca for immunologists. Dean Lewis Thomas was the person who insisted on the importance of immunology, and he attracted the world's leading immunologists to work at NYU, at a time when most other universities had a maximum of one person qualified as an immunologist. What a change today when immunology has moved to the forefront, impelled especially by the AIDS epidemic.

Many immunologists at NYU were then doing pioneer work. To name only a few, Baruj Benacerraf had started what became the first classic work on immunogenetics, the Poly-L-Lysine gene in guinea pigs; Jeanette Thorbecke was investigating the cellular aspects of immunology; Edward Franklin was exploring the structure of the IgG molecule; and Jonathan Uhr was experimenting on antibody production. Later, other distinguished immunologists joined the group, including Bernard Levin, Victor and Ruth Nussenzweig, Michael Lamm, Julia Phillips-Quagliata, Ross Basch, and Suzy Zolla-Pazner. It was wonderful to work with these brilliant scientists, to show them intriguing experiments, and to discuss problems with them.

It was at NYU that Baruj and I discovered the "carrier effect."

It was already known at that time that an antigen, a substance that stimulates the production of antibody, is made up of two elements (1) the relatively bigger segment, called the carrier, and (2) smaller segments on the surface of the carrier, called determinant. The determinant is the portion that is recognized by the antibody and for which antibody is produced.

In our experiments, Baruj and I used determinants that had been first created by Landsteiner. It was these artificial molecules that Landsteiner named "haptens."

At that time, not much was understood about antibody formation, though it was already known that when an antigen is injected into an organism, some lymphocytes develop into plasma cells and produce antibody. It was also known that in the secondary antibody production, i.e. when the antigen is injected a second time into the organism, a greater amount of antibody is produced than in the primary response.

With the carrier effect, Baruj and I showed that in order to have this secondary response, the same carrier must be used in both the primary and secondary injections. Our experiments also showed that the antibody-producing lymphocytes needed some sort of help in order to produce antibody. This pointed out that antibody production was a more complex event than was originally thought.

The carrier effect became one of the seminal experiments that provoked other researchers into looking more closely into the nature and process of antibody production. This led to the discovery that many other specific cells—T cells, mononuclears, dendritic cells, etc.—are involved in antibody production.

◆⌁◆

One day, a friend of mine who was working in the Department of Otorhinolaryngology came to me and said that he had recently attended some of my immunology lectures. He thought that I would be the right teacher for a friend of his who wanted to learn immunology.

The friend was not a scientist, he said, but she was determined to overcome this obstacle. She would pay well for the lessons, he added.

I became curious and eventually it was agreed that I would give the lady ten or twelve lessons of one or two hours each, every Wednesday from 5 to 7 PM, and that she would pay the honorarium to my grant and not to me.

I had a second-year medical student then, Ron Lee, who was working in my lab as a volunteer. He wanted to be present at these lessons. So much the better, I thought. He could tell me whether I was being clear enough.

When the lady arrived for the first lesson, I asked her why she wanted to learn about immunology. She replied that she was the sister of Mary Lasker, after whose husband the Lasker Award was named.

The award, given mostly to scientists in the biological sciences, was the most prestigious of scientific prizes in the United States. Those who won it often went on to win the Nobel Prize. The lady told me that she often helped her sister receive scientists, but she felt excluded when the guests began to talk about the sciences. She felt frustrated, she said, and wanted to understand what all the people around her were discussing.

I asked her how much she knew about science, as I wanted to know where to begin my teaching. "Oh, like everybody, a little bit," she answered.

"So," I said, "I guess you know that water is made up of two atoms of hydrogen and one of oxygen?"

"Fascinating! I had no idea!" she exclaimed.

Now I knew where I had to start. From scratch.

I soon found out that, however scientifically uninstructed, she was naturally intelligent. After the tenth session, she not only understood the basics of immunology, she would even volunteer apt and probing questions when I discussed our experiments with my student Ron. As Ron pointed out, she had learned not only the basics of immunology but, more importantly, how to think about it.

One day, I was in the elevator on the way to my laboratory when in stepped an old acquaintance from Rome, Giuseppe (Pippo) Vicari. He had arrived with his wife just a few days before on a fellowship at the Department of Microbiology. Pippo and I had met in Rome some fifteen years before, when I was still working at the Clinica Medica with Guido Biozzi. I wanted at that time to extend the observations I had made on rats to guinea pigs. The only laboratory in Rome that had guinea pigs was at the *Istituto Forlanini,* a medical center named after a great physician of the late nineteenth century who specialized in tuberculosis. Guido Biozzi knew one of the professors there, who put me in contact with his young student, Pippo Vicari. Whenever I went to the *Forlanini,* it was Pippo who would hold the guinea pigs while I injected them. We kept contact with each other and we met from time to time on my yearly visits to Rome. The Vicaris had a summer house by the sea near Formia where my sister had a house, and we would often go in the mornings to the same beach.

Our casual friendship became a close one during Pippo's stay at NYU. He would come over to my apartment for dinners of Italian food, where we would discuss our experiments or exchange the latest news from Rome. He went back to Rome two years later and worked at the *Istituto Superiore di Sanita,* Italy's equivalent of the National Institutes of Health. The institute had then attracted other excellent scientists, including Ernest Chain from England, who got the Nobel Prize with Alexander Fleming and Walter Florey for his work on penicillin; and an old friend from my days at the Pasteur Institute, Daniel Bovet, who got the Nobel Prize for his work on sulfonamides, antihistamine, and muscle-relaxing substances. The increasing migration of scientists from one country to another and the cross-pollination of ideas were breaking down international boundaries, even as the hippies, then an amusingly novel phenomenon, were listening to Beatles songs and experimenting with communal living in pursuit of universal brotherhood and peace. I made it a point to visit Pippo and Daniel at their laboratories every summer, where we would discuss our work, give encouragement, and update each other on the latest developments in immunology on both sides of the ocean.

Pippo became head of the institute's Department of Immunology and, upon his invitation, I held several seminars at the institute. One time, the institute director, Dr. Pocchieri, presented me with the *Medaglia dell'Istituto Superiore di Sanita,* its highest honor. I was certain that this had come about on the instigation of Pippo, who would later himself become head of the institute. I got a kick on learning that the medal was also being presented to Dr. Robert Gallo, a scientist whom I greatly admired. He later became a public figure as co-discoverer of the AIDS virus. But many years before this, he was already making one brilliant discovery after another, as an immunologist at the National Institutes of Health.

In 1963 my friends Kimishige and Teruko Ishizaka called me up. They were then both working in Denver and would soon become famous in the field of medical research for discovering IgE, the antibody responsible for allergic reactions. The Ishizakas wanted to send their first Japanese student, Tomio Tada, for a visit, so that he should learn from the source how to do the PCA reaction.

I soon found out I could not teach him anything in science, as he was already such an expert. However, it happened that we were just having our monthly concert at NYU, so I invited him to the concert. The day before he was to fly back to Denver, I took him to the Metropolitan Museum. His exposure to European art was virtually nil, but he was enthusiastic. I told him that for a beginning, I would like to show him only the start of modern European painting, and proposed the galleries of early Florentine art.

That was the start of our friendship. In the following twenty years, Tomio and I would go together nearly every summer, often with his wife Norie, to visit Italy and study its inexhaustible legacy of art. Tomio became such an expert on Italian art that he would often correctly identify a painting's creator and approximate its date even when the artist was unknown outside the specialists' field. We would refer to this as "making the right diagnosis." He then wrote a book in Japanese, *Italian Art Seen Through a Scientist's Eye*. I was touched to learn he had dedicated the book to me.

Tomio then tried his hand at writing classical Noh plays. One of them, *The Well of Ignorance*, is about a fisherman who is wrongly thought to be dead. His heart is given to a young woman, and this forces the fisherman's soul to wander in the world between life and death. Exploring the modern issue of organ transplantation through a classical Noh drama was a real innovation. *The New York Times* ran an article about its success in Japan, saying it had clearly touched a raw nerve (April 1, 1991).

Tomio then went on to publish a book on immunology for laymen, *Meanings of Immunity*, that became a bestseller and won the Osaragi Jiro Prize, the Japanese equivalent of the National Book Award. In the late 80's, Tomio founded the important journal, *International Immunology*, and the yearly international conference, Winter Advanced Course for Immunology and Infectious Diseases. I have attended these conferences nearly every year, and they have always been of the highest scientific standard.

At the 1995 International Congress of Immunology in San Francisco, Tomio was elected president of the International Union of Immunological Societies. A banquet was given to welcome him to his new post. As part of his acceptance speech, he had prepared a performance on the Japanese drum called *kotsuzumi*, an ancient musical art dating back to the 14th century. He said he wanted to share how the *kotsuzumi* helped him better understand the evolution of the human genome (the total set of chromosomes transmitted to an offspring). He explained how both the genome and the *kotsuzumi* had started out very simply, with just two elements, and then over time became longer, more varied and complex.

Using the podium as a substitute, Tomio started drumming and chanting, with barest simplicity at first, just uniform alternations between a beat on the podium and a drone of his voice. The guests became oblivious to the sushi and sake on their tables as Tomio's drumming and chanting filled the hall, becoming more complicated and intricate. As far as anyone knew, it was the first time anyone had ever linked the genome to drumming. It was an example of how music and science could complement each other.

· XX ·

a visit to the pallavicini palace

IN THE EARLY 1970's, I was in Rome on a visit to my sister, when Miss Tully arrived. She was staying in the city for a few days before going on to the *Festival dei Due Mondi*, the annual international music festival run by Gian Carlo Menotti in Spoleto. I asked her if she had seen the collection of the Princess Pallavicini.

"No," she told me, "but I've heard of it, and I've always wanted to see it."

The Pallavicini Palace contains one of the greatest private art collections in the world. In Rome, only two other similar collections exist, that of Prince Doria Pamphili (open to the public four days a week) and that of the Prince Colonna (open once a week). Of the Pallavicini collection, only one small section is open to the public, for one day a month: the Casino Rospigliosi-Pallavicini, the pavilion that stands apart from the main palace.

It was my chance to do something for Alice. Princess Elvina Pallavicini and I had maintained a warm, friendly relationship after I left Rome in the mid-fifties. I would always send flowers to her and her daughter, Maria Camilla, whenever I visited Rome; and they would always invite me for lunch or dinner. It was therefore easy for me to ask the Princess if I could bring Alice to see her palace and paintings. She invited us for tea and it was agreed that I would show Alice the palace beforehand.

We arrived early in the afternoon, as there were so many things I wanted to show Alice. We began our exploration with the suspended garden with its fountain and scores of orange and azalea trees. The garden stretched atop a building that was once a horse-and-carriage stable. At one end of the garden stood the Casino Rospigliosi-Pallavicini. The main hall of this pavilion was one of the wonders of Rome. Guido Reni, considered in his time the equal of Raphael, had painted on its ceiling his celebrated masterpiece, the *Aurora*, a huge fresco depicting the Goddess of Dawn, accompanied by the Hours as she spreads flowers ahead of the chariot of the Sun. With its delicate colors and classic restraint, the painting was widely acknowledged from the start to be one of the most splendid works of Italian painting. The adjacent halls of the pavilion were filled with other important works of the Italian *seicento* and *settecento*, including Reni's "Crucifixion" and "Andromeda." There were two equestrian battle scenes by Luca Giordano, whose sobriquet was Fa Presto, as he painted so unbelievably fast. The larger painting, all 15 by 25 feet of it, was finished in one day, and it was a masterwork!

I then took Alice through the garden into some small rooms connecting the garden and the palace. These rooms contained numerous scenes of Rome by Vanvitelli, as well as Italian *seicento* and *settecento* furniture. Rare porcelain from Meissen, Vincennes, Sèvres and Italy gleamed in several vitrines.

Alice was a connoisseur of the decorative arts of the period and it was not easy to hurry her on through these connecting rooms. I had to remind her that there were many, many other things we had to see. Of paintings alone, the palace had some 4,000 in its collection.

We soon entered the palace itself. In the first hall was the massive Papal baldachino, a canopy reserved for the Pope's use and one of only five that had been granted to Roman princes by the Vatican. On the walls hung biblical scenes by Domenichino and Guercino, a *putto* by Poussin, and numerous other *seicento* and *settecento* paintings, including major works by Mattia Preti and Bernardino Strozzi.

We then moved on to the ballroom. Its ceiling had been painted with the *Crepusculo* (Dusk) by Giovanni da San Giovanni as a companion piece to Guido Reni's *Aurora*. The *Crepusculo* disappeared in the 19th century. Princess Pallavicini told me that when she came to live in the palace she noticed that the ceiling of the ballroom was lower than that of the other rooms. She made an exploration and discovered another ceiling above the ballroom ceiling. This was how an overlaid masterwork was rediscovered, not with infrared or x-ray but with ladders, flashlights, and axes.

We then went on to one of the principal salons, which contained the harpsichord painted by Poussin. Only the frame with Poussin's pastoral scene remained, as the works of the instrument were lost. Another painting by a French master shared the salon, a framed landscape by Claude Lorrain. On three of the walls hung individual paintings of Jesus Christ and the twelve Apostles that the Marchese Nicolo Pallavicini had commissioned from Rubens.

We went through several other rooms containing family portraits, Neapolitan flower paintings, and Roman sculptures, as well as Princess Pallavicini's own collection of old English furniture, including a salon of Chippendales. In one vitrine lay the pearls Louis XIV gave to Cardinal Mazarin's niece, Maria Mancini, when she married the Prince Colonna. I recounted the affair of Louis XIV and Maria Mancini to Alice, and how Cardinal Mazarin terminated this romance by betrothing his niece to the Roman Prince Colonna.

We arrived at the rooms where the Princess actually lived. It was here that she hung the paintings she felt closest to: Rubens' portrait of his second wife, Helene Fourment (the household affectionately called the painting Madame Rubens), two works attributed to Velasquez (an Infanta and a group of men at arms called "The Brawl"), an allegory by

Lorenzo Lotto ("Chastity"), the "Burial of Saint Francis" by Lorenzo Monaco, altar pieces by Defendente Ferrari, and last but not least, four Botticellis, among them the Princess' favorite, the *Derelitta*.

An air of mystery pervaded the palace. We went through the rooms silently, as if unwilling to break some spell that had allowed the delicate works to survive the destruction of three centuries.

We finally reached the salon where the Princess was waiting for us. I introduced Alice, and tea was served.

Alice and the Princess conversed in French, still the traditional language of high social discourse in Europe.

"Thank you so much for the invitation and the chance to see the palace," Alice told the Princess.

"I'm glad you could come to see us," the Princess said.

"This has been one of the most amazing visits I've ever had in Italy," Alice told her.

"It's my great pleasure," the Princess responded. "Now, tell me, what else are you doing in Italy?"

"Well," said Alice, "I'm going to Spoleto to attend the *Festival dei due Mondi*."

"Oh!—Gian Carlo is a good friend of mine," the Princess told her. "An American lady supports him for these festivals, and therefore he is very warm and open to American ladies."

"That's very nice of him," said Alice.

"If you wish, I could very easily call him up and recommend you to him," the Princess offered.

"Oh thank you very, very much," answered Alice with a charming but mischievous smile, "but it is really not necessary, as I am the lady who supports him."

"It's an honor to have met you!" the Princess told her.

◄○§?○►

Here I should add a brief history of the palace and the Pallavicini family.

The palace was originally built in 1611, for Cardinal Scipione Borghese, the brother of Pope Paul V. Being the brother of the Pope and also a cardinal meant an enormous income at a time when the Papacy was the equal of kingdoms and empires in temporal affairs, a situation that has vastly changed along with the nature of the Church itself. Cardinal Borghese was a great connoisseur and patron of artists, especially of Bernini, who created the busts of the cardinal now in the Villa Borghese.

When Bernini presented the first bust to the cardinal, it fell and broke. Bernini repaired it, but the cardinal wanted a faultless bust, and Bernini carved a second one. The cardinal judged rightly that the first one was a more expressive work of art, and in the end kept both. This is the reason why we now have two marble busts of Cardinal Borghese by Bernini.

In the late 17th century, the palace passed into the ownership of Cardinal Giulio Mazarin, the Italian-born minister and adviser of King Louis XIV. In 1704, Cardinal Lazzaro Pallavicini, who was made Prince of the Church in 1669, bought the palace. Cardinal Pallavicini had a favorite niece, Maria Camilla, for whom he arranged an advantageous marriage to Prince Giovanni Battista Rospigliosi, the nephew of the Rospigliosi Pope Clement IX. As a marriage gift, he gave Maria Camilla paintings by Caravaggio, the Carracci brothers, Rubens and others. Later, the Pope himself added works by Bernini, Maratta and Poussin. These became the nucleus of the family collection.

Many of the successive descendants continued to add to the collection, especially Marchese Nicolo, in the 18th century. In the 19th century, some objects were sold, including the Rospigliosi cup, now in New York's Metropolitan Museum, and magnificent renaissance illuminated manuscripts, now in the Pierpont Morgan Library.

Cardinal Pallavicini had stipulated in the marriage contract that if Maria Camilla had only one son, the heir was to inherit both the Pallavicini and the Rospigliosi titles. If she had two, the first-born would take the Rospigliosi name, and the second, the Pallavicini name. In the event of a sole daughter, the names, titles, and possessions of both families were to be conferred upon her spouse. It was due to this elegantly simple provision that, while so many great renaissance families have long since died out, the Pallavicini-Rospigliosi family has survived.

· XXI ·

the fifth slave

CHARLES DE TOLNAY was another friend I took to meet the Princess Pallavicini. I knew she would be very interested in his ideas, as he was one of the leading art scholars of the time. Tolnay was himself Hungarian. I first met him in Rome when the Ambassadress Cerruti gave a luncheon to introduce us.

Tolnay's major opus was a six-volume study on Michelangelo, and he became known as the world's preeminent expert on the artist. It was also he who established that the Master of Flémalle and Robert Campin are the same person, confirming theories advanced earlier by other art historians.

I admired Tolnay's ability to find adventure in something as flat and square as a small piece of canvas. So I seized the opportunity to go with him to the Cloisters in New York and see the masterpiece of Campin, who worked in Tournai between 1406 and 1444 and who was the teacher of another great Flemish painter, Rogier van der Weyden. Campin's painting depicting the Annunciation had been the property of the Prince of Merode, who later sold it to Nelson Rockefeller. It was while the painting was still in the collection of the Prince of Merode, inaccessible to all but the family circle, that Tolnay first saw it.

The Merodes were an old Flemish family that inherited the painting from descendants of the Prince of Annenberg, who had obtained the painting at a sale in Bruges in 1820. Tolnay told me that two days after the Prince of Merode sold the painting to Rockefeller, the prince changed his mind and tried desperately to cancel the sale. However, Rockefeller refused to give it back.

Apart from its luminous beauty, Campin's work is revolutionary: painted around 1425, it is the earliest known depiction of the Virgin in a homely bourgeois interior, rather than on a pedestal or in an ecclesiastic setting. The Cloisters, New York's museum specializing in the arts of the medieval period, obviously realized what a treasure it had. It dedicated a whole room to the painting, and furnished the room with medieval objects seen in the painting, down to the basin and candlestick holders.

The painting is a triptych, with the Annunciation shown in the center. On its left is a panel depicting St. Joseph in his workshop. On the right is another panel with the portrait of the kneeling donor, just lately identified by historians as Ingelbrecht of Mechelen. Tolnay said that the donor was probably not yet married when Campin painted his likeness. It was only when the painting was almost done, or sometime afterwards, that the donor would have gotten married, because the portrait of his kneeling wife, squeezed in behind his, was painted over the grass in the background.

Tolnay showed me how Campin started a trend of realism, rendering each object with care, no matter how humble, such as the shining copper basin, the mousetraps, the just-extinguished candle with the spark still on its wick and smoke still rising, the Flemish street scene beyond the windows, and the passersby and people looking out of their own doorways and windows. He spoke of the symbols Campin evidently enjoyed placing everywhere, such as the rose bush and the red-breast robins for the Virgin Mary, the white towel for chastity, the copper basin and the lily for purity. Then there was the shaft of light coming through the roundel window without breaking it. Campin transformed this natural phenomenon into a symbol of the virgin conception by painting a minuscule image of a baby carrying a cross, floating down the shaft of light. There were allusions to texts by prophets and saints; the mousetrap, for example, recalled a sermon by Saint Augustine about catching the devil in a mousetrap. All these symbols and clues were fascinating, but regardless of them, the painting came across directly, through a distance of more than five hundred years, in its joy, detail, and warmth. We spent almost two hours studying the painting and didn't notice the time go by.

Once when I was on a visit to Paris, both Tolnay and the Ambassadress Cerruti happened to be there as well. We all went together to an exhibition of early renaissance sculpture at the Orangerie in the Tuileries. There we met an elderly gentleman whom Tolnay and the Ambassadress both knew, Bernard Berenson.

I was aware that Tolnay had openly challenged some of Berenson's attributions. Nevertheless, their conversation was remarkably cordial without the least hint of animosity. Two big intellects with equally big egos, who would be clashing anywhere else, knew how to bury the hatchet, at least for the while, in the presence of a great lady like the Ambassadress Cerruti.

Tolnay was professor at Princeton University when he published his six-volume opus on Michelangelo. Whenever we happened to be both in Italy, I would always take the chance to visit museums or churches with him. In Rome, for three consecutive days, we went to see the Moses of Michelangelo in the church of San Pietro in Vincoli, and we still felt we did not spend enough time studying it. The Moses sits in the middle of the monument of Pope Julius II, but Michelangelo originally meant it for the second story of an earlier, grander version of the monument. With its elongated torso, it was meant to be seen from below at a steep angle. Tolnay suggested that the way to see the Moses as Michelangelo had conceived it was in a crouching position.

I also had the privilege of seeing the Sistine Chapel with

him. I had fought my way through the throngs into the chapel so many times I thought I knew its ceiling well. I was mistaken. With Tolnay, many things I never even noticed suddenly became luminous, for example, how the postures and expressions of the *ignudi* (the nudes anchoring the central panels) reflected the scenes they surrounded. Tolnay recalled the tradition of nudity in religious art, based as it was on the idea that the soul is naked in the eyes of God. He pointed out how in the famous central panel, God is a bursting, convex form; Adam is passive, concave, like an empty bowl.

One day, Tolnay took me to a restaurant at the Via del Seminario, just off the Piazza Sant' Ignazio. It was a small, unassuming *trattoria* with animated locals seated at tables in long rows. As we dined, Tolnay told me he had been researching letters Michelangelo had sent to his patron and friend, Vittoria Colonna, when Tolnay learned that the sculptor used to eat in this restaurant. The restaurant still retained its name from renaissance times, *Di Due Colonne*, after the two ancient Roman columns that supported its vault.

On my yearly trips to Rome, I often visit the baroque Jesuit church, the Sant' Ignazio, to reacquaint myself with the superb ceiling fresco by Padre Pozzo, a tumultuous creation that shows Saint Ignatius ascending to heaven amidst a blizzard of souls, most of them scrambling their way up, and some less fortunate ones at the edges of the ceiling forever struggling to keep themselves from falling down. After the visit, I never miss passing by the nearby Due Colonne restaurant, compelled by some desire to see for myself if the two ancient columns are still standing.

Soon after Tolnay published his Michelangelo opus, he was asked to be curator of the Casa Buonarroti, the house in Florence where Michelangelo was born. The house had remained in the Buonarroti family for generations until they gave it to the city of Florence, when it became a museum and scholarly center on renaissance art, especially the Buonarroti legacy.

Thanks to Tolnay, I had the chance to sleep in Michelangelo's bedroom in a restricted area of the Casa Buonarroti. It was quite an experience, brushing your teeth, fumbling around for slippers, and doing other mundane activities in this earth-bound house of someone whom people usually imagine in the firmaments instead, or at least up on the ceiling.

One of Tolnay's most interesting studies concerned the "Fifth Slave." Soon after he took directorship of the Casa Buonarroti, he began making the usual courtesy calls to the other museum directors in Florence. When he went to see the director of the Pitti Palace, an unfinished sculpture caught his attention. It was standing in a brick niche in a neglected courtyard of the palace. It was a young male nude still trying to emerge from a chunky block of marble. One of its arms was missing and the other was resting on what seemed to be a tree trunk. It stood slightly contorted and its half-raised face had a mysterious expression, perhaps a plea or a smile. Tolnay thought that it was a remarkable sculpture in the style of Michelangelo.

As Tolnay knew, the Italian art historian Hugo Procacci had published an article in 1962 describing this statue as possibly from the workshop of Michelangelo. Upon closer inspection, Tolnay noted that it was made of the same Carrara marble and had the same dimensions as those of the "Slaves" Michelangelo made for the Tomb of Julius II.

I learned a lot about the "Slaves" from Tolnay, especially on the three days we studied Michelangelo's "Moses" at the Julius tomb in Rome's San Pietro in Vincoli. The "Slaves" were part of Pope Julius II's plan to build for himself the grandest tomb in the world. He commissioned Michelangelo to create a free-standing monument anchoring forty sculptures. The "Slaves" were to represent the dominions

Julius II acquired for the Papacy by war. However, Michelangelo himself became enslaved by the whole project. The Pope kept changing his mind and ordering new designs. Then finally he lost interest in the tomb. The project became one of the great frustrations of Michelangelo's life. In fairness to the Pope, no one could blame him for losing interest in his own tomb! But another explanation is that he had become consumed by a grander project, the rebuilding of St. Peter's Basilica under Bramante's direction. The tomb project ended up several decades later as a side altar in San Pietro in Vincoli, finished by other artists, a ghost of the original concept. However, Michelangelo's work on the Julius monument still produced some of the most stunning works ever made, including the "Moses" and the "Slaves."

The "Slaves" range from the highly finished early work, the "Dying Slave" in the Louvre, to the unfinished but perhaps even more sublime "Reawakening Slave" in the Accademia in Florence. The authorship of the "Slaves" has always been a cause of fascination and controversy through the centuries. Some historians attribute full authorship to some slaves only and argue that others, like the "Bearded Slave" in the Accademia, were mostly the work of Michelangelo's pupils.

At the time Tolnay visited the museum director at the Pitti Palace, six of these slaves were known to have survived. Michelangelo had given the earliest two, which were both finished between 1513 and 1516, to his friend Roberto Strozzi, when Strozzi was in exile in Lyons. Through various changes of ownership, these have now become two of the greatest glories of the Louvre.

Four other slaves, made later, have found their way to the Accademia. While researching his Michelangelo opus, Tolnay noted that Vasari described how he visited Michelangelo's studio in Florence just before the sculptor went to Rome in 1534. Vasari wrote that Michelangelo was working on five blocks of marble at the same time, and that these were all slaves for the tomb of Julius II.

The slaves, in various stages of completion, were in Michelangelo's possession at the time of his death in 1564. Michelangelo's heir and nephew gave them to the Grand Duke Cosimo Medici. Four slaves were later put in the grotto of the Boboli Gardens. Three centuries later, in the early 1900's, they were brought indoors to the Accademia. As for the "fifth" slave, no one knew what had happened to it.

Tolnay asked the director of the Pitti Palace if he could have the sculpture in the neglected courtyard of the palace to decorate the lobby of the Casa Buonarroti. He argued that it would then be inside a room and no longer exposed to weather.

Tolnay went to the archives and pored over the designs and variations Michelangelo made for the Julius monument. He examined the sculpture's posture in relation to the slaves and the monument designs. He noted that it had the same character and style as the "unfinished" slaves in the Accademia.

The sculpture was finally transported to the Casa Buonarroti in 1966. Tolnay published his paper soon after, attributing the sculpture to Michelangelo himself and describing it as the missing "fifth" slave. His paper argued that like the four other slaves in the Accademia, it was made for the 1532 version of the Julius monument and that it was probably meant to be placed on the left side of the facade, its head turned to the monument.

The "Fifth Slave," as it is now known, has become one of the major showpieces of the Casa Buonarroti. Its monumental form anchors the entrance hall, ushering the visitor to the other art works in the house that include the famous "Madonna of the Stairs." Some historians have come to consider the "Fifth Slave" as a work by Michelangelo himself, but later reworked by other hands. The renaissance art expert Frederick Hartt, in 1972, attributed it to Michelangelo's students, except for the head, which he considered to be by Michelangelo. I myself concur with Tolnay in taking it to be a fully authentic Michelangelo, although I have friends who disagree. Nonetheless ... what a fascinating exploration it has launched, this odd piece of stone, once forgotten in a neglected courtyard!

· XXII ·

the silver shop

For me London is a special place, for my childhood friend Eva lives there. As a little girl, Eva came to our house in Kolozsvar almost every day after her mother died, becoming practically a second sister to me. Her story, like that of many Hungarians of our generation, became an odyssey. During the Second World War, she fell in love with a man some fifteen years her senior. The man, Andrew Lederer, came from an extremely wealthy, aristocratic Jewish family. Even though his grandfather had converted to Catholicism, this did not make any difference to the Nazis, and his family lost everything during the Nazi occupation.

Among Andrew's relatives was the Baron Hatwany, whose grandparents had also converted to Catholicism. The Baron and I occasionally saw each other in Paris just before the Second World War. One evening, we were sitting on the terrace of the Cafe Dome at the Montparnasse. The Baron showed me a letter he had just received from his lawyer in Budapest. He pointed out the lines "Dear Baron, I must inform you that according to the decision of the authorities, though you are not considered a Jew, your lands are." Like Andrew and his family, he eventually lost everything.

When Eva first told me about Andrew, I said, "I understand that you have fallen in love. But take care. He has lost everything except his need for luxury and his taste." In any case, they got married. It was only later that I found out how Eva had fallen for Andrew.

Sometime before the Second World War, Eva's father

Miklos Krenner had become an important political writer in Hungary. He sent his two daughters Eva and Maria to study in Budapest. A common friend at their boarding house introduced them to Andrew Lederer. Andrew courted Eva, but she was interested only in boys her age. In 1944, the Nazis invaded Hungary. Eva's best friend and her mother were put under house arrest. They were of a well-known family of Jewish origin, though they were second-generation Catholic.

Andrew volunteered to rescue them. He was blond, tall, and spoke excellent German. It was still a grave risk, as the Nazis could detain him and find out that he himself was of Jewish origin. This did not stop him. He went into the house and told the guards, "These women are my friends. They are not Jewish and you should let them leave." The Germans gave up the women to Andrew and he was able to take them out of the house. Eva, who had been waiting outside in terror, embraced Andrew and told him, "I will love you forever!"

After the war, they escaped to Italy and lived in Rome for a time, where my sister and I saw them often. Finally they emigrated to England where Andrew, who had become a farming expert while managing the vast ancestral lands in Hungary, found work with a major agricultural concern. They had a son, Miko, who married a lovely English rose, Judy. When Andrew passed away, Eva took a job in a small shop selling antique silver. She became an expert, and if she came across a nice Georgian piece that was a bargain, she would buy it on my behalf.

I especially liked the classic, elegant style of Hester Bateman, a silversmith who was active during the reign of George III. Alice Tully, who had met Eva, also happened to know about my admiration for Hester Bateman. One Christmas, she gave me a lovely sauce bowl signed by Bateman. The card said, "From Alice and Hester to Zoltan."

I once told Eva that I had always wanted to see the Hermitage in St. Petersburg. This desire took on new life when Communism collapsed in the Soviet Union. One day, I got an urgent phone call from Eva. One of her Hungarian friends, who was working as a travel agent in London, was organizing a trip to St. Petersburg. Should she ask her friend if there was still a post open for me?

"Of course," I replied. "But for two posts."

"You're going with a friend?" Eva asked.

"Yes, as I'm inviting you for the trip." It was not difficult to persuade her.

We both loved the baroque beauty of St. Petersburg and the bounties of the Hermitage, which was especially rich in Italian and Northern renaissance works, Dutch masters, and French Impressionist art. We stood in rapture before such wonders as Leonardo's "Benois Madonna," Rembrandt's "Prodigal Son," and Canaletto's "Arrival of the French Ambassador in Venice."

Later, the same travel agent wrote to me that she was organizing a trip to Venice. I could not go, but I invited Eva *in absentia*, as Marcel Proust did several times with his friends. I enjoyed Eva's letters on her trip, as I felt she was traveling for me in this most dreamlike of places, this city I find the most beautiful of all.

One time I went to London for a visit to Eva. As soon as I arrived, I went to see her at the silver market where she was working. It was much easier then to go see her at the shop than to get her by phone.

Eva and I were discussing plans to go to the theater that evening when a lady dressed in worn-out, simple black clothes came in. It struck me that I had seen this lady before, but I just could not place her.

She asked Eva about a piece of eighteenth-century English silver, a small milk container. However, she found it too expensive and left, looking very regretful.

Eva's neighbor from the adjoining silver boutique came in as soon as the lady left. She asked Eva if she knew who the lady was. I piped up and said that I was sure I had met the lady, but I could not remember where or when.

"She is Birgit Nilsson," Eva's neighbor told us. "She loves antique silver. She always dresses in rags when she comes to my shop. She thinks it will help her get a bargain."

Indeed I had seen Birgit Nilsson before! In fact many times. But no wonder I could not recognize her this time, for I was used to seeing her only in all those resplendent costumes on the stage of the Metropolitan Opera, as the reigning Wagnerian soprano of her time.

I asked Eva to try to catch up with Miss Nilsson and to offer the milk container as a gift from an anonymous admirer. After a while, Miss Nilsson came back with Eva. She held my hand tightly and exclaimed, "Thank you so much! This is the most charming surprise I ever had!"

"It's nothing," I told her, "compared to all the joy you've given me through the years at the Metropolitan Opera … for instance, just two months ago!"

In the following years, whenever she sang at the Metropolitan Opera, I would always send her flowers and congratulate her after the opera ended. The first time I did this, the usher told me that I could only see her if I were on the list. He checked the list and said he could not find my name but he would check again. I was there, in fact on top of the list, and remained there in the years that followed.

Another time, I wanted to give Birgit Nilsson a small gift as a humorous remembrance of how we met. I went to Robinson on 57th Street, which was, along with Shrubsole, the best place in New York for antique English silver. There I asked for a small George III silver object. "Something like a marrow spoon or a coffee spoon or something like that … just for a joke," I told the English gentleman who was showing me around the vitrines.

"Oh, Sir," was his response, "Nothing can be for a joke, not even the most trifling object, when it comes to George the Third!"

◄►§ё◄►

One day, my friend Lloyd Old told me that there was such a vogue in organic foods that it would be reasonable to buy stocks in this commodity. Someone had given him the name of such a stock, which had the price of $100 per share.

I had a good friend, Paul Fabri, who was very fortunate with the stock market. His family had owned a major textile factory in Budapest. The family lost the whole fortune when the Communists took over Hungary, after which Paul fled first to London and then to New York. He had learned much about business and with shrewd investments in the stock market, had become comfortable again. The legendary general's widow, Mrs. Jean MacArthur, became one of his closest friends and, at dinners surrounded by his collection of antiques, he would at times exult on how "kind" the stock market had been to him and how it had helped him recover a fraction of the splendor he knew as a young man in Budapest.

As far as I was concerned, however, I had always been too preoccupied with other activities to even begin familiarizing myself with Dow Jones averages and NASDAQ indexes. However, when Lloyd called me about the stock offering in organic foods, I thought, Why not? So I bought 15 shares at $100 each, plus the commission.

A week later, I called up the broker and learned that the stock had gone up a bit, to $107 a share. I forgot about the stock for some six months. I called up the broker, and he asked me to wait a moment while he checked.

He came back on the phone and said the price of the stocks had fallen tremendously. It was now $15.

"What?" I complained, "Fifteen dollars for a stock I paid you a hundred for, just six months ago?!"

"No, Sir," said the broker, "It is $15 for *all* the 15 shares you bought." Then he added, "But with the commission, and a few other charges, you owe us $10."

"Sell everything immediately!" I ordered him.

That was my first and last adventure in the market. An incident like this could scarcely have deterred another person, but I myself was not inclined to take on the onus of following the fluctuations of something that gave me no direct inspiration. I was so busy with work and organizing the NYU concert series, I decided that life was full enough as it was.

· XXIII ·

serendipity

To be an immigrant in a country with a different language has its drawbacks: the disorientation, the biases you encounter, the need to start your life again literally from a suitcase. But it also has its advantages. A common "other" language brings extraordinary people into your life, whom you might never have met in the old country.

Among these extraordinary people was the physicist Leo Szilard, one of the greatest brains of the century. This Hungarian immigrant to the United States was the first to develop the idea of nuclear chain reaction. With Enrico Fermi he built the first nuclear chain reactor. The atomic bomb could not have been built without Szilard, one of the chief architects of the Manhattan Project. Without him, history, as well as consciousness as we know it in the second half of the century, would be unrecognizably different. (Szilard's life is well-described in his biography, *Genius in the Shadows*.)

Physicist by profession, he was nevertheless very much interested in the biological sciences, especially immunology. I first met him at a conference held by the FASEB (Federation of American Societies for Experimental Biology) in Atlantic City. He often came to the laboratory at New York University and, along with Baruj Benacerraf, we would hold long discussions on the sciences. Everyone was in awe of his intelligence. His brusque and superior manner was perhaps not surprising for someone who had discovered a way to destroy the world.

I actually never came face to face with Eugene Wigner,

the physicist who won the Nobel Prize in the early sixties for his research on the atom and its nucleus. One day, I read an interview he gave for a journal in which he said that he loved to read good Hungarian literature, and lamented that Hungarian writers had never been given their due recognition. I wrote to Wigner, who was then residing in New England, that I was taking the liberty of sending him some Hungarian books recently written by my friend Sandor Marai. Wigner wrote back thanking me for the books. This was the beginning of our correspondence that continued until his death. It was a friendship sustained by a mutual love of science and the novels of Sandor Marai.

I first encountered Sandor Marai in Paris during the late twenties when I was a medical student. His books fascinated me and I spoke about one of them to a friend of mine, Emanuel Boudot-Lamotte, an editor at the *Nouvelle Revue Française*. Boudot-Lamotte got interested in the book, an autobiographical work in which Marai described his early college life in Kassa (then in northern Hungary, now Slovakia). Boudot-Lamotte wanted to find a publisher for the book in French. I wrote to Marai in Budapest, and he answered that in a few weeks he would be in Paris and could we meet at the lobby of his hotel. Boudot-Lamotte and I went and met him. However, nothing came of the project.

I met Sandor Marai again in the late forties when he was visiting in Rome. Ambassadress Cerruti had invited us both for lunch for the purpose of introducing us to each other. This was when Sandor and I first became friends. He was worried about the increasing stranglehold of Communism on Hungary. A year or so later, he and his family left Hungary and started life again in Italy.

Sandor took up residence at Posilippo, a district of Naples with ravishing views of the bay. (That a dying Caruso wanted to be brought back to Naples so that his last view on earth would be the bay is perhaps an apocryphal story, but most people who have swooned over the scene themselves can have no doubt that it was the great tenor's last wish.)

I would visit Sandor in Naples every two or three months for the weekends, until he sailed with his family for the United States. When I myself moved to New York, I would see them for dinner every two or three weeks at their apartment on the Upper East Side, and when they moved to San Diego, I would go visit them at least twice a year.

Sandor wrote more than forty novels and some books of poetry. I consider him one of the century's greatest writers, even if most people outside Hungary and Germany, where many of his novels are available in translation, have never heard of him. Perhaps one reason why he did not get the recognition he deserved during his lifetime was his studious avoidance of social causes, *de rigueur* for East European writers who wanted to succeed internationally. Had he lived at the time of Jane Austen, he would have had a better chance. He became known among his readers for his penetrating chronicles of the lives of the Hungarian upper-middle class, or *bourgeoisie*, that ill-fated French term that has become one of the most attacked words in this century, from both the left and the right, by rebel and snob. But his stock continues to rise. The eminent Italian Adelphi press has just published Italian editions of two of his novels. The *Oxford History of Hungarian Literature* calls his *Egy polgár vallomásai (Confessions of a Burgher)* one of the greatest autobiographical novels produced in this century. The novel, which came out in 1934, is my favorite of his many masterpieces. It uses penetrating, often biting, social and psychological observation in depicting the fortunes of an upper-middle-class family in Hungary at the turn of the century.

In 1956, he wrote his lyric poem about the 1956 Hungarian uprising against the Communists, titled *"Mennyből az angyal"* ("Angel of Heaven"). I still treasure his handwritten copy of the poem with a dedication to my sister and me. It was a measure of Marai's standing in Hungary that even the Communist government, which he openly reviled, offered him its highest literary award for his life's work, an offer he vehemently refused.

◆⟩ჲ⟨◆

One of the luckiest Hungarians I knew was Janos Scholz. I met him in 1959 through Johanna Martzy, my violinist friend. Janos Scholz came from an old Hungarian family from Sopron, the western portion of Hungary. He studied at the Ferencz Liszt Academy of Music in Budapest. In 1932, he joined the Roth Quartet as its cellist. The quartet toured extensively, and then in 1933 emigrated as a group to the United States.

The Budapest Quartet is a Hungarian group with a similar story. Its original members all played in the Budapest Opera Orchestra before they formed the quartet in 1917. They gave their first performance in Kolozsvar. At that time, no one knew that the group would become the most successful quartet of the century.

The quartet, with its repertoire stretching from Bartok to Haydn, remained famous despite changing players several times, eventually losing all its original members but stabilizing in the mid-30's. At that point all four of the Budapest Quartet were Russian Jews.

A joke started making the rounds:—

Question:	What is one Russian?
Answer:	An anarchist.
Question:	What are two Russians?
Answer:	A conspiracy.
Question:	What are three Russians?
Answer:	A revolution.
Question:	What are four Russians?
Answer:	The Budapest Quartet.

The group emigrated to the USA in 1938, five years after the younger Roth Quartet. I heard them perform in New York during the early 60's, in the last years before they disbanded due to illness. I met the second violinist, Alexander Schneider, Sasha as he was called, through Albert Fuller; he was strikingly flamboyant and witty, on-stage and off.

The Roth Quartet, though not as renowned, continued to tour widely and successfully. Later, Janos Scholz left the group to start a notable career as cello soloist.

He met the Hungarian art historian Charles de Tolnay and they became close friends. Janos had such an instinct for art that just by visiting museums and conversing with Tolnay, he became one of the world's leading experts in Italian drawings of the renaissance and baroque periods. Both Columbia and New York University invited him to teach this subject, which he did for many years.

Janos liked to say that he arrived in the United States with "nothing but a suitcase and a cello." He started collecting drawings soon after, making his first purchase in Mexico. It was about a quarter of a century before widespread interest in drawings took off, a time when, in his words, one could buy an original Dürer drawing in a bookstore "for the price of a good dinner."

I would go every now and then with Janos, his second wife, and his son to concerts or for dinners at Alice Tully's apartment at the Hampshire House. He enjoyed showing me his collection of drawings, often exulting with childlike wonder at his luck in discovering so many masterworks for pennies, and in the most unsought places, like secondhand bookshops, country fairs, curio shops, even garage sales.

As a cellist, he had a keen eye for musical instruments. Once, he bought twenty old violin and cello bows from a shop in New York. It turned out that most of them were by François Tourte, who revolutionized bow-making in the late eighteenth century and became known as the Stradivarius of the bow. Janos paid twenty dollars apiece for bows that were later found to be worth several thousands of dollars each.

His serendipity extended to other objects. He found amazing bargains in rare books, early photographs, bronzes, Venetian furniture, and old carpets. Once, he bought an 18th-century Transylvanian *ladik* carpet for eighty dollars that was actually worth twenty thousand dollars in the auction market.

One night in 1977, he performed a cello recital at the Morgan Library and at the end announced that he was donating his collection of Italian drawings to the library. It consisted of more than 1,500 drawings from the 14th to the 18th centuries, and included works by Leonardo, Raphael, Titian, Tintoretto, Canaletto, Guardi, and Tiepolo.

The Morgan Library was not the only recipient of his beneficence. Among other donations, he gave 175 bows to the Smithsonian Institution.

For true serendipity, one may consider Janos' family relations. He married twice, and both his wives kept on good terms with each other. He had two boys from the first marriage and one from the second, and they all took care of each other as brothers.

la caravelle

THE FIRST TIME I went to the Caravelle was for a dinner Miss Tully was giving for eight. At the end of the dinner, I noted that Alice did not pay but just signed the bill.

For many young Americans, a world without credit cards is hard to imagine. But the time did exist not too long ago when most major establishments, the Caravelle included, accepted cash only. Not long after the dinner, I made a reservation at the Caravelle as I wanted to take a friend for a special night out. I did not want to be walking around with a lot of cash, therefore I asked the proprietor if I could have my signature deposited so that they should send the bill to my address.

The proprietor told me that I should give the names of at least two regular customers they could contact before deciding on my request. I told him I could do this and that the first person was Miss Alice Tully. "Oh!" exclaimed the proprietor, "We don't need another name. And you can start right now."

Every now and then, I would treat Alice to the Caravelle which, along with Four Seasons and Bouley, was one of her favorite restaurants in New York. One time, at the end of dinner, she erupted joyfully, "Oh Zoltan, you don't know what a thrill this is for me ... that someone else is paying the bill!"

Another lady who enjoyed dining at the Caravelle was Madame Pisart. I met her through my friend, the tenor Robert White. This Belgian lady, whose family once owned major uranium mines in the Belgian Congo, lived in a suite that occupied a whole floor of the Plaza Savoy Hotel on Fifth Avenue at 59th Street. When the hotel was demolished, she moved two blocks away to an apartment that occupied the entire 17th floor of the Regency Hotel on Park Avenue.

One Sunday afternoon, I went to the Frick Collection to hear Bobby White sing. Recitals and concerts at the Frick were gratis, but you had to come early to get a seat in the small auditorium. I arrived way ahead of time, got a ticket, then went to see some of the glorious paintings and renaissance sculptures housed in the Frick Collection.

I happened to see two ladies come in to get tickets. The younger one had a beautiful mink coat. The other, a lady of at least ninety years, wore a wornout, old-fashioned karakul coat even a homeless person would not be caught dead in. I knew karakul coats well, as my grandmother Polyxena had one. Before the First World War, the karakul, a special breed of Persian lamb with large tails, was very rare. Coats made of their fleece were more expensive and fashionable than mink or sable coats. Then karakuls went out of fashion after the war, when the breed was imported to Europe and raised in large numbers.

I surmised that the old lady in the antique karakul coat was this Madame Pisart whom Bobby White had told me about. She and her companion were complaining about not getting seats in the auditorium and were not relishing the prospect of listening to the concert through loudspeakers in the courtyard.

I approached them, introduced myself, and asked the old lady in the shabby coat if she was Madame Pisart. Yes she was. (And as it turned out, the lady in the elegant mink was her maid.)

I told Madame Pisart that I would gladly give her my seat in the auditorium so she could have the pleasure of seeing Mr. White sing. She was very grateful, and she later invited me several times to visit her at the Regency, oftentimes with Bobby White. She was hard of hearing and had misapprehended my first name, and instead of Zoltan, she called me Sultan. For some reason, no one ever saw the need to correct this nice old lady, myself included; and so she always called me Sultan.

Madame Pisart took Bobby White from time to time to have dinner at the Caravelle restaurant. One night as they went in, they noticed unusual activity in the dining room. The headwaiter, who knew that Madame Pisart was Belgian, told her, "Oh Madame, the king of Belgium is here, with his prime minister."

"Where is he?" Madame Pisart asked.

"At the back of the room," the headwaiter replied.

"Then I want to sit right here in the corridor," Madame Pisart said. The headwaiter obliged and chose a table in the corridor, the area of choice for people who just wanted a quiet meal away from the bustle of the main dining room.

Later, as the king and the prime minister passed the corridor on their way out, Madame Pisart looked straight at her plate, trying hard not to be noticed. The king whispered to the prime minister, "Look there on the left, the old lady is Madame Pisart."

Bobby White, who as a musician had acute ears, overheard the remark. As soon as the two men left, he said to Madame Pisart, "The king recognized you. He pointed you out to his prime minister."

"Of course he recognized me," Madame Pisart told him. "I spanked him often when he was three years old!"

Bobby couldn't help asking why she did not want to be noticed by the king.

"Look here, with my old rheumatic legs, it would be too painful to make a curtsy. Therefore it is much better to remain incognito!"

When I eat at the Caravelle or some other restaurant, I

sometimes ask, like other diners, that my leftovers be put in a "doggy bag." I don't know when this euphemism became institutionalized. It was certainly not so in 1926 during my second year as a student in Paris, when I went to visit the younger sister of my godmother Karola Bornemissza, the Countess Beldi, who was spending the Christmas holidays in Rouen. Countess Beldi, or Aunt Dudu as I called her, invited me to dine one evening at the restaurant La Couronne. The restaurant was in a medieval half-timbered house in Rouen's old market square. Having stood in the same spot since 1345, it was the oldest restaurant in the country of *haute cuisine*. It had not yet become a tourist trap, and was renowned as one of the best in all of France.

There was a guest book by the entrance, where I saw a quip written by the king of Spain's daughters:

Dinant à La Couronne, même Trotsky serait royaliste.[1]

> Beatrice Borbone
> Maria Christina Borbone

A quarter of a century later, their mother Victoria Eugenia became an occasional patient of mine on her visits to Rome. At that time she was residing in Paris with the exiled king Alfonso XIII, but every now and then would travel to Rome to see Beatrice, who was living in the Palazzo Torlonia with her husband, the Prince Torlonia. The exiled queen, a granddaughter of Victoria, was then in her sixties. No matter how sick she was, she would always meet me in the salon before we went back to the private quarters for the consultation. We spoke with each other in French, as I knew no Spanish, and every time I arrived, she would always clasp

---

[1] "Dining at La Couronne, even Trotsky would be a royalist."

my hands and exclaim with deep emotion, *"Oh docteur, c'est très gentil de vous de venir me voir!"* She always dressed in plain-colored clothes of simple cut. She appeared to be a woman at peace with herself, despite the loss of the crown, the well-known unfaithfulness of her husband, and her long years of exile.

I met her daughter Beatrice only once, at the Palazzo Torlonia, and very fleetingly, as she was rushing out for a lunch appointment. Shaking her hand reminded me of the quip she and her sister left at La Couronne when they were young girls, and of my dinner with Aunt Dudu that evening a quarter of a century ago.

For entrée, Aunt Dudu ordered *Oie Rôtie aux Marrons*, and I *Gigot d'Agneau*. We found out for ourselves why the restaurant was so famous. Aunt Dudu savored each bite of her *Oie Rôtie*. "It's simply the best goose I ever had!" she exclaimed. "It's so tender it melts on your tongue!"

She could not, however, finish her large serving, and she wanted to enjoy the leftovers at home. But at that time, no one eating in an elegant restaurant would ever dare to ask for leftovers. So Aunt Dudu called the headwaiter and told him that she would like to take the leftovers home for her little dog.

"But of course, Madame," the headwaiter replied, carefully taking away her plate but leaving the bread crumbs, for at that time it was not considered elegant to clean the bread crumbs off the linen.

"Such delicate cooking and such impeccable service!" Aunt Dudu gushed.

As we were finishing our cakes and *petits fours*, the headwaiter came out of the kitchen with a nice little package. He ceremoniously handed the package to Aunt Dudu and, with an eager smile, told her, "Madame, in addition to what you left, I put in some raw bones, as doggies love raw bones!"

The previous year, I also visited Aunt Dudu in Le Havre

for the Christmas holidays. On my first day there, she received some friends for tea. Among them was Madame de Grandmaison (who happened to be a first cousin of the writer-aviator Antoine de Saint-Exupéry). During tea, Madame de Grandmaison leaned toward us and said, in hushed tones, "It is rumored that Madame Lenormant, while strolling in the street, *greeted* Madame X!" Madame X was a Protestant.

Madame de Grandmaison put down her cup of tea and paused. "Well, I know Madame Lenormant very well. She would never do such a thing! All these rumors are nothing but calumny!"

When I visited Paris in 1962, having in the meantime moved to New York, I called Madame de Grandmaison, who herself had moved to Paris. She invited me for dinner, asking me to arrive early, as she was eager to hear my impressions of New York. I was the first guest to arrive. She showed me the table setting and told me about the other guests. "This one is a very talented painter," she said as she showed me one of the place cards. "And of course," she said, indicating another, "I also invited his lover, Monsieur Y."

· XXV ·

once upon a time

O N MY VISITS TO PARIS, I have always made it a point
to meet with my old friends there. Among them are Guido
Biozzi, my first collaborator in Rome in the early fifties, and
Henri Thibaudin, a former wine merchant, who is the very
personification of Gallic effusiveness. Until my friend Pierre
Habrekorn passed away, I would always see him and his
family. Pierre and I had been best friends at medical school
in Paris, and I was godfather at the baptism of his first child,
Claude. Pierre had originally planned to become a surgeon
but instead became a first-rate family doctor who made
home visits, the type that no longer exists. It was Pierre who
referred me to the director of the Valfleury, the convalescent
home for the needy, founded by the Blumenthals, where I
worked as physician-in-charge soon after the Second World
War.

Until Pierre married, he lived with his mother and brother in a *hôtel particulier* (town mansion, of a type built
mostly during the seventeenth and eighteenth centuries in
Paris) that they rented near the Bois de Boulogne. Pierre's
mother Henriette, sister of the novelist Charles Henry
Hirsch, who was then very popular in France, always welcomed me like a member of the family whenever I came to
visit. She was an elegant lady and was listed in the city's social register, a book that specified the days when she was at
home to receive visitors. Pierre's father, Gaston, who passed
away before I met the family, had been co-owner with the

director Edouard Fournier of the *Divan Japonais* cafe-music hall. They commissioned Toulouse-Lautrec to make posters for the *Divan Japonais*. These posters are now the only reminders, for most people, of the night spot that featured Yvette Guilbert and other popular singers of the day. Later, Pierre's father opened the *Bataclan* on the Grand Boulevard, the cabaret that launched the careers of numerous French talents, including the great actor Raimu.

Pierre and I shared a passion for art, and we often went to exhibitions together. He loved Toulouse-Lautrec and we regretted that his family had not kept any of the posters the artist had made for his father, as not many of the original Toulouse-Lautrec posters (generally printed in editions of 1,000 to 3,000 copies) had survived. I told Pierre how some of the original posters had made their way to Transylvania, after my father bought them on a trip to Paris, and how they unfortunately were lost when our summer home was burned down.

I had a couple of other friends in Paris, Jean Petain and Michel Girard, whom I met through my colleague at the Pasteur Institute, Andrée Hugo. Jean and Michel have also passed away, but I shall always remember their hospitality. Whenever I visited Paris, I always had an open invitation to stay at their place on the rue de Varennes, one of those elegant old Parisian streets whose sidewalks had no uniform width. A narrow part of the sidewalk running along a *hôtel particulier* meant the mansion was built earlier, i.e. before the late eighteenth century, when there was less pedestrian traffic. This was the case with Jean and Michel's place at 56 rue de Varennes. It stood opposite the Italian Embassy, which I had often visited before the war to pay my respects to the Ambassadress Cerruti. The massive seventeenth-century *porte cochère* (gate for coaches) at number 56, with its bas-reliefs of mythological figures and sea shells, opened to

a cobbled courtyard that led to a large private garden, a rarity in the heart of the Faubourg Saint Germain.

Jean and Michel, who were both almost seven feet tall,
liked to cook when they were at their country place in
Orgeval. One time, when I was enjoying their home cooking from a silver plate, I told them that I had recently seen
an exhibition in Paris of the surviving silver service of the
French Bourbons, very rare, as most had been melted down
in the Revolution, as well as during the times of Louis XIV
and XV to finance wars. I noted that their dishes looked very
similar to the ones in the exhibition. "No, not similar," said
Jean. "They are the same. I lent them for the exhibition."

Jean, whose family owned a food canning business, also
had a passion for antique French furniture. Some pieces in
his collection came from the former residences of Louis
XIV to XVI. There was a Louis XIV armoire in his bedroom, where he kept his clothes. Jean pointed out the sun
motif, the personal symbol of Louis XIV. Like the other
furniture of the period, the armoire was massive and ornate,
very much like the baroque ecclesiastical art and architecture
in Rome that returning French artists tried to emulate.

In the salon was a beautiful *bureau à cylindre*, previously
used by Louis XV. There were also some chairs and tables
from the period of Louis XV. A reaction to the heavy forms
of Louis XIV, these were lighter and more delicate. This
new style was curving, sinuous and organic; its decorative
leaves, water sprites, and bouquets asymmetrical, less formal.

Pompeii and Herculaneum were uncovered in the time
of Louis XV. The king's intelligent mistress, Madame
Pompadour, became seriously interested in the excavations.
Under her influence, furniture-making in France, then the
center of European taste, became more restrained. Symme-
try regained the dominance it had in the time of Louis XIV,
but in a lighter and more classical vein, resulting in what has

become known as the Louis XVI style. Decorations became bands of classical friezes, scrolls, and garlands. Furniture legs became fluted, delicately tapered columns reminiscent of ancient Greek and Roman architecture.

Jean pointed out the Louis XVI and XV pieces in the salon that were signed, and those that were unsigned. He gave me a rather esoteric but interesting lesson on signatures by furniture masters. He said that the furniture masters of the eighteenth century had to sign their pieces so that a tax could be levied on each piece they sold. However, a piece made for the king was tax-exempt, and therefore a signature was not obligatory. This was why many great pieces were not signed. Many of them were well documented, however, as it was customary for furniture to carry the motif found on the carved paneling of the room where the piece was to go.

Jean's friend Michel was a good amateur singer and had many friends working at the opera. Renowned talents of the Palais Garnier, like the Wagnerian sopranos Madame Lubin and Germaine Hoerner, liked to come for dinners at their place on the rue de Varennes, occasionally giving impromptu recitals.

With Michel, I often subscribed to the Wagner series given at the Palais Garnier in the spring by the troupe from Bayreuth. We always noticed the same gentlemen lost in rapt adoration as they sat in the first rows of the theater. They were very much like the opera and ballet fanatics one read about in the accounts of old Paris, the same sort of gentlemen who were already sitting there in the middle of the last century at the time of Napoleon III, when the first Wagner opera to be performed in Paris, *Tannhäuser,* was presented under the patronage of the Austrian ambassadress, the Princess Metternich. The first ripples of disgust and shock arose from these front rows during the *Tannhäuser* premiere when, for the first time in Paris, the second act of an opera did not begin with a ballet. It was the season's big scandal. The production was forced to close down after only three performances.

At the time I was attending the Wagner productions at the Palais Garnier, one of the regulars in the first row was a gentleman in his late seventies or eighties, Monsieur W, who owned a company that produced a popular French aperitif. One night, the gentleman went to Maxim's on the Rue Royale for an early dinner before going to the opera. In the restaurant, a young and pretty woman sat down next to him and proceeded to wink and throw meaningful glances at him.

"Mademoiselle, you must be making a mistake. I have a family," Monsieur W told her. "But that's not the point, mademoiselle. As you can see … I am far too old for that."

"That may be so, monsieur," she replied, "but not too old to pay!"

One night, a gendarme, knocking loudly on his door, woke him up.

"What is the matter?!" he asked the gendarme.

"I am sorry to come so late, monsieur, but I wanted to tell you that we just arrested a very old, horrible woman at the Bois de Boulogne. She was taking part in a big orgy in the bushes. The woman was using your name, monsieur, claiming she was Madame W."

"That's surely *maman!* Please tell me where I should go to fetch her!"

◈◦§◦◈

In Paris, I also always visited another friend, Mikolt Kemeny. She came from an aristocratic Transylvanian family, but she was now poor and earned her living working in an art gallery. She loved *haute cuisine* restaurants which were, however, beyond her means. It was therefore a pleasure for me to take her out to great restaurants like Taillevent and Grand Véfour whenever I happened to be in Paris.

Her father, the writer Baron Janos Kemeny, had been a member of our guest family. He was one of the founders of the writers circle "Helicon of Marosvecs," so named as the members held yearly gatherings at Marosvecs, the Kemeny's ancestral castle.

The Kemenys were one of those rare families, like the Banffys, that had a notable heritage system, one approved by the king for a few Hungarian families and similar to that established earlier in England. The eldest son got the great part of the fortune; the rest of the children had to strive, as they got only a minor part. The system had a Latin name, the *maioratus*. However suspect to egalitarian sensibilities, the *maioratus* had a simple purpose, to safeguard the destiny of the family, that the fortune should not be divided in the successions, and that at least one member should remain prosperous and be in a favorable position to help the others. The *maioratus* also carried the provision that if there were no male heir, the fortune would be inherited by the next closest male in succession (something that will not be taken lightly by today's feminist).

Janos Kemeny's father, Istvan, was far from the main branch and had no chance of inheriting anything. He enlisted in the army, where he became an officer in a select, aristocratic regiment whose duty was to be at the direct order of the King of Hungary. He was therefore stationed in Vienna where Ferencz Jozsef Habsburg resided.

One day, Istvan Kemeny's friend and comrade-in-arms asked him to vouch for a debt the friend had made playing cards. Istvan did so, but then it turned out that the friend could not repay the debt. So the young Kemeny was obliged to make good on his commitment. He wrote pleading for help to his rich and distant uncle who, being the titular of the *maioratus*, held the fortune.

The Kemeny family convened a council. It was decided that the uncle would pay the debt, but on the condition that the young man should abdicate his elegant military position and emigrate to the United States without any monetary help. "He should earn his living. He deserves this punishment and this will teach him for life," was the uncle's verdict.

So Istvan Kemeny left for the United States in the 1890's, where he worked at a menial job. He met and married a beautiful American girl and had three children, among them Janos. He never lost the yearning to go back to Hungary, but died before he could return. In 1904, the widow, Ida, impelled by her dead husband's dream, moved with her three children to Transylvania, where aunts and uncles gave them shelter. Afterwards, several successive and unforeseen deaths in the Kemeny family suddenly made her son Janos the successor of a childless uncle who had the *maioratus*.

So it happened that Janos Kemeny would be rich some time in the future. However, the First World War changed every expectation. After the 1920 Treaty of Trianon transferred Transylvania to Romania, the Romanian authorities expropriated the big estates owned by Hungarians. Now, after being "rich in the future," Janos lost his prospects. The Kemeny castle and the forest remained. However, the forest became non-productive, as the new government forbade the sale of any wood from it. And the castle, without any funds to back it up, became nothing more than a money pit, as castles usually do, being endlessly in need of maintenance. The Kemeny fortune, once one of the greatest in Transylvania, disappeared in a single blow. This did not seem to alter the good spirits of the young Janos. He had literary goals, inspired by the example of his great-great grand-uncle, Sigismond Kemeny, a famous Hungarian writer.

Janos was often at our house with the other members of the literary group "Helicon of Marosvecs" and it was there that he met his future wife, a lovely Scottish girl. This is yet another story.

My godmother, the Baroness Karola Bornemissza, had a

younger sister, Margit, an exceptional beauty. The sister, Aunt Dudu as we called her, was married to a Count Beldi. The count had a huge estate not far from Kolozsvar and was known to be one of the best cultivators of grain, sugar beets, and tobacco in Transylvania.

The Beldis, who were also part of our guest family, traveled every year and it became their goal to have visited each and every country in Europe. In 1913 they were in Greece when they met a Scottish gentleman, Mr. Paton, with whom a friendship rapidly developed. Mr. Paton told them that he had a young son who had just finished studying agriculture in Denmark, where it was reputed to be thoroughly modern. Mr. Paton thought it would be good for his son John to see for a while how agriculture was done in a less modern way.

"Send him to me," Count Beldi told him. "In my estate he will see how it's done properly, in the good old-fashioned way."

John Paton arrived in Transylvania in the spring of 1914. In the fall of the same year, the First World War began. Suddenly, the young Scottish man found himself trapped in Hungary, a citizen belonging to the enemy camp. However, the treatment in Hungary of the trapped nationals from the enemy camp (English, French, Russian) was different from that in most other countries in Europe. There were no concentration camps in Hungary, unlike in France and Germany, so John Paton was interned in the country house of Count Beldi; and when he came to Kolozsvar, he stayed in our house. It was indeed a civilized way of treating trapped civilians from an enemy country.

Another example was that of the dancer Nijinsky, who was caught in Budapest at the outbreak of hostilities. He had to stay for the duration of the war with his mother-in-law, the actress Emilia Markus-Pulszky. (However, there are probably those who would rather be interned in a prison camp than with their mother-in-law, especially one as authoritarian as Mme Markus-Pulszky.)

John Paton became close friends with his "captors," and soon after the war's end in 1918, he came back for a visit to Transylvania, bringing his young sister Augusta. She met Janos Kemeny in our house. They fell in love and got married.

John Paton himself later ended up harboring a person from the "enemy" camp. In 1938, he invited Mikolt, Janos and Augusta's eldest daughter, to visit Scotland, where he had married a well-to-do Scottish lady. Soon after Mikolt arrived, the Second World War broke out. A national of an enemy country, Mikolt was trapped in Scotland and remained with her uncle throughout the war. After the war, she moved to Paris where she found work looking after a small modern art gallery near the rue de Rivoli.

In Transylvania, Mikolt's father Janos, who had inherited the *maioratus* without the fortune after his uncle passed away in 1926, lived the life of an impoverished aristocrat. He and his wife Augusta, despite their reversals, remained generous, offering the use of the castle and forest to those in need of them, as a hiding place for Jewish friends during the Second World War and as a retreat for struggling writers. After the war, the Communists confiscated whatever had been left to the family, i.e. the castle and the forest. The Communists put Janos in a factory and forbade him to write and publish. After a few years, however, they relented and gave him their permission. He published many novels, fulfilling his deepest dream of becoming a writer like his great-great-grand-uncle.

Janos also wrote an autobiographical book, published posthumously, chronicling the saga of the Kemeny family (Bucharest, 1972). The title, *Kakukkfiókak (Children of the Cuckoo)* referred to the cuckoo's habit of laying eggs in another nest, an image recalling the way Janos and his sisters were reared by the Kemeny relatives when they moved to Transylvania from America.

Janos' wife Augusta and their daughter Mikolt corresponded regularly with me and they sent me copies of his books. I remained in touch with them until they too passed away.

◆ঌৄ৽◈

It was through Mikolt that I once found a tenant for a property I had in Italy. I was then planning to give a dinner at the Grand Véfour for Alice Tully and Hugues Cuenod, who both happened to be in Paris to see a Rameau opera directed at the Palais Garnier by Raymond Leppard.

I went to see Mikolt at the art gallery and invited her to the same dinner. Then a tall man came in and she presented him to me: a painter by the name of Cy Twombly. I was no fan of modern painting and had never heard of him. Before he left, he mentioned to Mikolt that he was looking for a house to rent on some coast in Italy.

I then told Mr. Twombly, "Why don't you rent mine? A view of the gulf of Gaeta, eight rooms, a garden, about a hundred orange trees and a hundred grapevines." The property had actually been my sister's country house until she passed away. It was in the town of Formia, on a hill a few meters away from a circular ancient Roman monument reputed to be the tomb of Cicero. The house had a big terrace with an unobstructed view of one of the most beautiful bays in Italy.

I gave Mr. Twombly the phone and address of an old friend, Helli Lodi-Fè, who lived at the Appia Antica in Rome.

When I arrived in Rome from Paris, Helli told me, "The country house has been rented to Mr. Cy Twombly, who by the way is quite a famous painter." Helli's husband Maurizio, after a career of producing films, including *Bread and Chocolate* and Bertolucci's *Il Conformista*, had gone on to become director of the Rome branch of the auction house Christie's, and therefore they had heard of Twombly.

Sometime after Cy Twombly left Italy, I realized that I really could not keep the house. Safety in Italy had not really recovered since the war. If one had a house in the country, robbers would break in as soon as it was left unattended. This happened to practically every one of my friends. One of the worst cases befell the nephew of my brother-in-law. His house near Viterbo, which the family had owned for many centuries, was completely emptied out when he and his family were absent for only two days. The robbers came as movers, and within a few hours took everything away in trucks.

But in addition to the generations of heirlooms that they had inherited and had now lost, the Casanovas of Viterbo inherited great strength of character. They were an intelligent, close-knit family who graciously weathered the loss and managed to put it in perspective. I tried to do my part in the recovery by giving them a precious painting by the *settecento* painter Rosa da Tivoli, which I had inherited from my sister.

When I realized I could not keep the house in Formia, I decided to give it to Isabella and Caterina, the two daughters of Helli and Maurizio. For me, Helli was like an adopted daughter. Though much younger than my sister, Helli had been her most steadfast friend. Like my sister, she was Hungarian (a direct descendant of the Empress Maria Theresia through her father, the Count Meran). They both lost their patrimony with the Communist takeover. They both married Italians. Helli's grandmother, Baroness Cornelia Wesselenyi, was from Kolozsvar and my grandfather was Baroness Wesselenyi's physician. When my sister became ill, Helli would come every day to visit her and sometimes sleep in her house. I was more than happy to give Helli's daughters the house in Formia.

Apart from the country house, my sister left me some beautiful objects, including some early 18th-century Kangxi porcelain, Louis XVI-period chairs made for the Palazzo Reale near Naples, ancient Roman glass bottles, and a pre-Columbian figure found on the day of her arrival as ambassadress in Bogota and later given to her as a thank-you gift by the Italian community. There were some family objects, saved from the ravages of the world wars and the Communist takeover only because my sister received them as wedding presents before she moved to Italy—a sixteenth-century chest of drawers with painted views of Italy from the Baroness Bornemissza; Persian and Caucasian carpets that had been in the family for hundreds of years; a Daum vase bearing a delicate design of red poppies that my father bought during a trip to Paris in 1904, as a present for my mother, then his fiancée. There was my mother's favorite silver piece, a sugar box in the shape of a coffer with fluted sides and adorned by a lion in repose. It had a lock because sugar was still a great rarity for which many ships sank, at the time the box was made in the seventeenth century. This box always sat in the middle of our dining table, gracing the daily dinners of the guest family, and now it had become for me a wistful reminder of all those old friends, most of them now departed, but once upon a time discussing art and science with such passion and joy.

As a tribute to my sister, I thought of giving an object to the Metropolitan Museum of Art. And so I went there with photographs of some Russian icons my sister had left me.

The curators politely turned me down, saying they were sorry they could not take any more icons. I accepted the decision but, before leaving, I asked if I could show the photos to them anyhow.

When I opened my envelope, both curators leapt out of their chairs. One of them started waving a picture. "Oh, we would like this very much!" he exclaimed. "It's a very rare type from the 17th century. And something we have long been looking for."

◆⟡◆

Recently, I received a photocopy, sent me by a second-nephew in Hungary, of a letter that had just been published in a book, a collection of essays on the Hungarian writer Zsigmond Moricz (*Zsigmond Moricz Between Us*, Bucharest). Moricz, who lived from 1879 to 1942, is considered one of the greatest and most influential writers in Hungary. With novels like his *Transylvania* trilogy, Hungarian literature solidly extended its reach from romanticism to realism. Moricz lived in Budapest most of his life, and whenever he went to Transylvania, he would always visit our house on Monostori Avenue. The photocopy was of a letter Moricz wrote from Budapest to his son. The son was traveling in the late thirties in Transylvania to solicit subscribers for a new magazine his father was editing. Part of the letter reads:

> There is something more. A family that you must look up. The head of the family is Elemer Ovary, a lawyer, not young, my age. Ovary Elemer has a son, Zoltan. He is an MD and lives in the house of his parents.
> To him you can say everything and empty your heart. He is a nice and enthusiastic boy. He was once in Budapest and came to see me at the publishing house. I took him to the Savoy and, if I remember well, you met him then. You will recognize him when you see him. Call up the Ovarys by phone and ask for Zoltan. Tell him that I wanted to present you personally to his parents but I could not come, so ask him to introduce you. He will fetch you and take you to the house on Monostori Avenue. Be gracious and charming as you always are!
> In their house, I am at home. In the house of Elemer

bácsi (Uncle Elemer) lives some sort of relative, Jolan. She is of splendid ugliness, but is extremely sensitive and cultured.

The mother, Olga *néni* (Aunt Olga), is the most profound person in the family. She will welcome you.

Great numbers of persons go to them. A lady, Baroness Bornemissza, is a woman of intense feelings and influence. I know that she likes me, and I am certain that she will help you out.

It touched me to read this letter that emerged from the past almost by chance.

Every now and then, I would lend books of Hungarian literature to Csaba, my laboratory technician. Working with Csaba gave me the rare chance of speaking Hungarian during working hours, right in the middle of Manhattan.

I met Csaba not long after we both arrived in the city. He was recommended to me by another Hungarian doctor when I was looking for a technician after the National Institutes of Health gave me my first grant. Csaba became my first technician, and stayed with me for twenty-five years.

He came from a prominent and wealthy family, the de Szalays, who had a big estate with beautiful gardens in the town of Szolnok, some forty miles southeast of Budapest. They lost everything when the Communists took over. Csaba became a student leader during the anti-Communist revolution in 1956. After the Russian tanks moved in and crushed the uprising, Csaba escaped to Austria, one of some 200,000 Hungarian refugees. He made his way to Belgium and then the United States.

I hired Csaba to be my technician even though he had no training in science. He was intelligent and easily became skilled in laboratory methods. With his patience and dexterity, he taught many of my students such demanding manipulations as the intravenous injection of laboratory animals and pipetting exact amounts of reagents.

Csaba had a green thumb. When he and his wife Helga moved out of Manhattan to Long Island, he grew a garden in his front yard. He nursed all kinds of trees, bushes, and flowering plants. Their scents brought happy memories of Csaba's ancestral home. Neighbors in Farmingdale would come to admire the garden and tell Csaba and Helga what a joy and privilege it was to live near them.

One time, I had a persimmon for dessert. At that time, this juicy, orange-colored fruit was very rare and expensive in New York. So I brought the persimmon stone to the lab and gave it to Csaba. I said, "You have such a green thumb, why don't you plant this?" It was really just a joke, as I did-n't think a persimmon tree, a warm-climate plant, could ever survive in an atypical environment.

Five years later, Csaba said to me, in the middle of an experiment, "Remember the persimmon stone you gave me? It's now a tree this high," raising his hand about five feet from the floor. "But it's just a tree, with no fruit at all."

Four years later, Csaba came to the lab with two plump persimmons.

"The stone you gave me is now a tree with many fruits. And here's the proof!"

I took the persimmons home. They were succulent. But I noticed they had no stones. So I told Csaba, "They couldn't have come from that stone. These fruits are stoneless!"

Csaba said, "I'm sure they did. It's the only one I ever planted. And you know what? The fruits are *all* stoneless!"

"How did that happen?"

"I have no idea!"

Somehow the persimmon mutated, perhaps the only way it had managed to survive. From then on, Csaba would come to the lab every summer carrying bags full of the sweetest plump persimmons.

· XXVI ·

students and teachers

I HAVE ALWAYS TRIED TO TEACH my students as much
as I could, not only about the medical sciences but also about
music and the arts. That's why I found it such a great privilege to organize the free concerts and recitals for the students at NYU. Often, I would also take students to other
concerts, especially those given in authentic-period style.
Many of the musicians were friends whom I liked to encourage and support. This was how many of my students found
themselves in concerts performed by Albert Fuller's Helicon,
Jim Richman's Concert Royale, Newell Jenkins' Clarion,
Andy Appel's Four Nations, and William Christie's Les Arts
Florissants.

Sometimes, I would suggest a trick to my students that I
learned when I was a young man in Kolozsvar. I would close
my eyes and imagine that the musician was playing for me
and me alone. This would help increase my concentration
and make me feel more deeply connected to the music.

Often, I would also take along close friends who are not
my science students but whom I consider my "students in
art," among them the teacher and psychotherapist David
Longmire; and Gil Quito, the TV writer and producer, who
has also collaborated on scripts for excellent films shot in
the Philippines and the United States. One of them, *Rites
of May,* is a story set against the medieval Holy Week rituals
in the Philippines, about a woman who searches for a lost
sister and finds herself being possessed by the sister's spirit.
It won a best picture award in the Asian Film Festival in

Sydney. The other, *'Merika,* is the story of an immigrant nurse in New York who decides to go back to the Philippines, turning her back on a well-paid job and a prospective husband. I have seen both of them only on video, but have found them to be very well-crafted and artistic.

On Sunday mornings, I would sometimes take a number of my students to see the illuminated manuscripts in the Morgan Library and the old masters in the Metropolitan Museum. Most of them might have visited the same galleries at the Metropolitan before, but I would call their attention to masterpieces they might have missed in the museum's embarrassment of riches, small paintings like Sassetta's "Journey of the Magi," Petrus Christus' "Carthusian Monk," and Pieter Bruegel the Elder's "Wheat Harvest."

Once, I had the fortune to look at the Bruegel with Charles de Tolnay. He pointed out the lush tree dominating the painting's center foreground. He told me that Bruegel had originally painted it as a simple stump. He said the stump certainly had some meaning for the artist, who had placed it in the most prominent position. Perhaps Bruegel wanted to contrast the stump with the exuberant harvest scene around it, perhaps he meant to portend the approaching bareness after the harvest.

In any case, some two hundred years after Bruegel painted his harvest scene, people could no longer grasp the beauty of a mere stump. For this reason, someone turned it into a full-fledged tree, adding trunk, branches, and leaves. The addition was, however, of a different hue and technique from those of all the other trees in the painting. It was this disparity that made Tolnay request scientific examinations of the canvas. It was definitely established that the tree branches and leaves in the center foreground were a later addition by another hand. But such was Bruegel's mastery, even this disfigurement failed to enervate this masterpiece.

I would take my students to see the Altman Madonna.

This marble relief, showing a seated baby leaning against the Madonna, is the best-preserved work by Antonio Rosselino, one of the greatest relief sculptors of the Italian renaissance, if not the greatest. The five Rosselino brothers were all accomplished sculptors, but Antonio surpassed them all. His Altman Madonna (named after its donor to the museum) is so delicately carved that one gets the feeling, as one examines the details, that the expressions of the Madonna and the child, far from being frozen in stone, are actually changing from one moment to another, from joy to sadness, bemusement to contemplation.

It gave me pleasure to teach my students the difference between early Sienese and Florentine painting. The Sienese were generally more narrative than the Florentines who, under the influence of Giotto, were more emotive and used color with greater restraint. I would describe the paintings in the Sienese gallery as a "wonderful orgy of colors." We would also explore the differences between Florentine and Venetian renaissance painting. Whereas the Florentines generally made clear outlines and designs before applying their colors, the Venetians took the more direct approach of using the paint itself to model and shape their subject, prefiguring the Impressionists by hundreds of years.

In the Impressionist rooms, my students and I would try out different ways of looking at the paintings. In front of Monet's "Porch of the Cathedral at Rouen," for example, I would suggest a general look first at the ordinary distance of one or one-and-a-half yards. Then I would urge my students to go nearer, until the forms disappeared and everything became flat: no more relief, no more contours, just an ecstatic mass of colors. Then I would suggest stepping backwards, way back, closing one eye, and forming with one hand some sort of tunnel to look through. Suddenly, everything would spring back to life, sun-drenched, sensuous, and solid.

One time, I took a couple of my students to the Metro-

politan's Costume Institute to see an exhibition of stage costumes used by prewar dancers like Nijinsky. I told them how
I had encountered Nijinsky once in Hungary in the 1930's,
when I paid a visit to the doyenne of Hungarian actresses,
Emilia Markus-Pulszky, who was the mother of Nijinsky's
wife Romola. I found it curious even then that Romola was
known the world over and her mother not at all, as Emilia
was in every way the much greater actress. In a corner of the
room on that day I paid my respect to Madame Markus-
Pulszky, Nijinsky sat hunched with a ghostly stare the whole
afternoon, no more than a demented ruin of the dancer who
had once dazzled the world.

With my students I discussed the works the costumes
were made for. The costumes on display included those created for *Le spectre de la rose* and *L'après-midi d'un faune.* I
asked them to imagine the scenes. How different the costumes would have looked on the soaring, smiling Nijinsky
instead of the dummy in front of us! An elderly lady with a
loud voice kept following us and asking questions like "Who
was this Nijinsky, anyway?" and, "How can anyone be sure
he's so great if no one can watch him any more?" She was
speaking so loudly she was getting on the nerves of everyone
in the gallery.

I tiptoed close to the lady, then whispered to her, "Don't
tell anyone. I AM NIJINSKY!"

She drew back from me with a mixture of surprise and
confusion.

She checked the exhibit label, then asked me suspiciously, "Really?"

My students and I said goodbye to her, disappeared into
another gallery, and had a good laugh.

Sometimes, the joke was on me. I was almost ninety when
I brought some students to the Metropolitan for the opening week of the renovated galleries of French Impressionist
and Post-Impressionist art. I pointed out a Toulouse-Lautrec

painting of a woman seated in a theater box, her back towards us. The sitter was Misia Sert and I mentioned that I personally knew her when I was a student in Paris.

My students began to joke about my age. "Didn't Toulouse-Lautrec also do your portrait?"

"No," another said, "It was Rubens who did it!"

Someone else said, "No, it was Titian. And moreover, it was a nude!"

"Yes," I answered back. "But the painting got lost in a VERY big earthquake." At least, I thought, my students were getting down their chronology of painters.

Regarding the Misia of Toulouse-Lautrec's painting, she was a girl from a leading artistic Polish family, the Godebskys. She and her first husband, Thade Nathanson, founded the journal *Revue Blanche*, which became famous for supporting the Impressionists when the establishment would have none of them.

A wealthy man, Alfred Edwards, fell in love with Misia. Edwards offered Misia's husband a job he couldn't turn down, but it would mean having to leave France to look for coal mines in Transylvania, including Kolozsvar where my parents met him. As Edwards knew all along, there was no coal in Transylvania.

When the husband came back to Paris, Edwards had already seduced Misia into marrying him. With her new wealth, Misia became not just an advocate but also a patron of the Impressionists.

Once, Renoir painted Misia's portrait. She sent a check for 20,000 francs as payment. Renoir was shocked when he received it. He returned the check with a note, "No living artist can take more than 10,000 francs for a portrait!"

By the time I met Misia in Paris in the 1930's, Edwards had left her and she had become the widow of her third husband, the painter Jose Sert. Like my students looking at the Toulouse-Lautrec painting of Misia in a theater box, I had myself first encountered her in the theater. But she was then already an old, tired lady, no longer the vibrant woman of the painting we were looking at.

On another museum visit, I was showing the Sistine Chapel to the famous Brazilian scientist Rocha e Silva, and explaining to him, in French, the stories behind Michelangelo's frescoes. Two nuns behind us were eavesdropping and obviously understood French. So I started telling stories about Michelangelo's sexual activities. I was thinking perhaps this might frighten the nuns away. On the contrary, they followed us more closely.

I couldn't help asking them why they were listening to the stories, as these weren't for nuns.

One of them answered, "But what you say is so very interesting!"

"And why do you keep making the cross?" I asked.

"When you tell these sinful stories, we ask God to forgive him in view of his unsurpassed talent!"

As in most other schools, the graduating class at the NYU Medical School devotes a few pages of its yearbook to jokes. I do not speak to my students about my exclusive clientele in Rome, but one cannot hide anything from students. In one yearbook, they published Clouet's famous portrait of the French king Francis I, with the sly-looking smile. The caption read, "I want to see Dr. Ovary."

I also played a joke on my students. At that time, the last session in the Immunology course was reserved for questions from students concerning problems they had not understood well enough. I was the professor designated that year to give the session. It happened that the written examination of Biochemistry was scheduled for the following day.

Biochemistry was a notoriously difficult and critical subject. This test in particular was known to be a pitfall. I therefore posted an announcement on the student bulletin board: "In view of the Biochemistry test scheduled the day after, I understand very well if you can't come to the last Immunology session reserved for questions. If only one student shows up, I will be there. However, if nobody comes, I shall remain in my laboratory doing research. I ask you therefore to think about it. There will be a sheet on the bulletin board in front of my laboratory. If you decide to come, please write your name on the sheet before 4 PM, and no later!"

Nobody signed up.

At 5 PM, I posted another announcement:

> Those who signed up for the Immunology session are invited to the Caravelle restaurant for dinner, date to be discussed. We are having oysters, caviar, *foie gras truffé de Strasbourg,* Dover sole, roast duckling, and *soufflé.* [My gastronomic imagination went wild.] For drinks, Champagne Dom Pérignon, year to be selected; Château Petrus and Château Lafitte Rotschild, both 1945; Chablis Grenouille 1959 and Château Yquem 1952.

Less than five minutes after I posted the announcement, students were rushing up the corridor looking for the sign-up sheet. I told them the list had been taken down as announced, at 4 PM.

· XXVII ·

isten hozta

ONE DAY IN 1984 my friends at the Department of Pathology in NYU, Jeanette Thorbecke and Suzy Zolla-Pazner, asked me to join them in the cafeteria. Over lunch, they told me that they were organizing a symposium to honor me for the work I had done, especially at NYU. I was touched to hear this, especially coming from two of the most accomplished scientists in our department. They said that Vittorio Defendi, the extremely capable and well-liked chairman of the department, had given his support for their project.

The symposium was held in November of that year. There were nine speakers, including Baruj Benacerraf, Tomio Tada, and Jeanette Thorbecke. All had published papers with me, except for my close friend Lloyd Old, who was then working at the Sloane Kettering Institute for Cancer Research. All the speakers dealt with various aspects of my field of specialization, experimental allergy.

The symposium lasted a whole day. An open reception followed. Three musicians from the Juilliard School, students of Albert Fuller, played baroque music on period instruments. It was not a concert, just some musicians playing music together in the tradition of the seventeenth and eighteenth centuries.

I was touched to hear this music, once forgotten, now giving joy again. I had long realized that my attraction to this music lay in part in my own losses. It almost felt like a personal victory whenever some beautiful composition, once seemingly lost forever, was recovered. It gave me a feeling that what we had lost, the vanished old world, friends and family who had passed away, the lost days and years, could be found again, if only through an act of the imagination. I also mused on the healing powers of art and music, different from medicine of course, but often effective in some strange way.

After the open reception at NYU, the main participants and special guests of the symposium went to the Century Club for dinner. Among the guests was Alice Tully, whom I learned was one of the principal sponsors.

As I also found out, the organizing committee had sent letters soliciting contributions for the symposium. It turned out that they had collected enough money to make this an annual affair. Since then, we have had one or two speakers every fall for the Zoltan Ovary Symposium. Jeanette, Suzy, and I decide on the speakers, making sure to invite scientists who are doing exciting research or have very recently made discoveries in the field of immunology.

Jeanette, Suzy, and Dr. Defendi decided to move the thirteenth symposium to April to coincide with my ninetieth birthday. It meant much to me that several of my former students flew in from other parts of the States, and from as far away as Italy and Japan, just to attend the symposium. My first laboratory technician, Csaba de Szalay, came with his wife Helga, who was the former technician of my colleague Baruj Benacerraf. There were more participants on stage than usual. Lloyd Old, Suzy Zolla-Pazner, and Jeanette Thorbecke introduced the speakers. Tomio Tada, Noel Warner, and Robert Tigelaar, all former students of mine, spoke about their latest research.

At the end of the symposium, I went up the stage and gave this little speech:

"I would like to thank you for coming to this symposium for my ninetieth birthday, though I don't want to be reminded that I am ninety years old. And really, I don't feel that old.

"I think of the famous piano teacher, Rosina Lhevine, who at ninety years of age was still teaching at the Juilliard. She would come into the classroom and tell her pupils, 'I feel so young today. I feel like eighty!'

"I first came to work at the New York University Medical School in 1959 and I have loved working here. I am grateful to the medical school for supporting my love of medical research, and for all the wonderful, extraordinary people I have met here.

"I'm Hungarian and was born in 1907 in Kolozsvar, the capital of Transylvania. Kolozsvar had the second oldest university of Hungary, named after the reigning king, Ferencz Jozsef. So as a token of gratitude, I would like to give each speaker and organizer of this symposium a gold coin with the picture of Ferencz Jozsef on one side and the coat of arms of Hungary on the other side.

"This coin has no circulating value, as the currency, like so many other things, has passed away. Almost all the speakers and organizers tonight have already spoken in previous symposia named after me. I have already given you a similar coin worth ten corona. This time, I am doubling the fee, by giving a twenty corona coin.

"I thank you very much for sharing your love of science with all of us."

◆◦§◦◆

Through my years of research, I have been fortunate in finding good laboratory student assistants. Some of them had just gotten out of high school before going to university. They were mostly eager to learn some basic principles in immunology, but I often also made them participate in the more advanced research I was doing. Most of the time, my students were medical doctors or even accomplished researchers themselves. A good many have come from Japan, sent by Tomio Tada or my former students who now have many students of their own.

My method of teaching is very personal. I begin by explaining the problem I am working on. Then I let the student develop his own ideas and plans for the experiments. For me, this freedom to explore and create is very important. Then we discuss his or her plans and, if necessary, I point out a better way.

It is important for me to develop close ties to my students. I learned its value when I was a small boy and my grandfathers were department chairmen at the University of Kolozsvar. It was a part of life then for professors, students, and their family members to develop ties beyond the laboratory and university.

I try not to let distance undo our ties. When I go in summer to Italy, I always see my former Italian students. And when I go in winter to Japan, I always see my former Japanese students. The past fifteen winters, I have gone there almost every year for the scientific conferences. It has become an informal tradition that every time, Takao Hirano would organize a dinner in a French restaurant and invite my former students from all over Japan, many of them now professors themselves. I am touched that they have always come together to attend my dinner.

I have gotten acquainted with the children of my Japanese students, among them Nauto, the son of Shuichi Furusawa. He was about two years old and was just beginning to talk when he arrived in the United States with his parents. They enrolled him in a nursery school where he learned English. He always spoke to me in English and called me his "third grandfather." With his parents, he normally spoke in Japanese. It became a source of amusement for everyone that he would use a perfect American accent with me, but whenever he spoke English with his father, he would use an impeccable Japanese accent. It took a real ear for dialogue, as well as music, I thought, for a little boy like him to do this.

His parents' best friends in New York were musicians: Mineko, a violinist, and her husband, Michael Hinton, a drummer. They were both members of the orchestra of the Broadway musical *Miss Saigon*. Mineko was also a member of the St. Luke's Orchestra, while Michael played as guest drummer in several classical music groups.

Nauto was fascinated by Michael's drum. He was always eager to visit Michael's place. Whenever he got there, he would go straight to the drum. Soon, he was playing the drum part of many classical pieces.

When his family went back to Japan, Nauto felt sad that he would no longer be able to play on Michael's drum. I wanted to support the love for music he had learned from Michael, the way I had always tried to encourage his father's creativity in science. So, soon after Nauto and his father left, Michael and I went out to find a classical drum to send to Nauto, that he would not forget his love of music.

⋆§⋆

Recently, my former student, Domenica Mancino who had become rector of the Università Due di Napoli, called me up and said the university would like to present me with a diploma in medicine *honoris causa*. I felt it a great honor to accept such an offer from a country where I had had so many of adventures, both in medicine and art.

So I flew to Rome, then took the train to Naples for the appointed date. Mimmo, as I called Dr. Mancino, picked me up at my hotel in Naples for the ceremonies. Besides me, Alan Eglin Heathcote Emery, a scientist from England, was being honored for his work in the field of genetics and clinical medicine. It made me happy to see what a long way Mimmo had come since I gave a lecture in Naples in the early 60's, and this tall young man approached me, asking if he could be my student in New York. I was able to arrange this, and he became one of my best students and friends.

The ceremonies were held at the Palazzo Reale in Caserta, near Naples, the palace of the Bourbons when they ruled Naples, and now owned by the university.

It pleased everyone that I delivered my one-hour lecture in Italian without notes. At the reception afterwards, someone asked what languages I spoke. "Italian, English, French and Hungarian, and a bit of German and Romanian," was my reply. Someone else asked what language I dreamed in. "All these languages," I joked, "and in color, but strictly pastel."

Over the past decades, I was asked many times to go to Hungary and accept a diploma of honorary membership from the Hungarian Association of Immunologists. It was a venerable association, one worthy of Ignaz P. Semmelweis, the mid-19th century Hungarian doctor who, with Pasteur, ushered in the modern age of sanitation and immunology when he proved that handwashing could prevent infections.

Throughout all the years that the Communists ruled Eastern Europe, I remained in touch with my friends in Hungary and Transylvania and anonymously sponsored Hungarian scholars in Transylvania.

But my reply to the invitations from the Hungarian Association of Immunologists was always the same: "I thank you very much, but I am sorry, I cannot accept anything as long as the country remains Communist."

When, in 1989, Communism finally collapsed, mostly under the weight of its own atrocities, the Hungarian Association of Immunologists sent me another letter: "You had many times turned down our invitation while Hungary remained Communist. And now?" it asked.

This was how I went back to Hungary for the first time since I left it almost half a century ago in 1944. The diploma

was presented at the annual congress of the Hungarian Association of Immunologists, held in 1990 in Debrecen, not far
from Budapest.

I gave a one-hour lecture in Hungarian about advances
in hypersensitivity research using the PCA reaction. Afterwards, many of the scientists came and grasped my hands,
warmly thanking me for the lecture and expressing their
amazement at hearing such pure and polished Hungarian.
"Of course it's very pure," was my response, "Don't forget
that I come from Transylvania, and there we took pride in
speaking the purest Hungarian."

After the congress, I stayed in Budapest for several days.
I visited the former home of my maternal grandmother
Paula, on Elizabeth Ring, across the street from the ghost
of the Abazia Coffee House, and just off the Andrassy Road
that led directly to the National Museum of Fine Arts. My
grandmother had owned the three-story building that com-
prised her apartment and eleven others. The Communists
expropriated it when they came to power. Three years after
my visit, I received compensation from the post-Communist
government for my grandmother's building. It was about
five percent of its value and in Hungarian currency, which
was useless outside the country. I wrote to my second-nephew Kond, the son of my paternal cousin whom a very long
time ago I had called "Big Margit" to distinguish her from
"Little Margit." In my letter, I told Kond, a physician, who
was living with his wife and three grown sons near Budapest, that I wanted to give him the entire compensation for
my grandmother's building. It would surely have been of
greater benefit to him.

After visiting my grandmother's former home, I went to
the National Museum of Fine Arts to see the works of the
great Hungarian painters of the second half of the nineteenth century, who definitely deserved to be better-known
outside Hungary. One of these, Pal Szinyei Merse, was ac-

knowledged to have developed an Impressionist style independent of, and earlier than, the French. A number of the *plein air* painters like Karoly Ferenczy (teacher of Vertes, who sent that inadequately-addressed postcard from Paris to my mother), Jozsef Rippl-Ronai, and Laszlo Paal, were as adept at capturing fleeting reality as their contemporaries elsewhere in Europe. The difference is that their paintings would not get a fraction of the untold sums that those of their more famous French contemporaries command in today's auctions.

With regard to museums, Budapest is known internationally more for its other major museum, the National Gallery of Art, which contains some exceptional treasures. These include a small, dynamic sculpture, by Leonardo da Vinci, of Francis I on a rearing horse; great Raphael paintings, including the unfinished "Eszterhazy Madonna"; and a number of El Greco masterpieces once in the collection of the Hungarian Baron Herzog, who played the major role in the stunning rediscovery during the late nineteenth century of an obscure artist nicknamed El Greco.

While in Budapest, I stayed at the Hotel Gellert in the old quarter of the Buda section. The Gellert, overlooking the Danube, was the best hotel in Hungary before the last world war, when it boasted a rooftop swimming pool with artificial waves. Through the cataclysms of the century, the hotel had retained its elegant trappings but, like a proud dowager, had not kept up with the times. There was an exceptional heat wave in Budapest when I was there, and all the guests were suffering heat stroke, thanks to lack of air conditioning. Still, the hotel's restaurant held on to its position as one of the very best in Hungary. It was there that I gave a dinner for the people in the country I still knew personally. About fifty guests came. We all enjoyed a four-course dinner laced with Hungarian red wine in the Hotel Gellert's chandeliered dining room. The entire feast for fifty people in one of Hungary's most expensive restaurants cost less than $150, or $3 a plate! Their prices have of course escalated in recent years.

By chance, my childhood friend Eva Krenner was in Budapest visiting from London. Also on hand were the son Kond (whom I have mentioned above) and the daughter Clara of my paternal cousin "Big Margit." Clara is the mother of the cellist Andras Fejer of the Takacs Quartet, which is widely considered to be among the best quartets in the world. Like the Budapest Quartet and Roth Quartet before them, they emigrated to the United States; they are now based at the University of Colorado in Boulder. They always come to New York on their annual tour, giving concerts in Carnegie Hall or Alice Tully Hall, so I am able to get together with Andras every year. Among the group's most renowned recordings is the Haydn Quartets opus 76, the set that includes the "Emperor," perhaps the most magisterial of Haydn's dozens of quartets. The recording occasionally turns up in lists of the best Haydn recordings ever made, including *Music* magazine's special Haydn record collectors survey. Most recently, the *New York Times* (3/29/98) named the latest CD of the Takacs Quartet as the best recording ever of the Bartok string quartets.

I was touched that some of my dinner guests that evening in Budapest came all the way from Transylvania. They included my friend Csaba Apor, some twenty years my junior, who brought along his wife and granddaughter. Csaba's ancestors were from the Szekely region in Transylvania, where the Szekelys, a people who claimed descent from Attila the Hun, had lived since the fifth century AD. The Apors were great Szekely Barons for more than three centuries, until their ancestral estate and castle were seized by the new government after the First World War. Later, when the Communists took over, they forced Csaba Apor to become a factory worker.

Then, some forty-five years later, the post-Communist authorities gave him back ten acres of the Apor lands. It was nothing compared to the old estate, but he felt a deep love for the land when he started cultivating it again. He organized other farmers, and they produced some of the best livestock and crops in Romania. He yearned for his son, who had escaped years before to Sweden. And now that Communism had collapsed, Csaba was eagerly looking forward to a reunion.

Also on hand was my former technician at NYU, Susanna. Some twenty years previously, a Hungarian man who had immigrated to the United States divorced his wife after seeing all their children through college. He went back to Hungary to look for a new wife and met Susanna, a striking beauty thirty years younger than him. Then he went back to New York, taking Susanna with him.

I met Susanna through my technician and friend, Csaba de Szalay, who told me that Susanna wanted to make some extra money. She was a lovely, hard-working girl and we got along very well. However, she was not happy in New York and never really learned English even after fifteen years here. Her mother also came to New York but decided to go back to Hungary. On her way back home, she did something that would always make me grateful. She went to Formia to visit my sister, who was ill. Then she stayed several months to take care of her. As for Susanna, she moved to Vienna with her husband when he retired. And when her husband died, Susanna returned to Budapest, where she had always felt she belonged.

It gave me joy to see so many of my old friends together. We talked about all the people we knew, in Transylvania, in New York and other places. Many of those we remembered had passed away. We spoke admiringly of their passion for excellence, and indulgently of their human weaknesses.

Two years later, the International Congress of Immunology was held in Budapest. It was the eighth congress, the first one having taken place in New York in 1968. The congress is held every three years, in a different country, and is the major international gathering for immunologists. Some 15,000 immunologists from all over the world attend its week of lectures, meetings, presentations, and reunions.

The organizers of the Budapest congress asked me to give a talk at the opening ceremony. My friend Michael Heidelberger, who never retired, had just passed away at the age of 103. This left me, at the relatively tender age of 85, the oldest known immunologist still working full time.

At the opening ceremony of the Budapest Congress, I found myself on the platform with the president of Hungary, the president of the Hungarian Academy, the mayor of Budapest, the president of the Hungarian Association of Immunologists, and the president of the International Union of Immunological Societies. I was the last speaker. My talk was the most applauded, no doubt because it was also the shortest.

I just said the following: "Because I am the oldest working immunologist and because I am of Hungarian origin— as I was born in Kolozsvar in Transylvania—I was asked to welcome you to this congress in Budapest. I embrace you with the old Hungarian greeting: *Isten hozta*—God brought you!"

One of the more common questions I was asked during the congress was why I hadn't retired. Actually, I had given some serious thought to the prospect of a leisurely, contemplative life when I reached the usual retirement age. However, I decided that continuing my medical research would be even more fulfilling. I was fortunate that the medical school at NYU, unlike most others (e.g. Columbia, Harvard), had no mandatory retirement age. I loved my work and I believed I could still contribute to the sum of medical knowledge. I was still publishing papers in scientific journals. I was still receiving papers from my students who wanted to co-publish with me. I believed that working was the best way I could show that I cared. For decades I had gone to my office and laboratory seven days a week. So why should I suddenly put an end to these activities? Why should I blindly follow the dogma that a man was too old to do something at a certain age?

So, all the histories and novels I have always wanted to read remain unread, temptingly lined up and stacked on shelves, tables, and closets in my apartment. For a man past ninety, reporting for work can be a real effort at times—for instance after a night of half-sleep full of dreams of old friends, many of whom have passed away, or during a snow-storm, trying to make sure that neither your cap nor your cane are blown away by the winds. Still, a quarter of a century since I turned my back on retirement, I cannot complain. I believe continuing my work has kept me alert. I still enjoy collaborating and exchanging ideas with my students and colleagues, at work and abroad, through the e-mail, phone, and FAX, in ways that at the time of my childhood, not so long ago, were the stuff of pure fantasy. Right now, I'm working on an experiment on cellular receptors and hypersensitivity, in collaboration with my associate Mike Marino in New York and former student Masato Yamada in Tokyo. And my curiosity remains as intense as that time at the dawn of this century when I used to listen to discussions about science by the guest family at my mother's dinner table in Kolozsvar as they questioned the dogmas of the time.

◆⟩§⟨◆

Not too long ago, I decided to go to the Galapagos Islands. I had heard a lot about the islands for years. They are fabled for the unique way their inhabitants have developed. For aeons, until the relatively very recent arrival of man, the islands have evolved without any large predators. As a result, the wild animals, reptiles, birds and marine life of the islands have grown without fear of other creatures. It was this exceedingly strange nature of the islands that made the first Spanish discoverers call them *"Las Islas Encantadas"*—the Enchanted Islands. What a contrast to our world and our century full of fear!

Friends warned me that some of the islands were rocky and dangerous, and they were not for a ninety-year-old person. Some said that I should not even think of going. I did not let fear stop me. For if there's anything that squeezes the adventure out of life, it is fear.

One day, my writer friend from the Philippines, Gil, told me he had always wanted to visit the well-preserved colonial city of Quito in the Andes. His last name happens to be Quito, and this was how he first heard about this far-away city.

The only way one could normally reach the Galapagos was by flying to Quito, the capital of Ecuador, which owns the Galapagos. I suggested to Gil that we could first visit Quito then make our way to the Galapagos. So one Saturday afternoon, we boarded the plane at Kennedy Airport and changed in Miami for the flight to Quito. In Miami, a tall and beautiful lady took her seat next to us. When we arrived in Quito, we helped her with her luggage. She thanked us and shook my hand, saying she was Diana Pickett.

I did not have my card so I just introduced myself. Suddenly, she exclaimed, "I know you! You are an immunologist. I kept coming across your name when I was a student. I have always wanted to meet you!"

She told me that she herself was an immunologist at the University of San Francisco in Quito. She said that she wished I could find time to give a talk at the university but realized I probably had no time to spare. "Too bad. For us, it would be a historic event," she said.

I told her that I had no slides, not even a decent suit with me. But I had been invited to give a lecture on the history and future of allergy research at the yearly meeting of the Japanese Society of Allergy in Tokyo in three weeks' time. I could easily talk about this and about Michael Heidelberger, Baruj Benacerraf, Guido Biozzi, Lewis Thomas, and many others who have made this century such a bold era of discovery. As for the slides, I said, I could easily replace them with drawings on the blackboard.

It was decided right then and there that I would speak on a Wednesday, and that she would call specifying the time she would fetch me in her car.

At the edge of the tarmac, there were officials in dark suits waiting for her. We found out that apart from being an immunologist, she was also the Spanish ambassadress to Quito. She said goodbye, as the officials escorted her away.

I told my friend "Now, you see, that with me, you should always be prepared for some extra adventures!"

INDEX

A

AIDS, 109, 176, 181, 185
Ady, Erde, 26
Allen, Betty, 141
Annunzio, Gabriele D', 66-67
Apor, Csaba, 250-51
Appel, Andrew, 235
Armenians, in Transylvania, 40-43, 128
Aschoff, Ludwig, 83
Aston Magna, 128, 147

B

Bach, Johann Sebastian, 51, 58, 109, 139
Bachauer, Gina, 141, 148
Bánffy, Baron Albert, 22
Bánffy, Baroness, 22
Bánffy, Denés, 22-23
Bánffy, Count Miklós, 35-37
Bánffy Palace, Kolozsvár, 11, 15, 16, 17, 42
Bartók, Béla, 26, 28, 29-30, 141, 159, 211, 250
Basch, Ross, 181
Bateman, Hester, 203
Beatrice of Naples, Princess (Queen of Hungary), 10

Beijing, China, 163-169
Béldi, Count György, 227
Béldi, Countess Margit, 217-19, 227
Benacerraf, Annette, 133-134, 144
Benacerraf, Baruj, xi, 96-98, 109, 131, 133-34, 177, 181, 208, 242, 243, 255
Bessarabia, 70-72, 76
Bier, Otto, 102, 104-5, 1097
Biozzi, Guido, x, xii, 82, 84, 85, 97-98, 100-1, 184, 220, 255
Biró, Géza, 11
Bleriot, Louis, 32-33
Blumenthal, George, 88-89, 149-50, 201, 220
Bonazzi, Elaine, 141
Borbone, Victoria Eugenia, 217-18
Borbone, Beatrice, 217
Bordes, Charles, 58
Bordet, Jules, 121, 143
Bornemissza, Baron Elemér, 32-33
Bornemissza, Baroness Karola, 3-4, 32-44, 72-74, 217, 226, 231, 233
Bornemisza, Baron Johan Heinrich Thyssen, 32
Borneo, 172-73
Boudot-Lamotte, Emanuel, 209
Bovet, Daniel, 54-55, 116, 1297 184
Bovet, Philomena Nitti, 55

Bridging hypothesis, xi, 127
Brin, Irène, 111
Budapest, Hungary, 132, 169, 203,
     206, 211, 227, 232-33, 248-53
Budapest Quartet, 211-212
Buonarotti, Michelangelo, 112,
     134, 196-201, 240
Buxtehude, Dietrich, 51

C

Campin, Robert (Master of
     Flémalle), 194-96
Carrier effect, xi, 181-82
Casals, Pablo, 28, 30-31
Casanova, Olindo, 231
Casati, Marchessa Anna, 87-88
Cerruti, Ambassadress
     Elisabetta, née de Paulay, xii,
     64-68, 80-81, 86-88, 94, 141,
     159, 194, 196, 209, 221
Cerruti, Ambassador Vittorio,
     64-66, 80
Chain, Ernest, 184
Charles III of Austria, Emperor,
     King of Hungary, 40
Charles IV of Austria, Emperor,
     King of Hungary, 35-36
Charles Robert of Hungary,
     King, 09
Child, Julia, 132-35
Christie, William, 235
Clinica Medica, Rome, 82, 86,
     93, 96, 184
Cluj, Transylvania (see also
     Kolozsvár and Transylvania),
     1, 69
Cocteau, Jean, 89
Colette, 25

Collegium Allergologicum
     Internationale, 115-16
Corvinus see Mathias Corvinus
Coty, 66-67, 165
Crespi, Countess Consuelo, 93
Cuenod, Hugues, xii, 56, 89, 127-
     31, 133, 139-40, 229

D

Dabell, Frank, vii, viii
Dakar, Senegal, 103
Dalí, Salvador, 111-13
Damascus, Syria, 110-11
Davis, Mark, 177-78
Debussy, Claude, 62-63
Defendi, Vittorio, 242-43
Detre, László, 99-100
Diaghilev, Sergei, 67
Dillon, Douglas, 149-50
Dohnányi, Ernst von, 26, 28-29
Donogán, Valeria, 2, 34
Dracula (Vlad Tepes), xiv
Dreyfus, Alfred, 26-27
Duncan, Raymond, 49
Dunn, Ambassador James, 86-87
Dunn, Ambassadress Mary
     Armour, 86

E

Ecuador, 254-55
Elisabeth, Empress of Austria,
     Queen of Hungary, 27
Elizabeth of Great Britain,
     Queen Mother, 116-18
Eschenbach, Christoph, 141, 143
Éva, see Lederer, Éva

F

Fábri, Paul, 206
Fadrusz, János, 11
Fahey, John, 121-22
Farkas-Savet, Ella *see* Savet, Ella
Farkas, Moses, 49-51, 52, 119
Fejér, András, 251
Fejér, Lipót, 169
Fekete de Nagyivány, Susanna, 251
Ferdinándy-Fejér, Clara, 250
Ferdinándy, Kond, 248, 250
Ferdinándy, Margit *née* Horváth, 15, 248, 250
Ferencz József, Emperor of Austria, King of Hungary, 27, 119, 225, 244
Ferencz József University, Kolozsvár, 1, 4-6, 8
Ferencz Ferdinand of Austria, Archduke, 45
Fiji, 169-71
Fleg, Carolyn, viii
Fleming, Sir Alexander, 53, 108, 184
Formia, Italy, 24, 184, 229-30, 251
Fourneau, Ernest, 54
Fragreus, Astrid, 109-10
Franklin, Edward, 181
Frick Collection, New York, 215
Friedman-Kien, Alvin, 176
Frugoni, Cesare, 82, 93
Fuller, Albert, xii, 127-28, 130, 133-34, 137-39, 171-74, 178-79, 212, 235, 242
Furusawa, Nauto, 245-46
Furusawa, Shuichi, 245-46

G

Garden, Mary, 62-63
George VI of Britain, King, 117-18
Girard, Michel, 221-23
Goldberg Variations, 58
Good, Robert, 163
Grabar, Pierre, xii, 102, 180
Graham, Martha, 147, 158
Gran Scena Opera, 155-56
Grandmaison, Madame Antoinette de, 219
Guggenheim, Peggy, 157-59
Guitry, Sacha, 155
Gulácsy, Irén, 37

H

Haar, Alfred, 169
Habrekorn, Claude, 220
Habrekorn, Henriette, 220-21
Habrekorn, Pierre, 220
Halpern, Bernard, 96-98
Handel, George Frideric, 51, 57, 58, 142, 148
Hatvany, Baron Lajos, 202
Heidelberger, Michael, xii, 102, 115, 124, 180-81, 252, 255
Helicon of Marosvécs, 36-37, 119, 225-26
Helicon Music Foundation, 128, 147
Hinton, Michael, 246
Hinton, Mineko, 246
Hirano, Takao, 245
Hitler, Adolf, 65, 76, 77, 116, 119

Horthy, Admiral Miklós, Regent
    of Hungary, 75-76
Horváth-Toldy, Margit, 15-16
Horváth-Toldy, Countess
    Rachel, 15
Houghton, Arthur, 148-49
Hugo, Andrée, 62, 63, 221
Hungarian Association of
    Immunologists, 247-48, 252
Hungarians, in the United States,
    118-19, 194-96, 208-13, 233-34
Hungary (see also Kolozsvár and
    Transylvania),
    after Communism, 247-52
    Arbitrage of Vienna, 69
    before WW II, 72-75, 118-19
    Communist era, 68, 141, 210-
        211, 233, 247
    during WW I, 72-75, 118-19
    literature, 26, 35-38, 118-20,
        209-211, 225-26, 232
    National Gallery of Art, 249
    National Museum of Fine
        Arts, 248-49
    nineteenth century Hun-
        garian painters, 248-49
    Treaty of Trianon, 40, 41, 46
Hunyadi, János, 9-10
Hunyadi, Sándor, 26, 37

I

International Union of Immuno-
    logical Societies (see also
    International Congress of
    Immunology), xv, 252
International Congress of
    Immunology, 169, 171-72, 176,
    186-87, 251-52

Irénke see Lázár, Irén
Ishizaka, Kimishige, 185
Ishizaka, Teruko, 185
Istituto Biologico, São Paulo, 104
Istituto Superiore de Sanità,
    Rome, 184-85

J

Jancsó, Jr., Nicolas, 83-84
Jancsó, Sr., Nicolas, 6, 83
Jenkins, Newell, 235
Jews in Transylvania, 7, 11, 27,
    49-50, 76, 119-20, 202-3, 228
Johns Hopkins Medical School,
    Baltimore, 63, 94, 102, 115, 121
    131, 143
Jolán see Stenzel, Jolán

K

Kabat, Elvin, 124-25
Kallós, Paul, 115
Kaplan, Melvin, 141, 160
Kaplan, Ynez, 160
Karush, Fred, 124-26
Kemény, Augusta, 228-29
Kemény, Ida, 226
Kemény, István, 225-29
Kemény, János, 225-26
Kemény, Mikolt, 224, 228-29
Kemény, Sigismond, 226
Klein, George, 178
Koch, Fred, 129
Kodály, Zoltán, 28, 31
Kolozsvár, Transylvania (see also
    Hungary and Cluj), xiv, 1-46,
    49-52, 69-70, 72-75, 118-20

Kolozsvár, *continued*
    and Arbitrage of Vienna, 69
    and Treaty of Trianon, 40,
      41, 42
    Holy Week rituals, 13-14
    St. Michael's Church, 1, 8,
      12-13
Koós, Károly, 25, 37
Kóry, Joseph, 51-52, 119
Kóry, László, 52
Krenner, Éva *see* Éva Lederer
Krenner, Mária, 203
Krenner, Miklós, 203
Ksesshinskaya, Mathilda, 67
Kyoto, Japan, 174-78
Kuncz, Aladár, 26, 37-38

L

La Caravelle, New York, 156,
    214, 216, 241
Lacretelle, Jacques de, 37, 38, 89
Lamm, Michael, 181
Landowska, Wanda, 57-59
Landsteiner, Karl, 124, 182
László, Éva, 41-42, 43, 130
László, Magda, 128-29
László, Marci, 16-18
Lázár, Irén, 21-22
Léderer, Andrew, 202-3
Léderer, Eva *née* Krenner, 21,
    202-5, 250
Lederer, Judy, 203
Lederer, Miklós, 203
Lee, Ron, 183-84
Leppard, Raymond, 128, 229
Levin, Bernard, 181
Lhevine, Rosina, 244
Lina *see* Pertrucellis, Lina

Lippi, Filippino, 10
Lodi-Fè, Caterina, 230
Lodi-Fè, Helli, 229-30
Lodi-Fè, Isabella, 230
Lodi-Fè, Maurizio, 229
Longmire, David, vii, 235
Louvre Museum, 57, 132, 199, 201
Luderitz, Otto, 108-109

M

Magura, Transylvania, 39-40
Mancino, Domenico, 246-47
Márai, Sándor, 118, 120, 209-11
Marfisi, Angelo, vii
Maria Theresia, Empress of
    Austria, King of Hungary,
    40, 230
Marie of Romania, Queen, 42
Marisa *see* Monti, Marisa
Márkus-Pulszky, Emilia, 227, 238
Martzy, Johanna, 132, 211
Mary of Great Britain, Queen,
    41-42
Mary Néni, 43-44
Mathias Corvinus of Hungary,
    King, 9-11
Mayer, Manfred, 102, 115, 121,
    123, 143
Metropolitan Museum of Art,
    New York, 138, 146, 148, 158,
    179, 182, 186, 201, 236-240
Michelangelo *see* Buonarotti
Milhaud, Darius, 89-90
Monet, Claude, 49, 154-55, 231, 237
Monod, Jacques, 55-56
Monteverdi, Claudio, 127, 128-29,
    139, 148
Monti, Marisa, 142

Móricz, Zsigmond, 232
Morphy, Paul, 16-18
Motomashi, Yoichi, 169
Müller, Paul Herman, 71
Musica Aeterna, 138, 146, 148, 150
Mussolini, Benito, 65-66

N

Nara, Japan, 174-76
Natali, Ambassadress Magda, *née* Óváry, *see* Magda Óváry-Natali
Natali, Umberto, 80, 85, 110, 112, 230
National Institutes of Health, 121-23, 177, 184, 185, 233
Nebrida, Vincent, viii
New York Chamber Soloists, 141, 147
New York University Medical School, 131-32, 136-44, 180-84, 208, 212, 240-41, 244, 252
Nicolle, Charles, 70, 78
Nijinsky, Romola *née* Pulszky, 238
Nijinsky, Waslaw, 227, 238
Nilsson, Birgit, 205
Nobel Prize, 55, 70, 71, 78, 97, 98, 108, 121, 124, 125, 143, 180, 183, 184, 209
Norman, Jessye, 147-48
Notes (music journal), 141-43
Nussenzweig, Ruth, 181
Nussenzweig, Victor, 181

O

O'Higgins, Patrick, 93-94

Old, Lloyd, viii, xiii, 133, 163, 206, 242, 243
Ormesson, Ambassador Vladimir d', 112-113
Osler, Abe, 121
Óváry, Elemér, 2-3, 16-18, 19, 33, 39-40, 45, 49, 52, 74, 119, 232
Óváry, Kelemen, 1, 4-5, 245
Óváry-Natali, Ambassadress Magda (Baba), 3, 6, 15-16, 21, 23-24, 33, 34, 44, 46, 72, 74, 80, 85, 91, 103, 110, 142, 203, 210, 229-31, 251
Óváry, Olga née Purjesz, 4, 5, 16, 19, 20, 23, 25-28, 33-34, 44-45, 52, 74, 231, 232, 253
    literary salon, 25-39, 52, 119, 232, 253
Óváry, Polyxena, 3, 5, 9, 12-13
Óváry, Zoltán, ix-xiii,
    New York University concert series, 141-43, 235, 241
    students, 143-45, 179, 183-84, 185-86, 235-46, 253
    bridging hypothesis, xi, 127
    carrier effect, xi, 181-83
    childhood, 1-4, 5-8
    citizenships, 69-70, 86-87
    experiments (see also PCA reaction, carrier effect, bridging hypothesis), x-xii, 61-63, 83, 125-26, 184
    family background, 1-46, 232-33
    honors, 185, 246-47
    lecture tour in China, 163-66
    medical education in Paris, 48, 53-54
    medical practice in Rome, 82, 84-88, 92-93

Óváry, Zoltán, *continued*
  medical practice in
    Transylvania, 72-75
  military sevice in Bessarabia,
    70-72
  military service in the
    Ukraine, 75-77
  Passive Cutaneous Anaphyl-
    axis *see* PCA Reaction
  return to Hungary after fall
    of Communism, 247-52
  work at Clinica Medica, 82-
    84, 98
  work at Johns Hopkins
    Medical School, 120-21
  work at Istituto Biologico,
    104
  work at New York University
    Medical School (*see also*
    New York University
    Medical School) ix, 131,
    43, 137, 181-83
  work at the Pasteur Institute,
    37, 57, 70
  work at Valfleury, 88-89, 159
  Zoltán Óváry Symposium,
    242-244

P

PCA Reaction, x, 98-102, 121, 122,
  124, 126, 180, 185, 248
Paestum, Italy, 122
Pallavicini, Princess Maria
  Camilla, 188
Pallavicini, Princess Elvina, xii,
  112-13, 188, 192, 194
Pallavicini Palace, tour of, 188-94

Paris, France, 48-68, 69, 89-91,
  96-98, 219-224
Passive Cutaneous Anaphylaxis *see*
  PCA Reaction
Pasteur Institute, 37, 54-56, 69-71,
  82, 91, 97, 99, 102, 105, 121,
  164, 184, 221
Pasteur Vallery Radot, Louis-
  Pasteur, 61-63, 96, 97
Paton, John, 227-28
Paul, William, 177
Paulay, Ede de, 66
Paulay, Elisabetta de *see* Cerruti,
  Ambassadress Elisabetta
Pecci-Blunt, Count Cecil, 88-89,
  92, 149
Pecci-Blunt, Countess Mimi, 88-
  89, 91, 92, 149
Pedley, Miss Helena, 8, 19, 23-24
Pétain, Jean, 221-223
Petrucellis, Lina, 85, 86
Phillips-Quagliata, Julia, 181
Picasso, Pablo, xii, 48, 49, 92, 95,
  112
Pickett, Ambassadress Diana,
  254-55
Pierpoint Morgan Library, New
  York, 11, 129, 158-61, 193, 213,
  236
Pisart, Georgette, 214-216
Polo, Marco, 111
Porter, Rodney, 125
Portier, Paul, 98
Poulenc, Francis, 89-91
Prausnitz, Karl, 115-16
Purjesz, Paula, 3, 5, 6, 8, 18-20,
  46, 100, 248
Purjesz, Zsigmond, 1, 4, 5-7, 18,
  46, 230, 245

Q

Quito, Gil, viii, 235-36, 254-55

R

Raphael, 151, 160-61
Rhédey, Countess, 41
Richet, Charles, 97, 98
Richman, James, 235
Rio de Janeiro, Brazil, 90, 103-104
Rogers, Michael, 141
Romania (*see also* Hungary *and* Transylvania), 5, 40, 41-43, 46, 50, 52, 69, 70, 72, 83, 226, 251
Rome, Italy, 80-94, 111-14, 188, 196-97, 217-19
Romanov, Grand Duke Andrei Vladimirovich, 67
Rosen, Charlotte, 180
Roth Quartet, 211-12
Rubinstein, Helena (Princess Gourielli), 93-95
Ryskamp, Charles, 158-60

S

São Paulo, Brazil, 104-6
Savet, Ella *née* Farkas, 49-53
Savet, Paul, 50-51, 118-20
Scarlatti, Domenico, 29-30, 137
Scelba, Interior Minister, 81-82
Schang, Janie, 146
Scholz, János, 211-214
Schröder, Jaap, 141

Schubert, Franz: *An Silvia*, 144-45
Sebestyén, Miklós, 119
Semmelweis, Ignaz, 247
Sepsiszentgyörgy, Transylvania, 41
Sert, Misia, 239-41
Shanghai, China, 165-66
Sihler, Andrew, vi, vii, 113
Sistine Chapel, 196, 240
Smith, Gregory, 139-40
Sorbonne University, 49-51, 53-54, 98
Staub, Anne Marie, 54-55, 105, 107-109
Stenzel, Jolán, 34, 233
Stephen I of Hungary, King, Saint, 9
Stetson, Chandler, 131, 180-81
Stoker, Bram, xiv
Svedberg, Theodor, 125
Szalay, Csaba de, vi, 233-34
Szalay, Helga de, 234
Szamosujvár, Transylvania, 40
Szendy, Árpád, 2
Szilard, Leó, 208

T

Tada, Norie, 178, 180
Tada, Tomio, viii, 171, 172, 174, 177-78, 185-87, 242, 243, 245
Takács Quartet, 251
Tamási, Áron, 37
Taniguchi, Masaru, 178-79
Teck, Duke Alexander of, 41
Teleki, Ádám, 35
Teleki, Countess Ágnes, 35-36
Tepes, Prince Vlad, xiv
Thibaudin, Henri, 220

Thomas, Lewis, 131, 136-37, 138, 140, 181, 255
Thorbecke, Jeanette, vii, 181, 242, 243
Tigelaar, Robert, 243
Tolnay, Charles de, 194-201, 206, 236
Török, Elisabeth, 31, 128
Transylvania (*see also* Kolozsvár, *and* Romania, *and* Hungary), xiv, 1-46, 72-75, 225-27, 250-51
Tully, Alice, xii, 138-39, 171-73, 188-91, 203-14
    Alice Tully Hall, 156
    New York University concert series, 139-42
    art patron, 158, 160-61
    music patron, 146, 147-49
    tour of apartment, 150-54
Turner, Thomas, 122
Twombly, Cy, 229-30

U

Ueda, Akira, 179
Uhr, Jonathan, 181
University of Paris, 46, 53, 54, 61
Univesity of Szeged, 82-83

V

Vastagh, György, 8
Végh, Sándor, 141
Venice, Italy, 11, 33, 34, 127, 139, 141, 154, 157-58, 204
Veress, Sándor, 29
Vértes, Marcel, 25, 249

Vicari, Giuseppe, 184-85
Vikol, Rosa, 128
Vikol, Simon, 42-43, 154
Vilcek, Jan, vii

W

Waksman, Byron, vii
Waksman, Selman, 184
Waldman, Alida, 146, 158
Waldman, Fritz (*see also* Musica Aeterna), 138, 158
Walter Reed Army Hospital, 121, 123
Warner, Noel, 243
Weisberg, Jay, vii
Wesselényi, Baroness Cornelia, 230
Westphal, Otto, 108
White, Robert, 142, 144-46, 214-16
Wigner, Eugène, 208-9

Y

Yourcenar, Marguerite, 89, 91-93

Z

Zeri, Federico, 112
Zita of Austria, Queen of Hungary, 35-36
Zolla-Pazner, Suzy, vii, 177, 181, 242, 243

ABOUT THE AUTHOR

Zoltan Ovary

was born in 1907 in Kolozsvar, Transylvania.
He is a professor and scientist at
the New York University Medical School.
The International Association of Immunologists
cites him as the world's oldest fully-employed immunologist.
Dr Ovary has published more than three-hundred articles
in professional journals, including *Science,*
Journal of Experimental Medicine, and *Notes*
(a periodical for musicians).
He is a historic figure in medical research for his
discoveries, among them the
Passive Cutaneous Anaphylaxis Reaction,
a breakthrough in the study of allergy and the
quantitation of antibodies.
In 1984, NYU started the annual Zoltan Ovary Symposium
to celebrate his work and inspirational role.
Dr Ovary resides in New York City.

The text of this book is composed in Adobe Caslon, Carol Twombly's recreation of the type issued in England in 1720 by William Caslon. Caslon's design has seen the longest continuous use of any typeface in the history of letterpress printing. Daniel Updike wrote in 1922 that Caslon was "beyond criticism from the point of view of beauty and utility"; but more recent students, in reaction to what they see as overpraise, have found much to criticize. Their charges of awkwardness, unevenness, want of proportion, and so on, are valid. But that only makes it the more remarkable that a page of text set in Caslon actually does have the virtues claimed for it by Updike: is sober and civilized, serious and graceful and, above all, inviting.

The chapter headings are set in Bitstream's Poster Bodoni. The ornaments are from Carter & Cone's issue of Matthew Carter's Galliard. The title page is set in Zapf Michelangelo (titling) and Zapf Aldus.